In Dialogue with Michèle Le Dœuff

Also Available from Bloomsbury

A Short Philosophical Guide to the Fallacies of Love, José A. Díez and Andrea Iacona
Justice and Love, Rowan Williams and Mary Zournazi
Ethical Experience, Susi Ferrarello and Nicolle Zapien

In Dialogue with Michèle Le Dœuff

Philosophies, Encounters and Friendship

Edited by Pamela Sue Anderson and Michèle Le Dœuff

BLOOMSBURY ACADEMIC
LONDON · NEW YORK · OXFORD · NEW DELHI · SYDNEY

BLOOMSBURY ACADEMIC
Bloomsbury Publishing Plc, 50 Bedford Square, London, WC1B 3DP, UK
Bloomsbury Publishing Inc, 1385 Broadway, New York, NY 10018, USA
Bloomsbury Publishing Ireland, 29 Earlsfort Terrace, Dublin 2, D02 AY28, Ireland

BLOOMSBURY, BLOOMSBURY ACADEMIC and the Diana logo
are trademarks of Bloomsbury Publishing Plc

First published in Great Britain 2023
This paperback edition published 2025

Copyright © Michèle Le Doeuff, The Estate of Pamela Sue Anderson,
and Contributors, 2023

Michèle Le Doeuff, The Estate of Pamela Sue Anderson, and Contributors
have asserted their right under the Copyright, Designs and Patents Act, 1988,
to be identified as Author of this work.

For legal purposes the Acknowledgements on p. xi constitute
an extension of this copyright page.

Cover image: Photo © The Courtauld / © Estate of Vanessa Bell.
All rights reserved, DACS 2022 / Bridgeman Images

All rights reserved. No part of this publication may be: i) reproduced or transmitted in any form, electronic or mechanical, including photocopying, recording or by means of any information storage or retrieval system without prior permission in writing from the publishers; or ii) used or reproduced in any way for the training, development or operation of artificial intelligence (AI) technologies, including generative AI technologies. The rights holders expressly reserve this publication from the text and data mining exception as per Article 4(3) of the Digital Single Market Directive (EU) 2019/790.

Bloomsbury Publishing Inc does not have any control over, or responsibility for, any third-party websites referred to or in this book. All internet addresses given in this book were correct at the time of going to press. The author and publisher regret any inconvenience caused if addresses have changed or sites have ceased to exist, but can accept no responsibility for any such changes.

A catalogue record for this book is available from the British Library.

A catalog record for this book is available from the Library of Congress.

ISBN: HB: 978-1-3501-3499-7
PB: 978-1-3502-6997-2
ePDF: 978-1-3501-3500-0
eBook: 978-1-3501-3501-7

Typeset by Deanta Global Publishing Services, Chennai, India

For product safety related questions contact productsafety@bloomsbury.com.

To find out more about our authors and books visit www.bloomsbury.com
and sign up for our newsletters.

Contents

Preface   vii
Kate Kirkpatrick

Acknowledgements   xi

Introduction   1
Pamela Sue Anderson

1. On feminist discourse   29
   Michèle Le Dœuff interviewed by Tetsuji Yamamoto and Nobuko Miyoshi

2. On *The Second Sex*   43
   Catherine Rodgers in dialogue with Michèle Le Dœuff

3. On style and experience   67
   Ulrika Björk in dialogue with Michèle Le Dœuff

4. On a twentieth-century French woman philosopher   83
   Penelope Deutscher in dialogue with Michèle Le Dœuff

5. 'Bringing us into twenty-first century feminism with joy and wit'   91
   Pamela Sue Anderson and Meena Dhanda with Michèle Le Dœuff

6. Women in dialogue and in solitude   115
   Michèle Le Dœuff

7. A bonny dialogue – for French studies   133
   Elizabeth Fallaize in dialogue with Michèle Le Dœuff

8. A jolly panel discussion in Nottingham   159
   Pamela Sue Anderson, Suzanne Dow, Alison Martin and Mark Robson in dialogue with Michèle Le Dœuff

9. On the sex of philosophy   179
   Aliocha Wald Lasowski in dialogue with Michèle Le Dœuff

10. Highly singular memories of '68, etc.   201
    Michèle Le Dœuff 'in dialogue' with her past

11. Occasionally the unforeseen happens   215
    Michèle Le Dœuff

| 12 | A joyful dialogue with Spinoza and others: Le Dœuff, Deleuze and the *Ethics*
Pamela Sue Anderson | 227 |
| 13 | Towards a new philosophical imaginary?
Michèle Le Dœuff | 241 |

Name Index   251

Preface

Kate Kirkpatrick

If we are to believe Hegel's *Phenomenology of Spirit*, a preface is a text that begins by 'explaining the end an author had in mind, the circumstances which gave rise to the work, and the relation in which the writer takes it to stand to other treatises on the same subject'. Moreover, he tells us, such explanations are extraneous: Why start with a sprinkling of superfluous statements when you could go *to the work itself*?

One reason, as Michèle Le Dœuff points out in *Hipparchia's Choice*, is that some subjects – such as hers, women and philosophy – require the adoption of 'the opposite principle': 'starting with scattered thoughts and proceeding by twists and turns'.[1]

I am neither the author nor the editor of this work; it is tempting to claim therefore that its aims and principles have nothing to do with me. In one sense, it would be true. But in another sense it would be an expression of gross ingratitude: as a translator I was a witness to this work in the making, but more importantly, in the process, I became a participant in the dialogical methods of both Pamela Sue Anderson and Michèle Le Dœuff. You will meet Anderson's invitation to 'Le Doeuffian dialogue' in her Introduction. But before you do I'd like to offer a glimpse of the joy, grief and questions that accompanied bringing this project to be. This work is the result not (only) of solitary reflection but of collective endeavour, and my hope is that representing the practices that produced it may contribute to the project of enlarging the philosophical imaginary.

Imagine an English summer. Three women met in a house in Oxford: one was a heavily pregnant twenty-something about to embark on postgraduate studies, and two were senior philosophers whose work was field-shaping in their respective subdisciplines. They were united by their interests in women and philosophy, feminism and metaphilosophy. For one of them, it was quite literally and conspicuously harder to fit at the table – but for hours we sat there, over several weeks, discussing draft translations. What collocations were lost in moving from French to English? What conceptual genealogies were no longer elicited? A discussion about the cultural significance of the word *pavé* (no, 'cobblestone' wasn't quite right!) led us away from the text to the memory of the events it described and then back again.

Over those weeks and the years that followed I learned that Anderson and Le Dœuff were critical of what they called the 'master-disciple' model of philosophical pedagogy. Le Dœuff considered it her good fortune to have studied with Vladimir Jankelevitch – 'who did not want to have disciples'. Anderson was concerned about this model's marginalizing effects for women in philosophy, especially in the Anglo-American philosophy of religion since, in that context, certain forms of Christianity still perpetuate unease at being alone with members of the 'opposite' sex.

Their friendship – like their conceptions of philosophy – was capacious. I never felt like an interloper or an acolyte. Instead, I was invited to enter into their dialogues with each other, with philosophical tradition and with feminist history to see 'the becoming of a woman in philosophy as an individual and collective experience'.[2]

They had had longer than I to reflect on the deficiencies attributed to women in the canon and in the philosophical imaginary; they had seen more women become philosophers, or face obstacles, or fail. They opened my young eyes wider to the importance of philosophical friendship – to their own project and to intellectual flourishing. I remember recoiling in disgust when I read Montaigne's claim that women are 'not normally capable of responding to such familiarity and mutual confidence as sustain that holy bond of friendship, nor do their souls seem firm enough to withstand the clasp of a knot so lasting and so tightly drawn'[3] – my life had already been generous with counterexamples. In Anderson and Le Dœuff I found two souls firm enough in their friendship to loosen the knot and welcome others in.

Seven winters later three women were again gathered in a house in Oxford. It was a different house – and Pamela was dying. It is a testament to her passion for dialogue and for women in philosophy that the words you are about to read are the last words I discussed with her, just two days before her death. This time, instead of sitting by a table with Michèle I sat by her bed with Liza Thompson, as we read and finalized this book's Introduction. Our work finished, I held her fragile body and said the word I had been dreading for so long: goodbye.

In the years between these scenes Pamela had been working on a project on love and vulnerability.[4] As she struggled with cancer, she faced her research questions in her own flesh: What projects are possible when your body has no strength? Is vulnerability a weakness to be overcome or a capacity that can enhance life? In health she had argued that 'facing vulnerability in mutual affection allows for a richer life'. Philosophy should not shut out our feelings and affections but rather become 'life-giving'.[5]

As her days dwindled dialogue with others remained one of Pamela's greatest – and life-giving – joys. But then and now – at the close of 2020 – it seems clear to me that there are several preconditions of its possibility and that the situations of individual lives – and deaths – render them more or less difficult to meet. Now that the dust of grief has settled, I have some worries of a different kind: about moving from particular lives to universal claims about philosophy; that what aims to include may serve nevertheless to exclude.

You will encounter the importance of Le Dœuffian autodidacticism in the Introduction: dialogue of this kind requires preparation, a readiness to learn from others that follows from learning alone. It also requires enough humour – if not humility – to take one's own lacunae lightly. It is easier to laugh at oneself in a context of positive regard and trust – with someone who understands your projects and your possibilities. But must friendship be a precondition of dialogue? Anderson writes that 'the movement in [Le Doeuff's] dialogical relations to philosophy is both creative and created in friendship, for new and longstanding friends, and here we find a passion for equality and mutual recognition amongst philosophers'. However, what this 'mutual recognition amongst philosophers' requires or how often it is achieved remains unclear to me: Can friendship be something we owe everyone with whom we enter into dialogue? Or is it something more particular, an achievement that results from the sedimentation of intimacy and ideas over time?

If the latter is the case, and dialogue is dependent on a certain kind of ethical and temporally extended relation, it seems to follow that it is not accessible to everyone – that a certain kind of situation is a precondition of its possibility and its perpetuation. Some may see this as a reason to reject it: I say let them see for themselves. For along with masters and disciples, Le Dœuffian dialogue rejects the problematic premise that doubt or disagreement implies disrespect. It is a feminist philosophy, after all, which does not presume on behalf of anyone 'to think in her place'.[6]

To the work itself, then! What does it mean to think in your place?

Notes

1 Michèle Le Dœuff, *Hipparchia's Choice: An Essay Concerning Women, Philosophy, etc.*, translated by Trista Selous (New York: Columbia University Press, 2007), first notebook, pp. 2–3.

2 Anderson, 'Introduction', to *In Dialogue*, p. 6.
3 Michel de Montaigne, *On Friendship*, translated by M. A. Screech (London: Penguin, 2004), p. 6.
4 Anderson's work on this project was published posthumously in a special issue of *Angelaki* (vol. 25, 1–2, 2020) and as a book edited by Pelagia Gioulimari, *Love and Vulnerability: Thinking with Pamela Sue Anderson* (Abingdon: Routledge, 2020).
5 'Remembering Enhancing Life Scholar Pamela Sue Anderson', The Enhancing Life project at the University of Chicago, http://enhancinglife.uchicago.edu/blog/remembering-enhancing-life-scholar-pamela-sue-anderson.
6 Dœuff, *Hipparchia's Choice*, p. 29.

Acknowledgements

Bloomsbury Publishing and Michèle Le Dœuff should like to warmly thank all those who contributed to this volume. Pamela Sue Anderson, who first started this project, is no longer with us; let this volume be a contribution to her loving and lasting memory.

These texts were translated and revised collaboratively: Chapters 5, 7, 9, 11, 13 by Pamela Sue Anderson and Michèle Le Dœuff; Chapters 1, 2, 3 and 10 by Kate Kirkpatrick, Pamela Sue Anderson and Michèle Le Dœuff; Chapter 4 by Penelope Deutscher and Michèle Le Dœuff; and Chapter 8 by Alison Martin, Pamela Sue Anderson and Michèle Le Dœuff.

Although some chapters appear here for the first time, others had been published in journals or books. Let their editors and present right holders, who kindly gave us permission to reissue the dialogues, know how much we appreciate their support.

The following works are reproduced in this volume with permission and their original publishers referenced here:

'On Feminist Discourse', interview by Tetsuji Yamamoto and Nobuko Miyoshi, Philosophical Designs for a Socio-Cultural Transformation, ISLA 1998 (© Michèle Le Dœuff).

'On the Second Sex', interview by Catherine Rodgers, L'Harmattan, 1998, now Editions iXe.

'On Style and Experience', interview by Ulrika Björk, *Australian Journal of French Studies*, special issue Autour de Michèle Le Dœuff, 2003, now Liverpool University Press.

'On a Twentieth-Century French Woman Philosopher', interview by Penelope Deutscher, *Hypatia, a Journal of Feminist Philosophy* n. 4, 2000, now Cambridge University Press.

'Bringing Us into Twenty-First Century Feminism with Joy and Wit', Pamela Sue Anderson and Meena Dhanda, *Women's Philosophy Review*, 2002, n.30.

'Women in Dialogue and in Solitude', Cassal Lecture, *Journal of Romance Studies*, 2005, 5, now Liverpool University Press.

'A Bonny Dialogue – for French Studies', interview by Elizabeth Fallaize, first published here with the kind permission of Alan Grafen and the Elizabeth Fallaize Estate.

'A Jolly Panel Discussion in Nottingham', interview by Pamela Sue Anderson, Suzanne Dow, Alison Martin and Mark Robson, Paragraph, vol. 33, n.1, 2010, Edinburg University Press.

'On the Sex of Philosophy', interview by Aliocha Wald Lasowski, from *Pensées pour le nouveau siècle*, Paris, Librairie Fayard, 2008.

'Highly Singular Memories of '68, etc.', Michèle Le Dœuff 'in dialogue' with her past, Sens public, journal on-line, 2009, now Université de Montréal.

The epigraph of 'A Joyful Dialogue with Spinoza and Others' is extracted from *The Philosophy of Simone de Beauvoir*, Critical Essays, edited by Margaret A. Simons, Indiana University Press, p. 13.

'Occasionally the Unforeseen Happens', Paragraph, vol. 37, n.3, 2005, Edinburg University Press.

We also thank Dawn Wilson for the photographs.

For Pamela Sue Anderson, completion of editing and translating the dialogues was made possible through the support of a grant from the John Templeton Foundation, via the Enhancing Life Project. The opinions expressed in this publication are those of the author(s) and do not necessarily reflect the views of the John Templeton Foundation.

Time regained, translated by Stephen Hudson (pseudonym of Sydney Schiff), first published by Chatto and Windus, London 1951; reissued, without pagination, by howtodo.rocks, Basel, no date of publication.

Introduction

Pamela Sue Anderson

In Dialogue offers its readers revised and newly translated texts for engaging with Michèle Le Dœuff, her philosophy and her development as both a philosopher and a feminist. Dialogue itself will become the method which brings together Le Dœuff's work and life in philosophy. Actual and 'virtual' dialogues will constitute a provocation for a philosophical world yet to be fully realized.[1] This world is becoming newly shaped for women equally as much as for men, with all of our graceful differences.[2]

This Introduction will urge readers to consider how Le Dœuff's dialogical relationship to the history of philosophy, to philosophical texts, to becoming a philosopher and to ongoing exchanges with women and men, including her future readers, leads her sometimes to write philosophy and/as autobiography.[3] Le Dœuff's self-critical pursuit of truthfulness, in dialogues with others (which become 'texts' for her readers) and with the self's relation to itself (in becoming 'a text', as a virtual[4] topic, for debate), produces wise and insightful fragments of philosophy as autobiography. In turn, these dialogues encourage Le Dœuff's readers to learn the very best skills in philosophy. Women in particular will be urged to practice 'autodidacticism', when necessary. A conception of self-taught philosophers derives from twelfth-century Ibn Tufayl's novella (about which Le Dœuff has sometimes written),[5] or possibly earlier; but, as I will illustrate further, Le Dœuff has focused her study of autodidacticism on how it is that a late seventeenth-century woman taught herself philosophy in dialogue with texts. Le Dœuff concludes that an autodidact is someone without formal education who has learnt philosophy in critical dialogue with philosophical texts for herself or himself. This might seem an obvious point. However, Le Dœuff retrieves her positive idea of an 'autodidact' from previous centuries, while implicitly rejecting Jean-Paul Sartre's abusive, twentieth-century caricature in *Nausea*, of the autodidact who only ever has superficial knowledge of books, without really knowing life.[6]

Le Dœuff's praise of autodidacticism does not mean that she herself lacks a formal education in philosophy; but she is self-taught on many topics, and notably, on women's place in the history of philosophy.[7] Le Dœuff shows the significance of learning for oneself in the autodidactic practice of imaginary dialogues which have been necessary historically, and often still today,[8] in order for women and non-privileged men to gain knowledge of philosophy and to develop their own philosophical skills; the latter generally have been – at least in western intellectual history – the province of elite men who had the leisure for, and access to, formal education in philosophy.

One of the aims of this Introduction is to demonstrate in what philosophically significant sense the philosophical texts translated and/or revised in the present book are autobiographical even while producing philosophy. Basically, I propose that autobiography is reflected in how Le Dœuff writes, rewrites and lives her philosophy. Her own autodidactic skills, especially in learning about women in philosophy, are constantly evolving with her thinking; we will follow the progress in what she discusses in the chapters to follow. When asked what is 'philosophy'? Le Dœuff has said, it is best to learn that for oneself. Yet very recently she has also argued that 'A woman engaged in philosophy may find it wise not to discuss the question [what is philosophy?] at all, and simply prove her existence by doing her job, just as you can prove the possibility of movement by duly taking a stroll'.[9]

Thinking in dialogical relations allows for originality and creativity in how the philosopher evolves. Readers will discover in dialogue with Le Dœuff how philosophical and feminist questions are raised for oneself and for others. It will also become clear how exactly Michèle Le Dœuff began, and continues, to think for herself as a woman in philosophy and as a feminist. In general, we become better philosophers in critical dialogue with a philosophical text and in ongoing debates with (other) philosophers themselves. At a minimum, philosophy becomes 'feminist' when a woman has the freedom to allow no one else to think in her place.[10] She is, then, allowed to think for herself about life and about relations of human beings to the world and to each other, including social and biological relations to human and non-human life. Le Dœuff also offers a good reason for being a feminist in philosophy here:

> [When one is] a woman and a philosopher, it is useful to be a feminist in order to understand what is happening to you. I use the term 'feminist' here in its most basic sense of someone who knows that something is still not right in the relations between a woman and everybody else, in other words men, other women, the supposedly impersonal agents of institutions, and anyone else: some hitch that is strictly potential, of course, simply liable to manifest itself, but which you must learn to identify in everyday situations and conversations.[11]

An autodidact: In dialogue and in history

Le Dœuff has frequently mentioned a woman's need for autodidacticism. She illustrates this need to be self-taught historically in her closely studied example of the seventeenth-century French woman in philosophy, Gabrielle Suchon.[12] Le Dœuff demonstrates with Suchon that a significant skill which had to be cultivated by women, in order to do philosophy, is teaching herself in critical dialogue with philosophical books. We know from her own written words that Suchon was largely taught philosophy by her own close readings of a text, by raising objections to the philosopher-author and formulating possible responses which that philosopher might give to her objections. In this manner, thinking is free to advance. Yet note that Le Dœuff's own dialogical relation to Suchon is both backward- and forward-looking. This means that, according to Le Dœuff, the history of philosophy is always in the making, when a philosopher is in dialogue with a philosophical text. Le Dœuff argues that women, who have been excluded historically from the social institutions for learning philosophy, have found it especially constructive to be self-disciplined in critical dialogues. Whether in solitude or in company, these women have found dialogue to be crucial for the advancement of their philosophical and feminist thinking within the long historical and collective experiences of philosophers.

Predictably, Le Dœuff mentions Plato's historical promotion of the Socratic method of dialogue, but she is not exactly following any one author in promoting 'imaginary dialogue'. In her words,

> [In] holding dialogues with various people and trying to establish what conditions make it possible to hold a debate [. . . Socrates's] aim is to discover the truth in the company of others.[13]

> . . . But all things considered, the Socratic dialogues went further with some interlocutors than with others. But Socrates seems to have needed them all. Those who write must [therefore] know that they are bound by imperfection. . . . [I]n recognising this imperfection, we know that we are asking a great deal of the reader and that the author does not automatically have the last word in the imaginary dialogue.[14]

Thus, gaining wisdom as women in philosophy requires that we 'get on with doing philosophy' for ourselves, even if we must imagine being in dialogue with a range of interlocutors.

Le Dœuff insists that dialogue has been – and still is – one historically significant way to teach oneself philosophy, especially (but perhaps not only), if following the tradition of the western history of philosophy back to Plato. Of course, we might like to question how it is that Le Dœuff can coherently claim women have and will become philosophers both in dialogue and in solitude![15] Is she playing with her terms – and with us – when she sets so much stock on the power of dialogue and of autodidacticism? Do we actually learn anything concrete, or objective, in dialogue with X when that person (X) is not in any sense actually present to correct, or disagree with, us? The 'voice' of the imaginary-dialogue partner is not heard or known through the senses of sound, touch or sight. At most the author might be 'heard', if the woman in philosophy imagines hearing another philosopher's argument as his or her text is read aloud. No doubt Le Dœuff might be implying something significant here about her distinctive conception of 'the philosophical imaginary'.[16] Yet isn't the very idea of a woman having a dialogue in solitude to be dismissed by the so-called man of reason (the straw man of reason, as Meryl Altman would put it) as sheer fantasy?[17] Surely, if imagining is close to fantasizing, our self-education in dialogue runs the risk of being dismissed by the great, and the good, philosophers whose disciples learn by becoming like them – and not on their own!

Nevertheless, our readers will discover that 'dialogue', as conceived and lived by Le Dœuff, aims to provide self-instruction, especially for those young women and men with no other access to formal, mainly elite, institutions of philosophy. Our assumption is that philosophical skills can be learnt even if not engaging with the social practices and in the social institutions of the great masters of philosophy. The (masculinist) sceptics might accuse us of extraordinarily wishful thinking – of creating a fantastic idea – to imagine that as women, we might teach ourselves philosophy. Nevertheless, Le Dœuff is not proposing either an easy ride or a fantastic story here. The singular woman, who turns in solitude to dialogue with the texts of those women and men who have engaged up to now in western philosophy, will have to be disciplined and unafraid of hard work!

The project and friendship

In reality it has been true, as Le Dœuff consistently demonstrates in *The Philosophical Imaginary* (2002), *Hipparchia's Choice* (1991, 2007), *The Sex of Knowing* (2003) and 'Women in Dialogue and in Solitude' (2005), that women in the history of western philosophy have become philosophers, at least in part, through self-education.[18] Now *In Dialogue with Michèle Le Dœuff*, we – Michèle, her translators and interlocutors – have completed a project, which found us working together, not only on translations but on our lives and work in philosophy, mainly in Oxford and Paris. In this way, our project *In Dialogue* has produced new friendships, plus new (feminist) strategies for writing philosophy, in personal and intellectual freedom. I might wager that, eventually with the help of our readers, we will have found a transformative strategy for refining philosophy's self-definition, in order that philosophy itself becomes far more inclusive, and not just 'western', not largely elite and not largely for certain privileged men alone. Dialogue itself has become crucial to our strategy for truthful self-development in philosophy for women, men, all of those whose gender orientations are yet to be defined. What (dare I call it) 'Ledœuffian' dialogue creates is a philosophical strategy for creating, and joining in, a self-critical movement of thought. This movement follows the arguments and asides in a text, as if part of a stream running through the ever-evolving history of philosophical discourse. Le Dœuff in refining her own dialogues for the present project has also continued to produce philosophy in retrospect, for the future and in active engagement with the words on the page, with her translators, with her readers and with a philosophical world as yet to emerge fully. Quite literally our project, *In Dialogue*, offers hope for creating a productive and transformative strategy for becoming individually and collectively better, which must mean for Le Dœuff more 'joyful' philosophers – and learners.

It was suggested at the outset of this Introduction that Ledœuffian dialogue becomes a critical method for autobiography in philosophy. It also appears to be writing philosophy as something like *autre*-biography.[19] By 'another' biography, I mean that we might – and why not? – want to formulate philosophical objections to creating philosophy in dialogue as merely one's own (auto)biography. It is completely clear that Le Dœuff's philosophy in *Hipparchia's Choice* includes both autobiographical elements such as her 'primal scene'[20] in philosophy and biographical imagery of a woman who first chose her 'study' (*l'étude*) for philosophizing rather than her 'loom' (*le rouet*) for spinning (as was the practice in an ancient world). In fact, *Hipparchia's Choice* is a marvellous example of a philosophical text by a woman who initiates us both into the world of twentieth-century philosophy and into the history of writing philosophy – by creating a conceptual persona – who literally emerges out of that philosophical history. This is a virtual image for a persona in philosophy which has emerged, but not without thinking which is hard work, that requires discipline and painful struggle; this image is part of a philosophical imaginary, and captures affections such as joy which appear especially suited to this Ledœuffian project of looking backwards and forwards for women in philosophy.

In Dialogue we have sought to articulate a Ledœuffian process in the making of a woman philosopher. The texts are not to be read as mere interviews of unreflective musings, or a set of off-the-cuff remarks, about a life in philosophy. Instead, these are dialogues on the move, in which philosophy is being created, even as we follow Le Dœuff's thinking back to her original exchanges which have taken on a life of their own in conversation and in print. The reader might allow our boldness in admitting that these dialogues have gained weight and gravitas from a project aimed at new meticulous translations, refined and expanded expressions of new ideas, with the help of genuine philosophical hindsight.

Le Dœuff's philosophy is 'on the move' precisely because it reflects her multiple engagements with the history of philosophy, with other feminist philosophers, saying something about twentieth-century philosophical and political issues. Crucially, the movement in her dialogical relations to philosophy is both creative and created in friendship, for new and long-standing friends, and here we find a passion for equality and mutual recognition among philosophers. This philosophical project intends to give confidence to new generations of women – and men – in philosophy. To conceive how this could be so, it is well worth recalling 'the conceptual persona', which Gilles Deleuze's himself discovered with joy in Le Dœuff's text. Deleuze imagined this persona being made and re-made by Michèle, his 'friend' and 'interlocutor' in *L'Étude et le rouet*.[21] To repeat lines from Deleuze's letter to Le Dœuff:

> Dear Michèle Le Doeuff,
> Your book is a joy. It has a strength which permeates its every tone of voice. You are renewing the whole problem of thought, tracking down a distinctively masculine cogito. Already you are sketching the outline of a thought which would be free from such constraints, and estimating its cost. I admire your book and am impatient for the next one. Think of me as someone close to you and be assured, if you will, of my friendship. (Gilles Deleuze)[22]

Today we have the opportunity to read and to renew what was anticipated by Deleuze: the becoming of a woman in philosophy as an individual and collective experience. As he insinuates, the uncovering of 'a distinctively masculine cogito' opened up philosophical horizons for revising our thoughts 'free from' imposed gender constraints, but also free for creating new concepts in friendship and joy.

Following Deleuze, readers in dialogue with Michèle Le Dœuff need to be prepared for her thinking in retrospect, but also in prospect, for what earlier dialogues will mean for the future of women in philosophy. Le Dœuff herself might call the dialogues, which are being introduced here, 'joyful'. In fact, this is a description she originally offered to me, 'In dialogue with Spinoza and others'.[23] Yet readers should not think that either Le Dœuff's joy or that of Deleuze is some superficial pleasure or fantastic experience. Witness the facts of our corporate, enduring project. Le Dœuff thinks carefully and rethinks again: this is what she expects us to do, too: to think – hard – and to articulate what we have not previously been able to say or write. There is work to be done in dialogue with a philosopher: so let us not be afraid to ask tough questions of this woman philosopher and her philosophy which moves us backwards, in order to move philosophy and philosophers forward; the tougher the initial philosophical questions posed to her text, the better for the becoming of (her) philosophy. Critical questions are to guide us 'in dialogue with Michèle Le Doeuff'; but they might equally guide each and every reader to express greater confidence in thinking for themselves, about what makes 'a philosophy', 'a philosopher' and 'a woman in philosophy'.

A woman in philosophy: Additional biographical facts

Michèle Le Dœuff is a twentieth- and twenty-first-century French philosopher whose incisive wit and political insight continue to make her an engaging partner in dialogue. When interviewed by the Australian philosopher Raoul Mortley, in 1986 Le Dœuff was the youngest star and, in a sense, '*la relève*' of an already impressive line-up of French philosophers. The other philosophers in dialogue with Mortley at that time included Emmanuel Lévinas, Monique Schneider, Michel Serres, Luce Irigaray and Jacques Derrida. Yet, in Mortley's dialogue with Le Dœuff, she admits not being 'a groupie' of any sort. This happens to be one of the first things I learnt about Michèle, as she explains:

> [A]t the Sorbonne, I became a student of the moral philosopher Vladimir Jankélévitch, a remarkable and very kind professor, who did not want to have disciples, a man who was keen on students going their own way. In short, I have been lucky: I have had professors, books, but no mentor. Some authors have, of course, particularly influenced me, and among contemporary writers Foucault and Deleuze must be mentioned, I suppose, although I have never been a groupie of any of them.[24]

Le Dœuff's characteristic resistance to heteronomy remains crucial to understanding her autonomy as a woman which, as will be seen, she describes as personal and intellectual freedom.

As already explained, *In Dialogue* conveys a project for creating a critical method – joyful dialogues in lively debate – about philosophical issues from the history of philosophy. Let us sum up what is it that makes Ledœuffian dialogue distinctive. According to the philosophical issues addressed by Le Dœuff in her major books and her range of published essays, dialogue has been one way for a woman, despite many other social, material and historical obstacles, to refine her philosophical skills; she follows a philosophical tradition of posing objections to the philosophical argument on a page and working out replies, which might be given by the philosopher-author of that argument in the text. The conceptual persona of a woman in philosophy and in the history of philosophy portrays someone socially excluded, yet nevertheless free, to become personally and intellectually engaged. This engagement in the texts of philosophy provides both the key and the freedom for thinking for herself. As revealed in Le Dœuff's conceptual persona, a woman in philosophy might have been blocked from the great institutions of philosophy by sexism, including oppressive material and other social conditions, nevertheless 'in dialogue' a woman has been – and continues to be – free to think in her own place; hence, she is free to create her own ideas in, and to develop her own capability for, philosophy.

Not only has there been a long history of social exclusion of women from philosophy, but time and inclination are both necessary for a woman to learn to do philosophy. Over the centuries, finding the time for doing philosophy has never been straightforward for men, but it would have been impossible for most women. Recall that Le Dœuff's imagery captures the ancient difficulty of finding time for philosophy when she expresses in her French title, for her second major work: *L'Étude et le rouet: des femmes, de la philosophie, etc.* (translated *Hipparchia's Choice: An Essay Concerning Women, Philosophy, etc*). The two terms, *l'étude* and *le rouet*, recall both the choice between the study and the loom, or philosophizing and spinning, which an ancient woman philosopher, Hipparchia, would have had to make. But if this choice of studying philosophy was made, how do we imagine a woman in the world of ancient Greece actually learned to philosophize? One way was to find a master, or lover, of philosophy who would mentor her as his disciple, or beloved. However, Le Dœuff remains emphatic: discipleship is definitely not the best model for learning philosophy – especially, but not only, for a woman then or now – at least, as far as she is concerned!

As quoted from Le Dœuff's dialogue with Mortley (above), she herself did not follow, let alone submit to, any mentor whether a great man-philosopher or not. Moreover, Le Dœuff is a feminist who has refused to be grouped with those women who have been known in Anglo-American academic and intellectual circles as 'the French feminists',[25] who were especially popular from the 1970s into 1990s. Unlike those French feminists of sexual difference, notably Luce Irigaray and Hélène Cixous, Le Dœuff's goal for women is not about establishing the sexual difference between a man and a woman, nor is it about 'becoming divine' women.[26] Just the opposite: 'Not a Goddess, She!' is Le Dœuff's response to any Irigarayan imperative for recognizing divine women.[27] Le Dœuff calls for women to learn for themselves, to gain their own confidence, to cultivate their own capability for philosophy, but women in philosophy are not more than human; instead, we are limited by our differences and imperfections.

We could question Le Dœuff's own refusal to be either 'a groupie' or 'a disciple': How is it possible for us to learn from Le Dœuff, if she does not advocate discipleship? Can she herself have followers (disciples)? Has this resistance to discipleship done damage to the reception of her philosophy? Whatever the answer, let us recognize Le Dœuff's distinctive brand of feminism within a collective historical experience.[28] It will remain a critical issue that Le Dœuff's philosophy does not lend support to the creation of philosophical disciples, demigods or demigoddesses. Understood in positive terms, although she does not encourage discipleship or groups of followers, it is my experience at least that Michèle welcomes friendship and friends – but not divas!

A solitary woman: The individual and the collective

In her inspiring book review of Le Dœuff's *The Sex of Knowing*, Meryl Altman captures a highly significant dimension of philosophical style:

> [Michèle Le Doeuff] is 'un-French' also in her explicit concern to inform and instruct rather than simply impress, and in her attention to pedagogy and the next generation. Her work shows that it is possible to be immensely sophisticated intellectually and still write like a human being.[29]

From my own experience of teaching undergraduates and postgraduates in philosophy at the University of Oxford, as well as giving lectures in the UK and 'on the Continent', I have most often found the writings of Michèle Le Dœuff discovered by women (and some men), who were struggling on their own, in order to articulate a philosophical idea or problem.[30] In solitude these women have quickly internalized Le Dœuff's belief that 'to read a philosophy book properly is to have a sort of dialogue or debate with the author . . . through the debate with the author, you will have grown ideas of your own'.[31] In dialogue with Le Dœuff herself and/or her writings, the female, and perhaps the male, interlocutors will gain confidence in critical thinking and self-expression. This is especially helpful for a solitary woman in philosophy who becomes an individual part of a collective experience in virtual dialogue.

In turn, Le Dœuff herself explains the sense of responsibility she has felt towards other women in philosophy, but also to men in the field:

> *J'ai d'abord conçu cette responsabilité comme travail en direction de femmes philosophes, mes élèves ou les collègues d'ici et d'ailleurs. Leur offrir, à elles, ainsi bien sûr qu'aux hommes du milieu, la possibilité de changer leur perception de ce qui est en jeu dans le travail philosophique.*[32]
>
> I first conceived this responsibility as a work for women philosophers, my students and colleagues from here and elsewhere. I wanted to offer to them (and of course to men of the *milieu* as well) the possibility for them to change their perception of what is at stake in philosophical work. (translated by MLD)

She clearly hopes that a common camp of autonomous thinkers, women and men, will take shape naturally in dialogue with (her) philosophical work.

As I seek to demonstrate here, in setting out the project of the present book, dialogue also significantly shapes the *collective* experiences of women, as much as men, in philosophy as both a historical and a contemporary discipline.[33] Implicit in the learning process of critical debate and philosophical reflection is the coming together across history and texts of individual and collective experience in the production of new ideas. Whether we consider the history of western philosophy, moral philosophy, philosophy of religion, political and feminist philosophy – and most recently, meta-philosophy (2016) – the critical challenge of Le Dœuff's philosophical writings generates not only food for thought but nutrients for rendering healthy crops of new ideas in various locations within and outside of philosophy.

Le Dœuff herself has long argued that women need to see themselves as a collective: each woman produces ideas of her own, yet is nourished by the common historical experiences of autonomous women thinkers.[34] In her first, and possibly most widely circulated, philosophical essay on the topic of women and philosophy, '*Cheveux longs, idées courtes*',[35] Le Dœuff already and unequivocally rejects the philosophical relationship of master and disciple. In fact, she illustrates historically the specific dangers for women of this relationship with examples drawn from the history of philosophy, including Abélard and

Héloise, Jean-Paul Sartre and Simone de Beauvoir. For instance, Le Dœuff has become known for having early on (before others would, and in the face of some opposition) defended Beauvoir as having produced her own ideas in philosophy. This is so even though Beauvoir remained unaware of herself as a philosopher, since for Beauvoir 'the Philosopher' is Sartre's title. Beauvoir remained intellectually faithful to Sartre, even though she was not monogamous in her love relationships (nor was Sartre). With this example, Le Dœuff articulates a philosophical problem for women in (the history of) philosophy which she calls 'the Héloise complex'.[36] The paradigmatic nature of the Héloise and Abelard and of Simone (de Beauvoir) and Jean-Paul (Sartre) examples, in which a woman has access to philosophy only via her (male) mentor – who is also to be her lover[37] – (to whom she remains faithful) has enlightened Le Dœuff's readers to various degrees and in various ways. The feminist challenge for the individual (a solitary woman) must be addressed by enlightenment of the collective in the historical experience which is (western) philosophy.

A philosophical skill and an epistemic practice

Let us return to the question of being in dialogue with a person or a text. *In Dialogue with Michèle Le Dœuff* takes very seriously a conception of dialogue as a distinctive method for doing philosophy: it becomes a philosophical skill and an epistemic practice in Le Dœuff's own writings. I have followed a lead from Le Dœuff herself to propose that reading, writing and engaging in dialogue is itself a method – both to learn philosophy and to gain knowledge. Dialogue is, in one sense, an ancient method which, as old as the Socratic method at least; but it is, in another sense, an epistemic practice. This latter is epistemic, since at the level of our conditions for knowing; and as a practice, it is the activity (in dialogue) of opening up a new future for knowledge in philosophy.

Le Dœuff's *Cheveux longs, idées courtes* was originally intended as 'a dialogue with women in philosophy'. As Le Dœuff herself later explains,

> [M]y essay [translated 'Long hair, short ideas'] is a sort of dialogue, too, in this case a half-imaginary one, between myself and my students. During the summer of 1976, I was preparing my seminar for the following year at an all-women institution, and thought it useful to write down a sort of theoretical contract; a minimalistic basis to offer my students, with the idea that people need to have a handful assumptions in common in order to begin to talk to one another.[38]

Le Dœuff makes clear that the question of 'what it is to talk to each other' is a philosophical issue for each and every philosopher, not only something for women in philosophy to learn.³⁹ Her 1976 essay already encourages this learning to take place, even when the women concerned are not physically present to her.

In her later public lecture, 'Women in Dialogue and in Solitude', Le Dœuff argues explicitly that it is not unusual to find women learning philosophy in dialogue and at the same time in solitude.⁴⁰ Why solitude? Can we have both solitude and dialogue? Le Dœuff insists that at least for those women and men excluded from the academic institutions of philosophy, dialogue and solitude need to be reconciled in order for them to develop their own philosophical skills. In 'Women in Dialogue and in Solitude', Le Dœuff notes that in 1977 Gilles Deleuze and Claire Parnet also present the encounters and becomings of philosophers both in dialogue *and* in a so-called populous solitude (Deleuze and Parnet [1977] 2012). So, we notice that the date of the Deleuze–Parnet *Dialogue* means that circulation of Le Dœuff's original French version of 'Long Hair, Short Ideas' occurred at a moment in 1976–7 Paris when, as Le Dœuff herself explains in retrospect, some men in philosophy seemed to have thought it was also urgent to restate their own existence in dialogue with 'their brand-new, not to say still to come' ability to talk with women.⁴¹ As for women in philosophy, then, to be in dialogue with philosophical texts as bodies of work existing exterior to a reading self is an absolutely crucial philosophical skill identified by Le Dœuff for those women and men who have endeavoured to make learning philosophy gender inclusive.

Le Dœuff singles out a second book published after 1976 in Paris by a French philosopher – that is, a man – in dialogue with a woman. In addition, to the publication of Deleuze and Parnet, *Dialogues II* in 1977 (Paris: Flammarion), Vladimir Jankélévitch and Béatrice Berlowitz publish their dialogue, *Quelque part dans l'inachevé* in 1978 (Paris: Gallimard). So, it is in retrospect that Le Dœuff asks, 'when was it that a French male philosopher had last spoken with a woman?' As far as she knew, the 1977 dialogue between the philosopher Deleuze and a woman Parnet was a 'first'. Is the dialogue between Jankélévitch and Berlowitz the last? This is a rhetorical question. No particular answer is required, but this urges women in philosophy to investigate the question itself.

In pursuing the meaning of 'dialogue with a text' in philosophy, it is important to consider the interlocutor, or interlocutors, who are in dialogue with Le Dœuff's philosophy. Concrete differences matter when it comes to locations in philosophy, from which 'partners' engage in dialogue; we are shaped by our locations, but also philosophers shape their locations with the imagery, narratives and asides in their texts. Le Dœuff is interested in the relationship between the abstract and the concrete questions of philosophy. In particular, she develops a highly distinctive practice of working out how imagery in the texts of philosophy impinge on practical reality, and this same imagery will come into play in the relationship between contemporary philosophical questions and past philosophical works. In other words, the philosophical imaginary, including the images, the stories and the unthought asides, in the texts requires careful study; these matter to the precise ways in which we read the history of philosophy and philosophical texts today.

In her work on the philosophical imaginary, it could be said that Le Dœuff works both outside and within the tradition of western European philosophy: so, where she finds herself in the history of philosophy matters.[42] To this end, in the 'Third Notebook', *Hipparchia's Choice*, she proposes that the history of philosophy should be reoriented.[43] In *The Sex of Knowing* she initiates a reorientation in philosophical thinking about the nature of knowledge and focuses in particular, on Suchon (in the seventh century). Le Dœuff first mentions Suchon in *Hipparchia's Choice*, but she explores Suchon's philosophy in substantial detail in *The Sex of Knowing*.[44] Three of the dialogues collected in the present book focus on the significance of Suchon for the history of philosophy and philosophers today.[45] Basically, an interlocutor in dialogue with Le Dœuff will find her referring back to imaginary dialogues she has had with (the texts of) Suchon.

For example, in her dialogue with Ulrika Björk, Le Dœuff explains how after much careful detective work, she concludes that a certain Jean-Jacques Rousseau had read Suchon.[46] If following Le Dœuff, then the writings of past philosophers are given a mediating role in a new reflective freedom for today's women in philosophy, but also for men and women in other fields such as theology, ethics, politics, history and literature. As the paradigmatic example, Suchon's writings contribute to not only philosophical reflection on intellectual freedom, independence of thought, the role of curiosity but also new understanding of 'original sin'. The latter had, for centuries, blinded thinkers to the importance of self-education, active pedagogy and autonomy for all. At the very least, according to Le Dœuff, we can learn from Suchon that original sin needs not make a dirty word of 'curiosity' or denigrate the desire to know. Just the opposite! The woman's (Eve's) sin was the lazy attempt to gain knowledge by an easy route: eating the (forbidden) fruit of the tree which gives bodily and moral knowledge. Instead, self-education and learning as a woman in philosophy is not easy: work is necessary for gaining sinless knowledge.

The centrality of the text as a conceptual image becomes a methodological focus in Le Dœuff's dialogue with Suchon's seventeenth-century philosophical writings. Le Dœuff discovers Suchon's two published works containing philosophical ideas otherwise left in virtual oblivion.[47] Le Dœuff has been rightly described as 'a female detective' – the Miss Marple of philosophy; with her finely tuned skills of logic, lucidity and wit, she carefully teases out the philosophical, as well as the political issues within the history of texts. Le Dœuff investigates Suchon, picking up significant pieces of history, anecdotes and political ideas in her writings with significance for men and women. So, Le Dœuff's own dialogues with these texts function as a mediator of philosophical thinking. As will be seen in the chapters to follow, the nature and role of Le Dœuff's anecdotal remarks add new philosophical ideas to the intrigue surrounding the dialogue with texts in a woman's self-education.[48]

With subtly crafted episodes, ripe for Le Dœuff as the Miss Marple of philosophy to pick up, dissect and debate, the history of that seventeenth-century woman as an intellectual remains in process. Gathering together Le Dœuff's claims concerning 'a woman philosopher' as part of a distinctive, collective history of women in philosophy, however, depends on what she crafts as a good story about what has happened to our history of such women in philosophy as Suchon. The rising and falling of the conceptual persona of 'a woman philosopher' in the history of western philosophy can be represented with waves, creating a distinctive sort of imaginary history for our conceptual persona.[49] The central figure often disappears only to re-emerge in a new shape, yet with familiar content. Elsewhere I have demonstrated how a reader can detect the imagery of waves – and of feminist positions on the crests of waves – in Le Dœuff's approach to the history of women's writings.[50] For example, in *Hipparchia's Choice*, Le Dœuff appropriates Virginia Woolf's argument in *A Room of One's Own* and Woolf's imagery from *The Waves* to help convey the centrality of reading philosophical texts for the history of feminism and patriarchy.

Freedom and its antinomies

At the mention of patriarchy, it is absolutely essential to be clear about Le Dœuff's feminist conception of freedom. I will discuss this; but before that, notice Le Dœuff does not advocate a feminist politics on the basis of women's natural (sexual) difference from men. Crucially, her originality is to claim that philosophy is for all thinking, autonomous women and men. Moreover, male scholars as much as, and at times more than, female scholars have taken seriously and engaged with Le Dœuff's sensitive yet critical approach to the history of philosophy.[51] The seventeenth-century historian David Norbrook offers a critically constructive assessment of Le Dœuff's philosophical enquiries concerning Suchon's autonomous thought:

> Until recently Suchon has barely figured in the history of women writers, let alone of philosophy, and Le Doeuff's readings are making clear how much we have been missing. . . . [The] process of independent thought, from the bottom up, was in the end more important in transforming women's situation than the occasional woman's managing to wield power within a profession.[52]

In brief, Suchon herself advocates a conception of what I have called here, 'a text': critical study of a text can function in the self-education and emancipation of a woman from various dimensions of oppression, including both internal and external deprivations. Although this is not unique to her, or to women, Suchon's explicit goal is two sorts of freedom: (i) the intellectual autonomy, allowing a woman to learn freely (and on her own) by reading and debating an author's ideas; (ii) the social-material autonomy, or exterior freedom, which gives the conditions (time and place) for a woman to read, learn, write and publish. Suchon articulates the former freedom as (i) intellectual autonomy under a pseudonym in a discussion of a woman's natural right (cf. Suchon, 1693). The latter, exterior freedom – or, social-material autonomy – is articulated in a second book under her own name in terms of the autonomy of a single life. This is a life in which a woman is not primarily defined either by a marriage or by a convent life.[53]

In her assessments of Suchon's seventeenth-century intellectual writings, Le Dœuff seems to agree with Suchon's social and material conception of autonomy for women in philosophy, as it is discussed and lived by this seventeenth-century woman. Insofar as a woman who professes an intellectual autonomy, Suchon remains the same as her contemporary male intellectuals. But here is the material point. In Suchon's seventeenth-century world, neither male nor female intellectuals are given any material, social or political value for their intellectual efforts. In short, no financial support is given to philosophical work. So they remain poor and must find other paid work unless they are independently wealthy. Nevertheless, for us the crucial, even astonishing, fact is that in the seventeenth century a woman philosopher, as a thinker-writer, could exhibit both social-material and intellectual autonomy. The additional significant philosophical point is that a woman has both the cognitive and conative capacities to become equal to any man. This point supports both the conceptual persona in Le Dœuff's text[54] and the philosophical argument that a woman, just as much as a man, possesses the capability for philosophy and so, can and should be developed.

Yet Le Dœuff admits that the level of cognitive ability will vary as a contingent matter from one woman or man to the next. In generalizing from Suchon, Le Dœuff does not only concern herself with a conceptual persona of a woman who is created, and then excluded, by the (male) philosopher. Instead, she seeks to demonstrate with her examples of actual women, each in their own historical context, that they have written philosophy – even though sometimes unaware of doing so, as in the case of Simone de Beauvoir.

Feminisms and Le Dœuff's singularity

Le Dœuff has not been like any of her own contemporaries in philosophy and in feminism. First, as already mentioned, she does not follow those women (or, men and possibly transgender persons) who advocate a 'feminism of sexual difference'.[55] This label applies to feminists who claim, roughly, that a woman is different from a man on grounds of her sexually specific cognitive, conative and affective nature, and more than frequently this difference is described either in negative terms as a woman's lack of rationality or in more positive terms as a woman's distinctive intuitive nature. In *The Sex of Knowing*, Le Dœuff makes an incisive philosophical remark about women and men, which characterizes her own distinctive point of view:

> Another disturbing corollary: in the guise of critique [of reason], all of this ends up once more flattering the masculine half of humanity, which takes comfort in the idea that there really is 'a man of reason', systematic and methodical, from whom women who really are women differentiate themselves. As long as the equation of a crude notion of a rationality with a class of individuals cursorily defined as 'masculine' is not exposed as a myth, there is no point in valorizing or rejecting this hollow idea of reason on the basis of this equation. 'Reason is masculine, and that's why I'm in favour of it' is as empty a declaration as 'Reason is masculine, and that's why I want no part of it'. Neither has anything to say about what the issue of rationality might be, and both base a completely fantastical division of the sexes on a set of ill-defined questions.[56]

Second, neither is it possible to place Le Dœuff's feminist politics under a 'feminism of equality'. This label tends to apply to a feminist who gives privilege to an abstract notion of formal equality between men and women. In contrast, Le Dœuff remains uniquely, passionately and actively engaged with the concrete lives of women and their political struggles in the present as much as the past. So, Le Dœuff's originality forces us to reject both of the two well-known feminist labels for her work.

To illustrate her singularity in feminist circles, Le Dœuff's detective work in the history of philosophy, and of women in philosophy, reveals both the concrete and the more academic dimensions of actual historical struggles by women. In developing her political and historical sensitivity to the locations of women in the history of philosophy, Le Dœuff does not have to choose either a feminist mandate for (formal) equality or a feminism of (sexual) difference. Instead, she rejects *both* the assumption of a fundamental difference between a man and a woman on the grounds of the innate seeds for knowledge in every human being *and* the belief that an abstract notion of equality alone has excluded women from politics or public life.

Most significant in the case of Suchon is that Le Dœuff digs up this woman's revolutionary, and possibly heretical, but certainly unorthodox account of 'original sin'.[57] It probably goes without saying, the huge obstacle for women across the millennium is posed by Eve (the woman) who leads Adam (the man) to sin, in order to gain the forbidden knowledge of good and evil. But according to Suchon, as explained above, the sin of Eve has more to do with laziness than concupiscence: to sin is not to lust, but it is to find a ready-made answer. Instead of cultivating fertile seeds of knowledge, the sin is to take the easy method of eating an apple in order to have knowledge. This account challenges the dominant view that sin is originally caused by a woman's inordinate desire for knowledge of right and wrong: sin is due to curiosity and, what is supposedly worse, lust. Suchon's crucial assertion that 'God gave us intelligence to force us to seek knowledge of things'[58] supports a woman's *natural* right of freedom to know and so learn for themselves. According to Suchon, this natural right gives to each woman the capability for learning. In other words, women have both the responsibility and the capability for self-learning. This natural right, then, depends upon the capability and the autonomy of every man and every woman.[59] The philosophical conclusion from Suchon's rereading of original sin is, in Le Dœuff's own words, 'knowledge of the tree should result from the reflections the human being would undertake, not by picking and eating the apple'.[60]

To conclude, I would like to take one last step beyond critical praise of Le Dœuff's diggings into the seventeenth-century life and text of Suchon as a paradigm case of a woman in the history of philosophy, for women in philosophy as they have been conceived by English-speaking and European philosophers. In addition, to learning anew from the past, I would like to stress the forward-looking dimension of Le Dœuff's dialogues – not simply in the revised texts and translations of the dialogues published here but also in the philosophical lessons she provides for the future. These include the centrality of reading, writing and revising philosophy. I have employed a concept of 'the text' for both a symbol and a source of philosophical dialogue and self-education. The forward-looking dimension of Le Dœuff's philosophical and autobiographical thinking seeks to promote human intellectual and socio-political autonomy for all. We can move forward the *vital* significance of a woman's material and intellectual autonomy, as well as the urgently needed *potential* for *a publically informed freedom* for every *woman and man*, in order to produce their own ideas, to read, to write and to be read – in the case of philosophy at least – informed by the lessons learned in the past. So we don't give into any desire to turn in on ourselves resisting both the capability and responsibility of our autonomous thinking together in the politically fragile global world of conflicts, unthinking dogma and fear rather than joy in our differences.

We remain at a moment in history when, despite any potential decline in reading philosophy (and other literature – due to global media disseminating 'information'), texts can still teach each of us much about the past, while providing the crucial focus on the future, in a dialogical learning relationship, for readers and writers. Contemporary women and men, not totally unlike Le Dœuff's seventeenth-century example of Suchon, face a world in which the social status of individual authors in philosophy is fragile, and perhaps, becoming more the case daily with the global dominance of sound bites: it is easier not to think philosophically but to accept random points on social media. The public imagination associates knowledge and power, not with reading and writing philosophy texts, whether past or present, but with electronic and global productions of knowledge in the form of sound bites and bald assertions. Increasingly we lack discursive forms of critical reflective thinking by either women or men. There are undoubtedly virtues in new electronic forms of knowledge production. Yet in the light of the dangers of passive learning – and violence propagated globally via the World Wide Web, we might be much closer to the seventeenth-century world of Suchon than we would like to think. Le Dœuff reminds us of the disinheritance of women's writings in philosophy, as well as the loss of male and female *intellectual autonomy*. Is the public forgetting the past and its lessons? Are we becoming uninterested in the hard work of self-education, in learning and in debating new ideas crafted by individual authors in solitude and in dialogue? If yes, then this has huge implications for the future of philosophy in general and for women in philosophy, in particular; but those implications are also grave for a global world which too often fails, even to try, to make sense of things.

In the end, I urge us to learn with Le Dœuff as an author, a reader of the history of philosophy and – most of all – a friend in dialogue. Is she asking us how reason, truth, study, interior and exterior freedoms might keep philosophy and us alive? Le Dœuff herself is brought into being as a writer, a philosopher and a feminist, by her formal education in France, but also by way of autodidacticism.[61] In learning from Le Dœuff's highly significant accounts of freedom and of knowledge, consider that 'There is no better way to represent access to knowledge as the exercise of a natural right whose strength comes from within than to make self-instruction central to the process.' Le Dœuff's critical method of dialogue in the present book is 'consonant with this idea' of self-instruction leading to knowledge.[62] However, the message of this Introduction is that we need both to cultivate a special, critical relationship to philosophical texts by both women and men and to engage in dialogues with philosophers in solitude and in company. Thus, *In Dialogue* directs Le Dœuff's readers to her philosophical skills and textual tools, in order to both recognize and eradicate the significant social barriers which continue to prohibit a woman's own knowledge and authority in philosophy from becoming public. In response, and with Le Dœuff, we can rightly insist upon active dialogue and self-education in relation to philosophical texts and to one another.

Notes

1 The meaning of 'virtual' in this sentence derives from the philosophy of the early-twentieth-century French philosopher Henri Bergson: virtual refers to a dynamic present which is always becoming past as it 'gnaws into the future' (Henri Bergson, *Creative Evolution*, translated by Arthur Mitchell (Mineola: Dover Publications, 1998), p. 4). For Bergson, virtual is real but not actual; what is virtual is always becoming. In turn, this dynamic conception of past present-future shapes Bergson's conception of life as a continuous – virtual and actual – process. I describe Michèle Le Dœuff's dialogues as 'virtual', in order to make the point that her (past-present-future) ideas are created and retained in collective memory, from where they can always be revitalized in actual time, that is, revitalized in dialogue for a shared future in philosophy. Giving this distinctive philosophical

role to dialogue depends on conceiving the life of ideas as a free, Bergsonian process (i.e. not static or atomistic ideas). For further background on Le Dœuff's reading of Bergson, see Pamela Sue Anderson, 'Se réorienter dans la liberté (bergsonienne), l'amitié et le féminisme' ['Reorienting ourselves in Bergsonian freedom, friendship and feminism'], in Audrey Lasserre and Jean-Louis Jeannelle (eds), *Se Réorienter dans La Pensée : Femmes, Philosophie et Arts, Autour de Michèle Le Doeuff* (Rennes: Presses Universitaires de Rennes, « Archives du féminisme » 2020).

2   The emphasis here is on 'differences' in the plural: our unique singularity allows for our 'graceful' or 'joyful' differences. Yet bear in mind that Le Dœuff is not a feminist of sexual difference (though she celebrates all of our individual differences), see Michèle Le Dœuff, *L'Étude et le rouet: des femmes, de la philosophie, etc.* (Paris: Éditions du Seuil, 1989); *Hipparchia's Choice: An Essay Concerning Women, Philosophy, etc.* translated by Trista Selous (Oxford: Basil Blackwell, 1991; second edition, New York: Columbia University Press, 2007), pp. 224–7f. For my own criticisms of sexual difference feminism, in rejecting Luce Irigaray's proposal 'to become divine women', along with my own alternative proposal to follow Le Dœuff, in 'Not a Goddess, She!', see Pamela Sue Anderson, 'Transcendence and Feminist Philosophy', in *Women and the Divine: Touching Transcendence*, edited by Gillian Howie and J'annine Jobling (New York and London: Palgrave Macmillan, 2009), pp. 27–54, especially 34n8–9.

3   Charles Taylor captures the dialogical nature of the social self with these words: 'we define our identity always in dialogue with, sometimes in struggle against, the things our significant others want to see in us', see Charles Taylor, *Multiculturalism: Examining the Politics of Recognition*, edited and introduced by Amy Gutmann (Princeton: Princeton University Press, 1994), pp. 32–3.

4   For the meaning of 'virtual', see footnote 1.

5   See *The Philosophical Imaginary*, Preface, and 'Irons-nous jouer dans l'île?' In *Écrits pour Vladimir Jankélévitch*, Paris: Flammarion 1978.

6   While 'an autodidact' is a name for someone who is self-taught, Le Dœuff takes autodidacticism to name a doctrine of learning philosophy for oneself, see Michèle Le Dœuff, *The Sex of Knowing*, translated by Kathryn Hamer and Lorraine Code (London and New York: Routledge, 2003), pp. 34–6. In contrast, a pejorative caricature of an autodidact is created by Jean-Paul Sartre in his philosophical novel, *Nausea*, translated by Robert Baldick (original French text 1938), with an Introduction by James Wood (2000). London: Penguin Books, 1965; 2000, especially pp. 13–14, 54–7, 150–77. Wood describes Sartre's autodidact as 'a soft-headed humanist' (ix) who is made to look foolish by learning or gaining knowledge only from a superficial reading of library books in alphabetical order.

7   For my reflection on a fragment of Le Dœuff's philosophy as autobiography – that is her own 'primal scene' in her education as a woman philosopher in twentieth-

century France – see Pamela Sue Anderson, 'Michèle Le Dœuff's "Primal Scene": Prohibition and Confidence in the Education of a Woman', *Text Matters: A Journal of Literature, Theory and Culture* 1 (2011): 11–26.

8 Le Dœuff, *Hipparchia's Choice*, pp. 33–4.
9 Michèle Le Dœuff, 'Mini-course Abstract', Essex University, 11–13 May 2016; https://www.essex.ac.uk/philosophy/news and seminars/minicourses/.
10 Le Dœuff, *Hipparchia's Choice*, p. 29.
11 Ibid., p. 28.
12 Michèle Le Dœuff's interest in Gabrielle Suchon appears in at least three major pieces of work, namely *Hipparchia's Choice*, *The Sex of Knowing* and 'Women in Dialogue and in Solitude', a Cassal Lecture delivered at the University of London in 2004 and published in the *Journal of Romance Studies* 5, no. 2 (summer 2005).
13 Le Dœuff, *Hipparchia's Choice*, p. 33.
14 Ibid., p. 34.
15 Michèle Le Dœuff, 'Women in Dialogue and in Solitude', *Journal of Romance Studies* 5, no. 2 (Summer 2005): 27–54, cf. Pamela Sue Anderson, 'A Joyful Dialogue with Spinoza and others: Le Doeuff, Deleuze, and the Ethics', *Paragraph: A Journal of Modern Critical Theory* 37, no. 3 (November 2014), chapters 6 and 12 of this volume.
16 Towards a new philosophical imaginary, a keynote lecture presented by Michèle Le Dœuff at the SWIP conference held at All Souls (Oxford) 2014.
17 Meryl Altman, 'Waiting for Lady Reason', Review of The Sex of Knowing by Michèle Le Dœuff, *The Women's Review of Books*, November 2004, 22, no. 2 pp. 14–5.
18 Le Dœuff, 'Women in Dialogue and in Solitude'.
19 Le Dœuff, *Hipparchia's Choice*, pp. 142–8.
20 Ibid., pp. 142–8.
21 For this translation of Deleuze's 24 June 1989 letter, see 'Epilogue (2006)', in *Hipparchia's Choice*, second edition, p. 319.
22 Ibid., p. 319.
23 Anderson, 'A Joyful Dialogue with Spinoza and Others: Le Doeuff, Deleuze and the Ethics', 341–55, chapter 12 of this volume.
24 Raoul Mortley, *French Philosophers in Conversation* (London and New York: Routledge, 1991), p. 83. Note that Le Dœuff's supervisor Vladimir Jankélévitch might have, nevertheless, indirectly influenced Le Dœuff's Bergsonian-like conception of 'virtual' which was proposed above, sec footnote 1, but also for Jankélévitch's account of Bergson's debt to Spinoza's understanding of 'joy' (again, Le Dœuff might have drawn more from Bergson than at first apparent), see Vladimir Jankélévitch, *Henri Bergson*, translated by Nils F. Schott, edited by Alexandre LeFebvre and Nils F. Schott (London: Duke University Press, 2015), pp. 204–10.

As for the influence of Gilles Deleuze, Le Dœuff's own expression of an intellectual joy owes much to Deleuze's appropriation of freedom and joy from the seventeenth-century philosophy of Spinoza, see Gilles Deleuze, *Spinoza: Philosophie pratique* (Paris: Presses Universitaires de France, 1970); *Spinoza: A Practical Philosophy*, translated by Robert Hurley (San Francisco: City Lights Books, 1988). For a reference to Deleuze's own expression of joy, see footnote 21 (above).

25 For an argument concerning the construction of the label 'French Feminism' in the mid-1970s in the United States, see Claire Moses, 'Made in America: "French Feminism" in the United States Academic Discourse', *Australian Feminist Studies* 11, no. 23 (1996): 17–31.

26 Anderson, 'Transcendence and Feminist Philosophy', pp. 27–54. Le Dœuff must be clearly distinguished from all of those contemporary feminists who define themselves in terms of sexual difference, female subjectivity and becoming divine (women); she also has a distinctiveness, which resists being lumped together with a feminism of formal equality. For her own early subversive criticism of a feminism of sexual difference, as well as a feminism of formal equality, see Le Dœuff, *Hipparchia's Choice*, pp. 222–30. For a discussion concerning the controversy surrounding the term, 'French feminism', in feminist debates on religion, in particular, see 'Introduction', Morny Joy, Kathleen O'Grady and Judith L. Poxon (eds), *French Feminists on Religion: A Reader* (London and New York: Routledge, 2002), 1–10. For further critical discussion concerning the idea of 'becoming divine', see Judith L. Pozon, 'Corporeality and Divinity: Irigaray and the Problem of the Ideal', in *Religion in French Feminist Thought: Critical Perspectives*, edited by Morny Joy, Kathleen O'Grady, and Judith L. Poxon (London and New York: Routledge, 2003), pp. 41–50.

27 Le Dœuff, 'Not a Goddess, She!', Weidenfeld Lecture, University of Oxford, 2006.

28 See pages below. For criticism of lumping the three 'French' feminists Luce Irigaray, Hélène Cixous and Julia Kristeva, or 'the holy Trinity', under one label, see Kelly Oliver, 'Importing "The French Feminists" and Their Desires', in *Reading Kristeva: Unravelling the Double-Bind* (Indiana University Press, 1993), pp. 163–80.

29 Altman, op. cit.

30 According to Marguerite La Caze, this has been the case in Australia where *The Sex of Knowing* has been energetically received by the Australian Society of Continental Philosophy (8–10 December 2004 – cf. Marguerite La Caze, personal email correspondence, November–December, 2004).

31 cf. Deutscher, *Hypatia* (2000): 241.

32 Michèle Le Dœuff, 'Actrice sociale', *l'émilie*, décembre–janvier 2004–2005, 6.

33 Le Dœuff's own definition of a philosopher is someone who does not allow anyone to think in her place; she is an autonomous thinker. But this is basically Le Dœuff's definition of a feminist, too. See Le Dœuff, *Hipparchia's Choice*, pp. 10–11, 16–17 and 24–9.

34 For references to Le Dœuff's conception of a collectivity of autonomous women thinkers each in her own historical context, see Michèle Le Dœuff, 'Cheveux

longs, idées courtes'. Recherches sur l'imaginaire philosophique (Paris: Payot, 1980); translated by Colin Gordon 'Long Hair, Short Ideas', in Michèle Le Dœuff, *The Philosophical Imaginary*, (London: The Athlone Press, 1989; Stanford: Stanford University Press, 1990; London: Continuum, 2002), pp. 100–28. Also, *Hipparchia's Choice*, especially pp. 126–8.

Other useful sources include her own entry and the entry on 'Le Dœuff', in Edward Craig (ed.), *The Routledge Encyclopedia of Philosophy* (London and New York: Routledge, 1998; hard copy and online); *The Australasian Journal of French Studies*, the special issue, 'Autour de Michèle Le Doeuff' XL, no. 3 (September–December 2003) and 'Le Doeuff', in *Encyclopedia of Modern French Thought*, edited by Charles John Murray (New York: Routledge, 2005).

35 In the summer of 1976 in preparation for a seminar which she was to teach at Fontenay, Le Dœuff wrote '*Cheveux longs, idées courtes*' and the manuscript was circulated among her students, friends and colleagues. However, Le Dœuff herself was initially unaware of the life which her approach in this essay was to take on, and this fairly quickly. In the hands of *Radical Philosophy* editors, the text was prepared for an English translation (by Debbie Pope) and for publication; Le Dœuff was quite surprised when told that proofs were ready, and would she come over to Oxford to check the translation as she and the editors read these proofs together? She did and, as a result, when she presented an abridged version of it as a keynote at the *Radical Philosophy* conference, University of Bristol, May 1977, the printed version was available, fresh from the press: 'Women and Philosophy', *Radical Philosophy* 17 (summer 1977): 2–11. It continued to be reprinted, see Michèle Le Dœuff, 'Women and Philosophy', *French Feminist Thought*, edited by in Toril Moi (Oxford: Blackwell, 1987), pp. 181–209 and 'Long Hair, Short Ideas', pp. 100–28 et passim.

36 Le Dœuff, 'Long Hair, Short Ideas', pp. 100–28 and *Hipparchia's Choice*, pp. 59–60, 162–5. For the contemporary relevance of this complex, in the field of philosophy of religion today, see Pamela Sue Anderson, *A Feminist Philosophy of Religion: The Rationality and Myths of Religious Belief* (Oxford: Blackwell, 1998), pp. 50–2, 64n59, 223, 237–8.

37 Women philosophers and others who struggle with the question of 'the erotic' and their role as women thinkers might also consider Le Dœuff's account of the desire for knowledge. Le Dœuff argues with the support of Gabrielle Suchon that a woman's desire to know has been falsely connected with 'original sin'. Le Dœuff points out that women thinkers today should recognize, as Suchon did in the seventeenth century, that the sin described in Genesis is 'laziness', not desire. Adam and Eve's, our first fore-parents, sin lies in their failure to seek knowledge by way of their own thinking and reflection. Instead, they take an easy path by simply picking and eating an apple – to try to have ready-made knowledge; cf. Le Dœuff, *The Sex of Knowing*, pp. 31–9.

38 Le Dœuff, 'Women in Dialogue and in Solitude', cf. Le Dœuff, 'Long Hair, Short Ideas', pp. 100–28; *Hipparchia's Choice*, 2007, pp. 33–4.
39 Le Dœuff, *Hipparchia's Choice*, p. 33.
40 Le Dœuff, 'Women in Dialogue and in Solitude', Ibid.
41 Ibid.
42 This leads some of us to ask for more examples of how moving outside the tradition might enable more sustained, feminist rereadings of such traditional philosophers as Descartes, Rousseau and Spinoza. Le Dœuff's Cassal Lecture, 'Women in Dialogue and in Solitude', illustrates the move outside the tradition's rather exclusive focus on Descartes with a reading of his near contemporary Gabrielle Suchon (see Le Dœuff, 'Women in Dialogue and in Solitude'). Now, in the light of Suchon, what about a new (feminist) reading of Descartes? Or Rousseau? A new reading which women and men in philosophy could discuss would seem appropriate to add to Le Dœuff's contributions to the history of philosophy.
43 Le Dœuff, *Hipparchia's Choice*, pp. 198–207.
44 Ibid., p. 206; Le Dœuff, *The Sex of Knowing*, pp. 13–14, 17, 33–49, 54–5, 62, 162, 175, 222n16, 224–225ns54–65.
45 See Dialogues with Deutscher, Björk, Anderson and Dhanda, pp. below.
46 See Michèle Le Dœuff in dialogue with Ulrika Björk, *Australian Journal of French Studies* XL, no. 3 (September–December 2003): 354. See below p. 71.
47 Michèle Le Dœuff, *Le Sexe du savoir* (Paris: Aubier, 1998), pp. 355n13, n20; *The Sex of Knowing*, pp. 222n16, 224–225n54–65.
48 Ibid., p. 75f; p. 36f.
49 Pamela Sue Anderson, *Re-visioning Gender in Philosophy of Religion: Reason, Love and Epistemic Locatedness* (Aldershot: Ashgate Publishing, 2012), chapter 1.
50 Ibid., pp. 16 and 17.
51 Gilles Deleuze offers praise along with his warm support of Le Dœuff's philosophy – and in particular, her creation of a conceptual persona, and I might suggest her conception of the individual and the collective.
52 David Norbrook, 'Autonomy and the Republic of Letters: Michèle Le Doeuff, Anna Maria van Schurman, and the History of Women Intellectuals', *Australian Journal of French Studies*, 'Autour de 'Michèle Le Doeuff XL, no. 3 (September–December 2003): 276; cf. Le Dœuff, *Le Sexe du savoir*, pp. 53–87.
53 See Le Dœuff, *Le Sexe du savoir*, pp. 80–2, 358n60 where she refers to Sonia Bertolini, '*Gabrielle Suchon: une écrivaine engagée pour une vie sans engagement*' (Genève: Faculte des Lettres, 1997); cf. Gabrielle Suchon, *De célibat volontaire ou la vie sans engagement* (Paris: J. et M. Guignard, 1700).
54 For her own response to this question of conceptual persona, originally raised by Gilles Deleuze's reading of *L'Etude et le rouet*, see Le Dœuff, *Le Sexe du savoir*, p. 345f; cf. La Caze, 'Michèle Le Doeuff and the Work of Philosophy', *Australian*

Journal of French Studies 'Autour de Michèle Le Doeuff' XL, no. 3 (September–December 2003): 245n4.

55 The Belgian-French psycholinguistic theorist Luce Irigaray and her followers are among the most prominent feminists of sexual difference with whom Le Dœuff simply disagrees – and this is a fundamental philosophical disagreement. Also, see footnote above.

56 Le Dœuff, *The Sex of Knowing*, pp. 8–9.

57 Ibid., pp. 33–9.

58 Gabrielle Suchon as G. S. Aristophile, pseud., *Traité de la morale et de la politique, divise en trois parties, savoir: La liberté, la science et l'autorité* . . . (Lyon: B. Vignieu, 1693), vol. 2, 7.

59 Two other key assertions, one by Le Dœuff and the other Suchon: 'the will to know did not cause the Fall, but the punishment was ignorance' (Le Dœuff, *The Sex of Knowing*, p. 34) and 'God gave us intelligence to force us to seek knowledge of things' (Suchon, *Traité de la morale et de la politique*, vol. 2, 7).

60 Le Dœuff, *The Sex of Knowing*, p. 34.

61 Le Dœuff, *The Sex of Knowing*, p. 36. Cf. Suchon, *Traité de la morale*, vol. 2, 23, 268.

62 Le Dœuff, *The Sex of Knowing*, p. 36. But also, on the deprivations which prohibit this freedom to know, see Ibid., pp. 36–9. Le Dœuff extends the significance of this claim to the situation of the contemporary (philosophy) student, to repeat, 'we should advise young people to add as much self-teaching as possible to the curriculum', see Anderson and Dhanda, 'Bringing Us Into Twenty-First Century Feminism', *Women's Philosophy Review*, p. 23.

Bibliography

Primary texts in French English translation

Beauvoir, Simone de. *Le deuxième sexe*. I–II. Paris: Editions Gallimard, 1949. *The Second Sex*, translated by Constance Borde and Sheila Malovany-Chevallier. London: Jonathan Cape – Random House, 2009.

Beauvoir, Simone de. *Mémoirs d'une jeune fille rangée*. Paris: Gallimard, 1958. *Memoirs of a Dutiful Daughter*, translated by James Kirkup. London: Penguin Books, 1963.

Le Dœuff, Michèle. 'Feminism Is Back in France – Or Is It?' *Hypatia: A Journal of Feminist Philosophy*, Special Issue: Contemporary French Women Philosophers, edited by Penelope Deutscher 15, no. 4 (2000): 243–55.

Le Dœuff, Michèle. 'Gabrielle Suchon', in *Routledge Encyclopedia of Philosophy*, general editor Edward Craig, 211–13. New York and London: Routledge, 1998.

Le Dœuff, Michèle. *L'Étude et le rouet: des femmes, de la philosophie, etc.* Paris: Éditions du Seuil, 1989. *Hipparchia's Choice: An Essay Concerning Women, Philosophy, etc.*, translated by Trista Selous. Oxford: Blackwell, 1991; second ed., slightly revised translation, with a new Epilogue 2006, by the author. New York: Columbia University Press, 2007.

Le Dœuff, Michèle. *Le Sexe du savoir*. Paris: Aubier 1998. *The Sex of Knowing*, translated by Kathryn Hamer and Lorraine Code. London and New York: Routledge, 2003.

Le Dœuff, Michèle. *Recherches sur l'imaginaire philosophique*. Paris: Payot, 1980. *The Philosophical Imaginary*, translated by Colin Gordon. London: The Athlone Press, 1989; and Stanford: Stanford University Press, 1990; reprinted London: Continuum, 2002.

Le Dœuff, Michéle. 'Women in Dialogue and in Solitude', *Journal of Romance Studies* 5, no. 2 (Summer 2005): 1–15.

Suchon, Gabrielle. *A Woman who Defends All the Persons of Her Sex: Selected Philosophical and Moral Writings*, edited and translated by Domna C. Stanton and Rebecca M. Wilkin. Chicago: University of Chicago Press, 2010.

Suchon, Gabrielle. *Du célibat volontaire ou la vie sans engagement*, 2 vols. Paris: J. et M. Guignard, 1700. *Du Célibat volontaire ou La vie sans engagement 1700*, Tome premier, 'Introduction' et notes de Séverine Auffret. Collection Des femmes dans l'Histoire. Paris: Indigo & coté-femmes éditions, 1994.

Suchon, Gabrielle (G. S. Aristophile, pseud.). *Traité de la morale et de la politique, divise en trois parties, savoir. La liberté, la science et l'autorité*. . . . Lyon: B. Vignieu, 1693; Part I, reprinted in Severine Auffret (ed.), *Traité de la Morale et de la Politique 1663: La Liberté*, Paris: Des femmes, 1988.

Secondary texts

Altorf, Marije. 'After Cursing the Library: Iris Murdoch and the (In)visibility of Women in Philosophy', *Hypatia* 26, no. 2 (Spring 2011): 384–402.

Anderson, Pamela Sue. *A Feminist Philosophy of Religion: The Rationality and Myths of Religious Belief*. Oxford: Blackwell, 1998.

Anderson, Pamela Sue. 'A Joyful Dialogue with Spinoza and Others: Le Doeuff, Deleuze and the Ethics', *Paragraph: A Journal of Modern Critical Theory* 37, no. 3 (November 2014): 341–55.

Australian Journal of French Studies, 'Autour de 'Michèle Le Doeuff'' XL, no. 3 (September–December 2003).

Anderson, Pamela Sue. 'An Epistemological-Ethical Approach to Philosophy of Religion: Learning to Listen', in *Feminist Philosophy of Religion: Critical Readings*, edited by Pamela Sue Anderson and Beverley Clack. London: Routledge, 2004, 90–102.

Anderson, Pamela Sue. 'Michèle Le Doeuff's "Primal Scene": Prohibition and Confidence in the Education of a Woman', *Text Matters: A Journal of Literature, Theory and Culture* 1 (2011): 11–26.

Anderson, Pamela Sue. *Re-visioning Gender in Philosophy of Religion: Reason, Love and Epistemic Locatedness*. Farnham, Surrey: Ashgate Publishing, 2012.

Anderson, Pamela Sue. 'Transcendence and Feminist Philosophy', in *Women and the Divine: Touching Transcendence*, edited by Gillian Howie and J'annine Jobling, 27–54. New York and London: Palgrave/Macmillan, 2009.

Deutscher, Max (ed.). *Michèle Le Doeuff: Operative Philosophy and Imaginary Practice*. New York: Humanity Books, 2000.

Kail, Michel. 'Une philosophie à l'oeuvre', *Les temps modernes*, juin–juillet 2002, 144–62.

La Caze, Marguerite. *The Analytic Imaginary*. New York: Cornell University Press, 2002.

1

On feminist discourse
Michèle Le Dœuff interviewed by Tetsuji Yamamoto and Nobuko Miyoshi

Your work on women's philosophy is very rare and precious. As for philosophers in France, in the past there were Simone Weil, Simone de Beauvoir and today, there is you. Speaking in general, what would you say about philosophy by women; what are essentially the differences compared to philosophy by men?

MLD: Permit me, instead, to explain how you can end up asking the question concerning women and philosophy or how such a question could stand out to me. As a young assistant professor of philosophy, I was astonished to see that the community did not show congeniality towards women, and that the equality of women and men in philosophy was not at all a *fait accompli*. In preoccupying myself with this aspect of the question, I was led to raise diverse problems touching the discipline, and you can find some of them in a piece written in 1976, 'Women and Philosophy'.[1] But it was still the 1970s, the epoch when French women launched a large political movement which was not necessarily or solely intellectual. Just think that the major practical objective was to fight for access to reproductive rights, as we say today – that is to say contraception and the possibility of recourse to abortion. This movement also took charge of challenging domestic violence. It was the first time, in France, that marital violence was named as such, criticized as such and exposed to the public for the scandal it is. In this very active movement, we were not only intellectuals. There were women of every social milieu and of every level of education. For me the

---

This interview took place in Paris, France, 17 September 1997, and was published as Michèle Le Dœuff, 'Du discours féminin', in *Philosophical Designs for a Socio-Cultural Transformation: Beyond Violence and the Modern Era*, edited by Tetsuji Yamamoto (Printed in Japan for ISLA, Philosophical Designs for a Socio-Cultural Transformation, E.H.E.S.C, 1998), pp. 369–78. Translated and revised by Kate Kirkpatrick, Pamela Sue Anderson, and Michèle Le Dœuff.

story started like this, with two – frankly, fairly separate – dimensions. During the week, I tried (among other things) to understand why philosophy didn't seem open to women, as it should be. Then came Saturday – militant, mass movement Saturday – when I went to demonstrations and meetings, when I mixed with women from milieux other than my own, when I learned an enormous amount.

Uniting these two aspects was far from easy. And yet, it should be possible both to treat problems linked to the status of women in philosophy – analyse the masculinism of Sartre, Montesquieu or Rousseau; retrieve women philosophers of times past and see what these grandmothers thought – *and* to find a larger perspective. This latter could give a theoretical form to the indignation which was ours vis-à-vis domestic violence, sexual harassment at work or the injustices to which women are subjected and which always have an element of violence. It is never pure, cold injustice to which we are subjected; there is always an element of aggression or violence. This is what I tried to do in *Hipparchia's Choice: An Essay Concerning Women, Philosophy, etc.*: to find a form of thought which reflects the malaise of women in traditional styles of intellectual interaction and which could make apparent the moral and political questions that are important for all women.

What is the status of women in philosophy?

MLD: The typical status is to be excluded or else to be the admirer/lover of a philosopher who expects to be great or already entertains delusions of grandeur. But you must differentiate a bit between periods of philosophy. Greek antiquity seems to have been less closed off to women than subsequent periods. Ancient philosophical sects were, in any event, marginal or set apart from society overall. These groups lived differently and accepted – in a certain manner and with many nuances – that some women would join them in the enterprise. In the seventeenth century, Gilles Ménage wrote a book that compiled the bulk of the evidence (or the legend) about these women philosophers of antiquity. Unfortunately, only some small fragments from or about them were extant. My favourite is Hipparchia: criticized by an imbecile who accused her, as a philosopher, of neglecting her housework she responded, 'I have devoted to study all of the time which, according to my sex, I should have lost at the wheel.'

The last of the women philosophers of antiquity was called Hypatia. Very brilliant, she taught mathematics and Neoplatonist philosophy in Alexandria at the beginning of the fifth century AD. She was assassinated on the order of the bishop of the city, who would not put up with a woman shining in philosophy or being a teacher. He sent his monks to assassinate her (I will spare you the details of the cruelty they showed her). I interpret this as the mark or symptom of the historical tragedy it was, and still is, for women in Christianity, or rather in a certain form of Christianity, understanding that there may be others. This form of Christianity hardly recognized the distinction between religious and civil life; it was the monastic type of Christian life, that is to say, centred on communities of supposedly chaste men living in brotherhood and locked away in monasteries which were beginning to monopolize the transmission of knowledge or the instruction of the young, while pagan antiquity continued to consider the transmission of knowledge in schools or in the family. That a woman thought for herself and taught publicly was something intolerable, at a time when all manner of free philosophical thought, inherited from the pagan world, whether conducted by men or by women, was the object of persecution itself anyway.

Mr Yamamoto, I have read your reflections on the East and the West, and the necessity of questioning the fixed or frozen character of the duality that lies between them.[2] I think that this idea is very important, and I believe that feminist women intellectuals who find themselves living in Europe, or let us say West of something or other, have an important role to play today in the refusal of a frozen duality between 'Orient' and 'Occident', a duality which, in the West, always operates in favour of a certain western boastfulness. So you hear it said more and more that the West has always shown itself to be kind, just and liberal with respect to women, or to have recognized emancipation a long, long time ago, while the Islamic world will never liberate them, or that the East could not think of liberation, and so on and so forth. Geographically speaking, 'the Orient' is an unstable figment in the European imagination. From my point of view, this duality is false, perfectly false. I also think that if the feminist intellectuals here undertake to show how the tradition called 'Occidental' could be atrocious with respect to women – so if we are (and we are) insistently self-critical of the culture of the West – we could then begin to destroy a sentiment of cultural superiority that exists here too, in particular vis-à-vis the Islamic world. And yes self-criticism, or lucidity with respect to the faults and evils of the local culture, is the beginning of learning and tolerance and openness to other worlds. When you are self-satisfied, you clam up in a very absurd sense of superiority. A person like Hypatia must be brought out of oblivion to show how the Christian Middle Ages began with the assassination of an intelligent woman.

And in the Middle Ages?

MLD: In the Middle Ages, as far as I know the only woman who was really initiated in philosophy was Héloise, whereas when at last you reach the fifteenth century, and the Renaissance, you find a nice collection of women initiated into the world of letters and philosophy. Thus Christine de Pizan, who wrote the marvellous *City of Ladies*, which is a little like a feminine version of Plato's *Republic*. Currently, I am very interested in a woman of the seventeenth century, Gabrielle Suchon. She lived in a small city in Burgundy, and she wrote two books: *A Treatise on Morality and Politics* and *On Voluntary Single Life* [or, 'The Celibate Life Freely Chosen'].[3] The argument of this second book is that, at the time of writing, there were only two possible situations for a woman: marriage or the convent. Suchon argues that there should be a third, for women who have neither the vocation for the cloister nor for marriage, to be single within normal civil life. And quite right, too! Convent life was a terrible privation of liberty, and marriage was equally terrible: a woman must obey her husband; when the husband is reasonable, the simple fact of having to obey is still painful, but, what is more, how many women have a reasonable husband? On the other hand, voluntary singleness (celibacy freely chosen), which can agree with those who have no inclination for marriage or the convent, could be a good thing for women and also for society. Because, single women potentially represent great wealth for society, as they are likely to take charge of a long list of significant social activities. And singleness would be a great good for women themselves, for it would represent a freedom which is also the condition of true access to knowledge. An extremely interesting philosopher, this Gabrielle Suchon, who wrote marvellous pages on 'freedom of movement and place' (*la liberté de lieu*), that is to say the right to travel and to live where you wish. But for the moment it is not easy to gain knowledge of Suchon's corpus of writings. Only certain parts of her work have been edited in French by Séverine Auffret.[4]

Do you have a complete list of women philosophers?

MLD: If you like, I can give you another woman philosopher from the first half of the seventeenth century, one Anna Maria Van Schurman, who lived in Utrecht, taking part of a group, including Voetius, Descartes, Huygens. Anna Maria was an excellent logician.

Do you think there is a fundamental difference between masculine philosophical discourse and feminine philosophical discourse?

MLD: I have already confessed my lack of interest in dual perspectives and fixed dualities. I prefer not to employ the categories of 'masculine discourse' and 'feminine discourse' for the following reason: if you make use of them you posit them as radically different, or even, perhaps, as irreconcilable; and when you apply them to philosophy, you assume that philosophical discourse results from the chromosomes of a person, without reference to history, without reference to the diversity of cultures. I prefer therefore to employ the category of 'feminist discourse' – discourse conveying a body of thought that seeks the equality of the sexes, mutual respect, community and liberty for everyone – while 'misogynist discourse' is that which wants to maintain the structures of domination. We can assume that some men have tried to engage in feminist discourse, or that they could try to in the future. We can assume that women have good reason to hold or understand feminist discourse, because they have the daily experience of subjection and humiliation. Unfortunately, there are many women who condone sex domination. Occasionally, feminist discourse seems to be there as a discourse which is available but which no one takes up, whereas at other times it is a perspective thinkers of both sexes alike accept. There is clearly not a preordained official agent of feminist discourse, even if it is clearly something vital for women to consider it falls to them to take the initiative or to continue the reflection. But if you separate the sexes in respect to philosophical discourse, you may never understand why, in Plato, you can find quite respectful pages on the equality of women and men in intellectual life, access to philosophy and to the governance of the ideal city. And since today one speaks of the feminism of Pythagoras, sometimes without looking too closely, if you posit a duality of nature or substance between men's discourse and women's discourse, you'll have to imagine transsexualism! For my part, I prefer to construct my object in the following manner: there is a long philosophical tradition of male domination, that is to say a tradition assuming that the subjection of women is something normal, desirable, even something to be increased. There is another tradition which seeks to challenge it. My task is to reread the debates between these two traditions and try to describe how perverse the first one is and how insufficient the second may prove to be. History invites one to push reflection further.

Many feminists say though that Plato was not for women.

MLD: In an *oeuvre* as vast as Plato's, you necessarily find complex things – different from one another. It is certain that the model he employed most was a practice of philosophy which took place between adult men, or between adult men and younger men; the dialogues establish an interpersonal link often charged with male homosexuality. It is very useful to be cognizant of this, because in the ordinary life of universities or places of research, this aspect is far from being obsolete. Nevertheless, you can also take into account the more utopian Platonic texts in which Plato perceptibly separates himself from the social reality of his time, texts which show that, for him, in an ideal state of things, philosophy is a practice open to women as well as to men. Thus, in *The Republic*, this remark: 'You mustn't think that in what I have been saying I have had men in mind any more than women – those of them born with the right natural abilities.'[5] Access to philosophy and to functions of government is the matter he addresses here. Certain commentators pay particular attention to a passage from *The Apology of Socrates*, which describes the 'unimaginable happiness' there may be in practising philosophical debate in Hades, to speak and argue with 'thousands of men and women'. In real life, in Athens, you could not philosophize in the street with women, these commentators claim, because women scarcely had the right to be outside. Whereas philosophy took place outdoors, on the Agora, the public square, in the market, while walking or feasting – banquets being clearly part of public life too. As a result, unless you read this location of philosophical dialogue as a ruse to buttress a deliberate exclusion of women from the space of philosophizing, based on social norms, one can consider that the absence of women from debates was, according to Socrates, something contingent.

Feminism today is no longer that of the 1970s. What would you say about current French feminism? Are you satisfied with it? In Japan, for example, I know of a group of intellectual women who created their group because each had left a job after getting married and then found it difficult to work again. In Paris, there is an organization for Japanese women, but the impression is of no longer having a very clear idea of where we stand.

You are right, but the intellectual women of my generation who were active during the 1970s will always retain some nostalgia for that time. We have lost the excellent togetherness with women of other social milieux. For me at least, this constituted a most precious aspect of the 1970s: the dialogue with some women who had not done university degrees was both possible and great; within militant groups, we found knowledge and reflection that none of our studies had prepared us to acquire – issues about which a woman who had only completed some academic studies had no idea . . .

Today apparently, but only apparently, the debate is limited to intellectual women. That, I am glad to say, is not always true. It does not take much for more vast and open meetings to exist. In 1989, I organized a conference at the Sorbonne to celebrate the fortieth anniversary of the publication of *Le deuxième sexe* with a few friends from Family Planning and other associations, without a budget, neither subsidy nor a large amount of publicity. We had distributed some flyers in the streets, and I had just managed to have it announced on a radio programme two days before – but when it took place the auditorium was packed with a perfectly diverse audience.

One constantly feels that very little would be enough for a large movement to get off the ground again, in one year, in ten years. Moreover, feminism today continues to exist in the social movement of organizations involved in addressing practical issues and endeavouring as best as they can to dialogue with various governing bodies. What militant associations have lost is the visibility in, and access to, the media. And they would have access to the media, if a big feminist movement was visible, for example, in the streets.

Through the loss of contacts which feminist intellectuals and activists used to have with and within a mass movement, we also lost something like the historical and political point of reference given by it and held in common. As a result, we are somewhat unstable and scattered. What sort of issues or points should our speech take up as essential today? Or rather, what are the points which are trying to emerge among women's consciousness and lives, and which are seeking a way into our speech? What is still failing to be properly heard and taken into account? Perhaps we are in an in-between, in which case intellectuals' main responsibility is to continue to work and to propose some ideas or reflections, and – quite important in my view! – good portions of knowledge, all in all, to produce a culture which the next wave of feminism will take up or leave aside. At any rate, while carrying on thinking for oneself and for the audience we still do have, we may have ambition to help younger women (and women who are not our younger sisters) to develop stronger and well-furnished minds.

You mentioned that a group of Japanese women found it a problem not to be able to carry on working when married or, later on, to resume work. In France, I have heard of a similar project, run by the Ministry of Social Affairs, which was called '*Retravailler*'. Women who stop being employed for fifteen years (while bringing up their children) have then to relearn all the basic habits. Through this programme, the State helped them to retrain into a structured routine.[6] Now, from a more general point of view, there ought to be a consensus today about the fact that women are keen on maintaining their economic independence and their place within the public sphere of work. But, whereas many women do value independence and economic independence in the first place, this is far from being self-obvious to many men. Some men understand and some don't want to hear about it. As it were, automatic mental resistances release themselves in an astonishing way – not just words, not a single line of argument, but like the springing up of fright. When my institution became co-ed and my first male students arrived, I was astonished to see how this mechanism functioned, and this even with the nicest of them. It was enough to state that sex inequality in the labour market is a real issue, to unleash an emotional reaction, which sent shivers down their spines. 'But you don't dispute the right of women to be mothers at home, do you?' We are not at the level of reasoning here, but rather at the level of association of ideas, which made them assume that the fundamental right of women is to be 'mothers at home'. As if any right granted to women could prove a threat to their own mums' right to have been a mother completely available to them. By the way, if some young men assume that having had a 'mother at home' is what propelled them into success, they are apparently wrong. Statistics seem to show that 75 per cent of male or female students admitted into French top-level *Grandes écoles* had mothers with a job.[7]

If some young men, charming, intelligent and embarking on the beautiful study of philosophy, can prove to be closed to reasoning on certain topics, although not on all topics, perhaps we could formulate one line of questioning: What is it that many male politicians do not understand? What is it that the classical men philosophers failed to understand? And so on. This might not be the most direct way to reply to your question about a difference between men's philosophical discourse and women's philosophical discourse, but it is a way.

In your opinion, what is the current meaning of Simone de Beauvoir?

MLD: She speaks directly to younger generations. High school girls, and without necessarily being told to by their teachers, read on their own initiative – as a book for them, which touches them – Simone de Beauvoir's *Memoirs of a Dutiful Daughter*.[8] In this they are demonstrating their literary taste, since it is the book in which Beauvoir invested most. It is carefully and deliberately written as a monument to the girl she was and no longer is. And one can understand that this book, in which Beauvoir describes her childhood in a narrow-minded and traditional petit bourgeois milieu, and her own liberation from it, how she found a life of her own, may well capture the attention of today's young women. It is the story of a journey, and every young woman has a journey of this kind to complete.

As for *The Second Sex*, it is more important than ever for theoretical debates. Beauvoir did not presuppose that there is an essence of woman or a substance that is woman. One is not born, but becomes, a woman.⁹ This has been on the agenda for years, in terms of intellectual debates, to question the wave of essentialism that dominates today.

Currently Michelle Perrot works on the history of women, Hélène Cixous, Luce Irigaray and Julia Kristeva on écriture féminine: What do you think of their work?

MLD: There is, between Hélène Cixous, Luce Irigaray, Julia Kristeva and me, a discrepancy of training. Their training was literary and psychoanalytic, and in fact they belong to a certain tradition of literary exegesis in France, a school which has always sought to make links between literature and psychology, or, for those at the end of the second half of the twentieth century, between literature and psychoanalysis.

As for me, I was trained in philosophy, and perhaps more still by my engagement with activist associations, so the questions I am interested in are different. The project of systematically searching for a 'feminine writing' in the work of women, even if such an idea may work for certain texts, is not at all applicable to what interests me: there are works by women which completely rule out the idea of a '*écriture feminine*', and they must also be taken into consideration, especially when they tell us important things. If you read women philosophers you will not find a desire to cultivate that which could pass for feminine writing, a notion which itself does not make much sense when women before the eighteenth century are in view. Gabrielle Suchon, whom I mentioned earlier, had another concern in mind: she called for solid style, rigorous argument – as opposed to the glittering, the pompous, the delicate. Indeed, she left aside 'the politeness of speech' recommended to all men and women by '*les maîtres de l'élégance française*', the Academie Française. Mary Wollstonecraft, a century later, declared that she refused to bother polishing her phrases with politeness and writing prettily like a woman. These two women philosophers seem to have seen in questions of style a straitjacket from which it was necessary to be free. As for Anna Maria Van Schurman, she presented her thought as a 'logical exercise', in the form of syllogisms. She therefore chose a very restrictive form, to arrive at a conclusion she hoped would be binding for reasonable minds, namely that parents must educate their daughters. Here are three women who tried to think of enlarging the possibilities offered to women, without bothering about pleasing.

You speak of 'masculinist philosophy'[10] and of violence. There would then be multiple forms of violence expressed in masculinist discourse. In your opinion, can these forms of violence be overcome?

MLD: I certainly hope so. If not, what is the good of working towards that end? Textual violence is a question which has not yet been completely explored, taken as the destruction or incitement to destruction of the other, possibly of this other person who is the reader. It is not so much that the text expresses violence, but that it sets itself up as an act of violence when aimed at a woman reader.[11] Christine de Pizan described this very well in *The Book of the City of Ladies* (1405),[12] where she puts herself in the same situation, reading by chance a little book by Matheolus (an author who was already obscure at the time and all but forgotten today).[13] His is a nasty book, alleging that women are unworthy beings, and so on. Now Christine lets herself become engulfed in sadness, remembering that practically all celebrated authors speak, in one manner or another, evil of women. Very fortunately, Lady Reason intervenes, and says to her, 'Christine, what have you done with your sense?', showing her that she has all the reasons in the world to know that what she had read was neither true nor honourable. I think this is an apt description. Even when one knows the author is not honourable, and one is able to know that what he says is untrue, there is nevertheless an effect on one's subjectivity, when nasty comments are made with respect to women in general, demoralizing or even destroying the person to the point where she can no longer judge sanely or clearly. Violence is often calculated and designated to break the person's capacities for resistance or expression, inhibiting her judgement even to the point of preventing her from knowing it to be violence as such.

A phone call arrives at a domestic violence hotline. 'I am calling because . . . my husband, no, he's not violent, but I am worried because I wonder whether he could become so. Last night, I told him I didn't want to make love, then he went to look for a knife in the kitchen, he put it up to my throat and forced me to make love like that. So I thought that he is in danger of becoming violent.' This woman didn't recognize violence as violence, even though she was a victim, because it is forbidden to women to judge men and to have a critical opinion of them. This sort of paralysis of judgement is cultural, but I suppose that one would find it, in diverse forms, in many cultures. I think there is a vicious circle of violence, the end of which is to inculcate an acritical attitude or the prohibition of response. When this attitude is interiorized, then acts of violence themselves become invisible. In any case, any act or discourse which posits the other as incapable of response, or of analysing what one does to her/him or what one says of her/him, is of the order of violence. And this is true even in philosophy: when Sartre writes 'Slime is the revenge of the In-itself. A sickly sweet, feminine revenge . . .',[14] hence assimilating 'the feminine' with the In-itself, with sickly sweetness, with slime and with underhanded revenge, he presupposes that no one will answer back. In one fell swoop, he issues a *communiqué*[15] which he imagines cannot be contested, for example, by a woman, and he enmeshes 'the feminine' in a web of metaphors which connect it to abjection. More globally, in philosophical discourse, the subject of a seeing, of a knowing, of an action is routinely designated as masculine, while women are relegated to the side of the topic being discussed; they are seen but do not speak. Take Merleau-Ponty. He endeavours to show that the body of another is not perceived as an ordinary object; perception is inhabited by a more secret perception which accentuates the erogenous zones of the visible body, and as a result will set 'the movements of the masculine body' in motion. There you are! In this passage of *The Phenomenology of Perception* Merleau-Ponty speaks about the visible body in general, and of the perception of that body by a normal subject, and then suddenly it appears that the visible body is the body of a woman, seen and reshaped by the look of a man, according to a personal sexual schema belonging to him as the perceiving subject! What this text says is not just that the seeing subject is necessarily a man, and the seen body necessarily that of a woman, but moreover that the gaze (or seeing) (of a man on a woman's body) can legitimately refashion what it sees, to accentuate the erogenous character. A violence of seeing is legitimated here.[16]

There is, in the philosophical heritage, another aspect of violence with respect to women: patriarchal philosophers address themselves to the powers of the world, to political authorities, to the fathers of the family, to significant people in civil society. And when they thus play the counsellor, they may recommend violence, insensitivity or oppression. Thomas Aquinas, in *Summa Theologica*, writes that the father of a house must never smile at his daughter. . . . Many are the philosophers who have considered that the husband legitimately possesses a 'right to correct' his spouse; in the context of the eighteenth century, Rousseau wrote that little girls did not like learning to read and that women must be kept apart from political life: a generation later, the French Revolution took place, and its principal actors had read Rousseau. And they had read Montesquieu, who wasn't any better. I am not in the process of saying that it was philosophy that invented violence between the sexes, but that philosophy has often supported it, and that consequently philosophy is not in itself, not *ipso facto* at any rate, a good school for unlearning violence.

You asked if violence can be overcome philosophically. One may find, even in the philosophical tradition, some elements – to be sure, neither numerous nor adequate – which point towards less violence. Compare the pedagogy of attentive and patient dialogue with another, like that sketched as the Socratic ideal, to the revelationist pedagogy presented in the texts of the *Corpus Hermeticum*, which dates from the end of Antiquity. A person who supposedly knows everything appears to teach 'the truth' to someone, consistently bullying him and calling him stupid. The question of pedagogy, violent or gentle, seems to separate two types of relation to what one can call 'knowledge'. It is dogmatic knowledge, ready-made, and which has only to reveal itself to a person designated at the outset as imperfect, which calls for violent pedagogy. By contrast, you may occasionally find the idea of a gentle pedagogy, respectful of the student, but calling for activity on his or her part: this is associated with a conception of knowledge as yet to be found, as something which no one yet possesses. In Bacon, the pedagogy of scientific research, the learning of the sciences by those whose task will be to further knowledge, is presented as gentle.

I am working on Schiller and, currently, on one of his essays, 'On Grace and Dignity' (1793).[17] *According to Schiller, grace is connected to a feminine principle, dignity to a masculine principle. While men dominate, fight, oppose (others) and affirm self, grace convinces with charm, not with the will to dominate, and so on. And so, any sense of opposition disappears completely with grace. Schiller would have wished for the rule of grace, but he considered this difficult to achieve. So, he was obliged to recognize a necessary role for dignity.*

MLD: In that case, there is a book which should interest you, *Politics and Grace* by Christian Meyer, especially the pages devoted to the Greeks and grace (χαρις, *charis*). Meyer describes grace as a virtue that is necessary for politics. Now, if you connect this need for grace to the wish not to dominate others, you can create the image of politicians – both women and men – who will not seek to dominate others, which would be quite a nice change, don't you think! As for me, I would not support any drastic distinction between dignity and grace. Moreover, I would be even less likely to pin such a distinction on the duality of sexes. To defend one's dignity, while resisting the domination that other people exercise, or seek to exercise, is in no way incompatible with the idea that we can have of grace.

What are you currently writing?

I am completing a book which will have the title, *The Sex of Knowing* (*Le Sexe du savoir*).[18] The subject has proven to be more difficult than I had thought, but I am incredibly happy to be working on it.

Notes

1 Michèle Le Dœuff, 'Women and Philosophy', *Radical Philosophy* 17 (Summer 1977); later English version, 'Long Hair, Short Ideas', in *The Philosophical Imaginary*, translated by Colin Gordon (London: Continuum, 1989), pp. 100–28.
2 Tetsuiji Yamamoto, *Cho ryoiki no shiko e: Gendai purachikku-ron (Akuto sosho)* (Nihon: Edita Sukuru Shuppanbu, 1988). Tetsuiji Yamamoto, *Shohi no bunsuirei: Hito to mono no atarashii kankeigaku* (Sankosha: Shohan edition, 1990).
3 Gabrielle Suchon, *Traité de la morale et de la politique* (Lyon: Imprimé aux dépens de l'Auteur, Chez B. Vignieu, 1693); and *Du célibat voluntaire, ou La vie sans engagement* (Paris: Jean et Michel Guignard, 1700). Cf. Gabrielle Suchon, 'On the Celibate Life Freely Chosen, or Life Without Commitments', in *A Woman Who Defends All the Persons of Her Sex: Selected Philosophical and Moral Writings*, edited and translated by Domna C. Stanton and Rebecca M. Wilkin (Chicago and London: University of Chicago Press, 2010), pp. 229–300.
4 Gabrielle Suchon, *Traité de la morale et de la politique*, edited by Séverine Auffret (Paris: De Femmes 1988); *Du Célibat volontaire ou La vie sans engagement*, edited by Séverine Auffret (Paris: Indigo – Coté femmes, 1994).
5 '*Ne crois pas que ce que nous disons s'applique plutôt aux hommes qu'aux femmes.*' For English version, see Plato, *Republic*. Book, vii, 540c. Translated by Tom Griffith (Cambridge: Cambridge University Press, 2000), p. 250. Cf. Michèle Le Dœuff, *The Sex of Knowing*, translated by Kathryn Hamer and Lorraine Code (New York: Routledge, 2003), p. 221n3.
6 I am not sure it is still extant: it may well have been merged into the manifold retraining programmes for the long-term unemployed people.
7 See Actes de l'Université d'été de Lizieux des 24 et 25 août 1999, p. 63.
8 Simone de Beauvoir, *Memoirs of a Dutiful Daughter*, translated by Jame Kirkup (Harmondsworth: Penguin Books, 1963).
9 Simone de Beauvoir, *The Second Sex*, translated by Constance Borde and Sheila Malovany-Chevallier (London: Jonathan Cape, A division of Random House, 2009), p. 293. The origin of this sentence could be something in Erasmus: 'one is not born, but becomes, a human being', that is, one needs education. But one may also remember of Brillat-Savarin's remark: '*On devient cuisinier mais on naît rôtisseur*'.
10 For masculinism, see Michèle Le Dœuff, *Hipparchia's Choice: An Essay Concerning Women, Philosophy, etc.*, translated by Trista Selous (first published 1991; second edition, New York: Columbia University Press, 2007), p. 78: 'By masculinism in general, I mean the assertion of masculine dominance over the feminine.' Also, see Le Dœuff, *Hipparchia's Choice*, pp. 44–5, 78–9, 96, 97, 139, 165.
11 In French, the feminine noun *lectrice* is used, making it clear that this potential audience is female.

12 Christine de Pizan, *The Book of the City of Ladies*, translated by Rosalind Brown-Grant (Harmondsworth: Penguin Classics, 1999).
13 For more on Matheolus, see Le Dœuff, *The Sex of Knowing*, pp. 135 ff.
14 For more on the sickly sweet, feminine revenge, see Le Dœuff, *Hipparchia's Choice*, p. 80.
15 In French, the word *communiqué* is contrasted to 'dialogue', with the former having connotations of being a one-way message.
16 For more on Merleau-Ponty, see Le Dœuff, *The Sex of Knowing*, p. 79ff.
17 Friedrich Schiller, 'On Grace and Dignity', *New Thalia* 2 (July 1793), translated by George Gregory (Schiller Institute Inc., 1992) at www.schillerinstitute.org/educ/aesthetics/Schiller_On_Grace_and_Dignity.pdf.
18 Translator's note: this work was subsequently published, Michèle Le Dœuff, *Le Sexe du savoir* (Paris: Aubier, 1998); *The Sex of Knowing*, translated by Kathryn Hamer and Lorraine Code (London: Routledge, 2003).

2

On *The Second Sex*

Catherine Rodgers in dialogue with Michèle Le Dœuff

CR: In *L'Étude et le rouet* [*Hipparchia's Choice*][1] you write that reading *The Second Sex* in the 1960s helped you in two respects: to turn the unease felt in being a woman into something to be connected with an objective reality and to understand how this unease is also experienced by other women.

MLD: That's right but perhaps one could add this: when I was a student, *The Second Sex* was actually little read among my fellow students. When it was read it was more as a source of information. My friends and I would read this book to endeavour to learn, at last, something about our bodies. You must imagine a lively group of young women who had been admitted to the *École Normale Supérieure* at Fontenay, thanks to their already sound knowledge of philosophy, French literature and possibly Latin, who – for the most part – had no ideology-free understanding of the basic biology of menstruation and had never had the occasion to discuss the [biological] facts about their bodies with anyone.

At the time, there were no manuals of sex education – or hardly any, to speak of. They would indeed proliferate a little later, in the early part of the 1970s, for better and for worse, some more informative than others, some more concerned to preach traditional morality in sex life than others. But in 1966, I had never seen in any bookshops a book capable of explaining what menstruation, puberty or menopause could be. In *The Second Sex* we found factual information about [woman's] biology and, above all, a message, an extremely important one: one can speak of biological issues and also, more generally, of the facts of life including the social ones; one has the right to know about and reflect on them.

Catherine Rodgers, *Le Deuxième Sexe de Simone de Beauvoir, un héritage admiré et contesté* (Paris: L'Harmattan, 1998), pp. 233–65, translated and revised by Kate Kirkpatrick, Pamela Sue Anderson, and Michèle Le Dœuff.

CR: All the same, the perception of women's sexuality in *The Second Sex* carries the marks of amazing disgust! This disgust must have done a lot of damage at the time.

MLD: When I reread the book today with (I hope!) the eyes of an adult, it occasionally happens that I exclaim under my breath, 'Honestly! She could have done better, she could have avoided using such and such a negative term. . . .' But at the time it didn't strike us as negative. Quite simply, I did not notice the negative analyses which she sometimes put forward. I never memorized them.

CR: While the women students who attend my courses and read *The Second Sex* are immediately struck by the negative aspects of her perceptions.

MLD: That's because they already know everything *The Second Sex* had to say about the sexual processes of women's bodies, and they no longer need the symbolic permission – which the book gave – to have knowledge of things to do with sex. Whereas we were extracting information from the text, and receiving its permission to gain sexual knowledge. The negative overtones escaped us. But then, we had already internalized other representations (or images or perceptions) which were frequently even more backwards. I remember a conversation with a friend, a conversation in the course of which she said: 'And as Simone de Beauvoir has explained, menstruation corresponds to a form of disappointment for nature – the body had got ready for pregnancy and then feels it was unnecessary!' I was totally astonished. Having periods as a disappointment, and of not being pregnant? Come on!

CR: The account doesn't correspond to my reading of *The Second Sex*, either.

MLD: But that's exactly what's surprising – my friend projected onto the text a negative evaluation which cannot be found in *The Second Sex* but which some prevailing ideology had whispered to her, I suppose. But what this explains is that *The Second Sex* had the power to do us good, because we had even more negative things in our heads. And yet we also had much that was far more positive in our experience. We were a generation who, in the space of a few years, had got rid of a number of taboos. For example, we had discovered tampons and with them the ability to swim during menstruation. A cultural revolution which goes beyond what we can imagine. Just think that our mothers had told us all not even to dip our toes into the water. Some years after puberty, we knew that menstruation didn't have to hinder movement, that our mothers had inculcated superstitions worthy of the age of dinosaurs: as a generation we had a mental independence compared with the discourse of Beauvoir, and already the pride of having discovered something ourselves; we felt strong enough to be autonomous and not dependent on all of the details of a view held by a woman who was our elder. At the same time, we knew that we didn't know everything (far from it!) and therefore we plunged ourselves into *The Second Sex* to increase our knowledge, as we pleased. From this point of view, I read the book selectively. When there were things that didn't please me, it didn't bother me much – I slid over them.

CR: Do you remember what displeased you?

MLD: Not precisely; I pushed it aside so well that I can't give you a single example. I picked and chose, which, by the way, is not the worst method in the world. With regard to a text written by a woman of a former generation, two approaches are possible: the most common, sadly, consists of reading until one *finally* finds a point of disagreement and then shouting, because in fact one was looking for this, wanted to see the elder in the wrong, wanted to rediscover a reason to challenge a discourse produced by a woman. The opposite attitude, eclectic and optimistic, consists of reading everything, in gliding over weaknesses or what one doesn't like, and in retaining nothing but the positive contribution of a text. Neither of these methods can pretend to be a theoretically refined approach, even if – in a reading that presents itself as sophisticated – one can sometimes sense one or the other of these versions. It takes a lot of time to learn to read while simultaneously straining to understand how a constructive debate is possible in conversation with a work.

To return to the question of puberty: there is an obvious link between what Beauvoir says about it in *The Second Sex* and the manner in which she invokes her own puberty in *Memoirs of a Dutiful Daughter*. One could say that she lived this turning point in her life rather badly, and that we must take the intention of *The Second Sex* not so much as a theoretical attempt but as an autobiographical element, and nothing more. But, yet again, the fundamental message comes through: one can speak of puberty in general, and of hers in particular. One has the right.

CR: In *Hipparchia's Choice* you reproach her for a certain number of things which derive from her liberal, individual-centred perspective: her own construction as a unique subject, which caused her not to see certain things; not having found important women in the past or minimizing their contributions; but also the way she found it impossible to imagine a community of women, collective solutions;

the fact that she underestimated the effects of institutions of socio-legislative structures in the oppression of women, which ultimately drove her to blame – a bit too rapidly – women who, according to her, did not seize the opportunity to transcend their situation.

MLD: I criticize, indeed, certain aspects of her *oeuvre* after having reread it many times. This doesn't mean that I *reproach* her with anything. . . . Of course, if a feminist wrote today, as she did, as if she was the first woman to have reflected on the question, there would surely be reason to object. One can easily find books in a bookshop or library; this was not so much the case in her day. I do regret, for example, that in *The Second Sex* there isn't a real familiarity with Virginia Woolf, but must acknowledge she would have had a hard time getting hold of *A Room of One's Own*.

CR: She briefly mentions Virginia Woolf.

MLD: Yes, but it is not certain that she had already read her when she wrote *The Second Sex*; because what she says of her is quite vague. Years later, she was to whisper: I'm not a virtuoso like Woolf. She didn't know about the existence of Mary Wollstonecraft, but then who did in France at the time? She apparently had not heard of Marie de Gournay, though she quotes from Poulain de la Barre. One could even go so far as to say that she can be credited with the rediscovery of Poulain de la Barre. But she did not look to find women thinkers of olden times, which today constitutes one of the weaknesses of *The Second Sex*. At the same time, I try to put myself in her place: engaged in writing a book on women, in Paris, in the post-war period – that must have been a formidable challenge. There were so many taboos to overcome.

CR: Could her 'omissions' perhaps be linked to her methods of working? At the Bibliothèque Nationale, she most probably read many secondary texts which had not recorded the existence of these women.

MLD: Have you noticed the extent to which we really lack documents about her method of work? The writing of *The Second Sex* spread out over many months, but we do not have a single confidence about how she did her research, whereas her correspondence contains a lot of information about the genesis and development of several of her other works like *L'invitée*, for example. It's very strange! The book seems to have come out like Minerva, already with her helmet on.

CR: Have you arrived at an explanation for this lack of information?

MLD: No, and the genesis of the book still intrigues me. Have the letters where she speaks of it been omitted from the edition of her correspondence? Or, did she deliberately choose not to speak of it, either because it seemed preferable to keep a total intimacy with her book-to-be, or because it was difficult for her to discuss it?[2]

CR: In reading *Hipparchia's Choice* I felt that you had a lot of sympathy for Beauvoir. At the same time, the sentence which concludes the Second Notebook, which is dedicated to *The Second Sex*, seemed negative:

> 'But what exactly were you looking for in *The Second Sex*? A theory, or the voice and support of a big sister?'
>
> 'What are we looking for in any philosophical text if not the theoretical support of a forerunner. Although, of course, we may not find it'.[3]

I had the impression that you had been disappointed by *The Second Sex*.

MLD: No, although there is something in what you say, I found philosophical support in *The Second Sex*, but not such support that I could dispense with thinking for myself, which was a blessing in disguise. You know, it's important to encounter a little bit of disappointment. One doesn't have the right to expect that a book will provide precisely what one is looking for. That would be to behave in a truly tyrannical manner towards authors, to behave like a spoiled child, and this must be deemed below our dignity as readers. Or it's that one simply wants to experience infatuation, which is worse. Our dignity implies, on the contrary, that we work with disappointment; this is at least what I suggested in my first feminist essay, 'Long hair, short ideas', while trying to find out how disappointment structures the philosophical position. It is because one had hoped to find in an author something that one sought, and that, alas, one didn't completely find it there, that one is condemned to work oneself. The narratives that Socrates and Descartes each gave to their becoming-philosophers [*devenir-philosophes*] emphasized disappointment.

CR: Disappointment is therefore generative.

MLD: It brings you to push reflection further.

CR: Your conclusion was not, therefore, as negative as I thought.

MLD: It's a negativity which is dialectically positive and tremendously positive to boot! All the more so because disappointment itself is not guaranteed, either!

CR: You have written that *The Second Sex* was 'the Movement before the Movement'. Could you explain what you mean by this?

MLD: What we were to find in the Movement was the possibility of exchange, of sometimes pungent discussion, of progressing thanks to one another, of setting ourselves into motion and clarifying our ideas. Because really to understand that we found ourselves in a situation that was not of our making was in itself wonderfully liberating. Blocks of anxiety or guilt were gradually chipped away as we explored questions and frequently an analysis produced by one of us took the weight off the shoulders of others. What *The Second Sex* had brought me, before the experience of the Movement, was a similar benefit: I read the book in dialogue with its author, and I believe that those of my student friends who read it at the time also found this in it: an opening, elements of information, a fashioning, an untangling of questions, an objectifying of problems and the possibility of debating with someone. A dis-interiorization, finally, which made one feel lighter.

CR: Do you think that *The Second Sex* is the source of the Movement in France?

MLD: The Movement, I think, started without a direct connection to Beauvoir, otherwise it would have got off the ground in the 1950s, I should think![4] I must acknowledge that I did not join it until November 1971, that is, fifteen months after it emerged. Fifteen months late: I could make no claim to the title 'historic feminist',[5] which some give me, far too kindly. As a result I cannot give you a personal testimony of what happened at the very beginning. But at any rate, the Movement got under way with the famous 'happening' organized at L'Étoile in August of 1970, to show interest for an American demonstration of the same date.[6] I think, therefore, that the women's movement began under an Anglophone influence, not as a result of books, and not as a purely cultural event, but with practical aims in view from the outset. Then came Spring 1971: it was the 'Manifeste des 343'[7] that launched the Movement properly into being a mass movement. If one looks at it more closely: the majority of those who were the first driving forces, women such as Christine Delphy or Anne Zélinsky, had no special interest in the work of Beauvoir. Of course there was, from the very beginning, Delphine Seyrig[8] – a great reader of Beauvoir. Several years later I heard her recount her enthusiasm for *The Mandarins*, which she had devoured hot off the press. It was Delphine, moreover, who took responsibility for going to see Beauvoir, to ask her to sign the 'Manifeste des 343'. Simone received her with much warmth and of course gave her signature. She joined the Manifeste in April and then, in November 1971, she joined the demonstration for the right to abortion and contraception and generally made herself available for the Movement. But this is not to imply that younger women rushed to read or reread *The Second Sex*. The Movement was not very bookish in the early years; instead it was carried by activism. It was a movement which also retained a leftist reflex against stars. It also considered – and with good reason, I think – that everyone must, in the context of a collective reflection, discover that even the most simple and the most ordinary of their own experiences have worth, and that a woman can analyse them – even things like who in a couple brews the morning coffee. In the first years of the movement I don't think we had the instinct to go and look in books, nor did our fervour ignite interest in reading, in the least. That came a little later.

CR: Many of the claims in *The Second Sex* would, though, be taken up by the Movement, even if a direct link was not established.

MLD: It's not surprising; when women reflect on the condition which is imposed upon them, they see the same reality and finally come to many of the same conclusions. You know, it often happens that I discover in sixteenth-century texts things that I have thought for a long time!

CR: Françoise Picq, in *Liberation des femmes: Les Années-Mouvement*, gives two principal sources of the Movement: revolutionary thought and *The Second Sex*.

MLD: That is perhaps, at least partly, retrospective. One can certainly think that having read *The Second Sex* several years earlier prepared some of us not to refuse to address the question from the outset, not to refuse to hear it spoken of at all. But all the same, I remember a filmed interview we had in 1986, just after the burial of Beauvoir. The project was to record tributes (of her life from those who knew her well). Among those interviewed, Christine Delphy said that she had never accorded much importance to *The Second Sex* – the works of Andrée Michel had much more influence on her; Anne Zélinsky asserted that her reading of *The Second Sex* had taught her nothing, but then nothing at all – which can all the same seem quite extraordinary; Delphine Seyrig referred to *The Mandarins* above all; I, who alone defended *The Second Sex* and Liliane Kandel, too deeply in grief to speak.

CR: In your experience, *The Second Sex* was never discussed?

ML: At the beginning of the 1970s, I had never heard the name of Simone de Beauvoir pronounced as that of an author whose books were read or widely thought worth reading. Not in the Mouvement de Libération des Femmes nor at Mouvement pour la liberté de l'avortement et de la contraception. It was uttered only as the name of a famous woman, a feminist, who generously helped us. But everyone knew that she was famous because of what she had done, as a woman writer and this a generation before us – she had accomplished what we were doing in another way. And it pleased us immensely that she was *with* us.

Personally, it was around 1975 when I plunged back into her work, once the *loi Veil*[9] was voted in, in fact, a vote which lessened the intense urgency of activism. Just think that until then, we – who also had full-time jobs – had so much to do, organizing demonstrations, editing and distributing tracts, not to mention the more serious undertaking of helping women who requested abortions and organizing travel to England or Holland. In any case, when I began working on *The Second Sex* I experienced many negative reactions, not from the militants to whom I felt close, but from certain parts of the Movement, those who also said with their pens that Beauvoir was outdated. They assured me that now it was Irigaray whom one must read! It must be said that Beauvoir never took up the mantle of psychoanalysis, whereas the Paris of the 1970s was atrociously psychoanalytic. I thought her a little antiquated, but this did not bother me. When 'Long Hair, Short Ideas' appeared, in which I speak a bit about Beauvoir, but also of Héloise and Hipparchia, all three were viewed equally as archaeological references. One had to be very stubborn to get over the idea that a feminist work – whether Irigaray, Cixous or Kristeva – didn't render everything which preceded it obsolete. Far from it!

During this time, a small group formed around Beauvoir herself, for the section 'le sexisme ordinaire' in *Les Temps Modernes*. It is surely there one must look for the best intersection between the Movement and Beauvoir's thought. Otherwise, since the Movement spoke especially about abortion and contraception, and since *The Second Sex*, despite its good intentions, considered the fight had been won on these fronts, it would have been a little difficult for us to make the link.

CR: Elsewhere, in *Hipparchia's Choice*, you make reference to some incredible sentences from *The Second Sex*, where she wrote 'we have won, the battles are behind us'.

MLD: She needed to say that to herself, after having shown the extent of the damage.

CR: Do you recommend reading *The Second Sex* today?

MLD: Of course! But it is no longer necessary to recommend *The Second Sex*; it recommends itself. Many French teachers read *Memoirs of a Dutiful Daughter* with their pupils, and you hear schoolgirls say that the book touched them; they also frequently make reference to *The Second Sex*. Furthermore, it seems that young people are finding their own way to these books.

CR: *The Second Sex* is a long text, difficult to read.

MLD: Yes, and the beginning is more arduous than the end, as if Beauvoir's pen was unleashed in the process of writing, or as if she wrote the Introduction last of all, in a more synthetic mode. If the young, despite everything, find their way in *The Second Sex*, it is probably those who have already read *Memoirs of a Dutiful Daughter*. Already being familiar with the person, they find the way to approach her theoretical work.

Another thing gives me an agreeable surprise: despite the attempts of many to defame Beauvoir over the years – a campaign which aimed to discredit the person but also to disqualify her work – the young continue to read her, as if this campaign left them neither hot nor cold. Their great independence of mind continues to look for nourishment in the work of Simone.

CR: In *Hipparchia's Choice* you write that Beauvoir did not really find an original explanation for the oppression of women, and that it was this void that pushed her to produce 1,100 pages of text. You are not convinced by the 'historical' explanation she proposes, which centres around reproduction?

MLD: She says that society recognized more value in the sex that risks its life in war than the one which brings children into the world. But since she didn't develop this explanation, one suspects that she herself hardly believed it. Moreover, must one seek to give an explanation? When I wrote *Hipparchia's Choice* I thought that it was as good to float the question because hypotheses about the causes of this oppression have every chance of being mythical. Today, my opinion has changed somewhat. If one wants to transform the situation of women in this world, one must have hypotheses at least about the causes of this oppression, just as, generally speaking, in order to remedy anything you must undertake to know something about the aetiology. The question thus has an obvious practical interest. But it is possible to reason backwards, in evaluating how certain victories made by women at least in this part of the world have, little by little, undone certain aspects of oppression. We have not yet been able to measure all of the positive effects of reproductive rights, but we have begun to see that the mastery of fertility has prodigious effects on the manner in which women perceive themselves, on mother–daughter relations, on the possibility of higher education and delaying or avoiding marriage, having a job without being inadvertently trapped by a birth, leaving violent partners, posing the question of marital rape: these victories, which have undone great swathes of oppression, have offered us better understanding of how the oppression is constructed. When our great nieces have truly achieved the revolution and created perfect equality between women and men, they will know. In the meantime, our most urgent responsibility is to bring to the women in developing countries the same things that have permitted us to advance a few steps. Like contraception. But frequently we also hear about great initiatives spontaneously taken by women of the poorest areas of the world and if we are invited to back them, let us back them!

CR: The problem, if one puts pregnancy at the origin and centre of the oppression of women, is that as long as men won't get pregnant . . .[10]

MLD: But pregnancy is not the same thing if one is speaking of two or three children who were *wanted*, planned at a good time of life, in a convenient environment . . .

CR: Which doesn't really exist . . .

MLD: Which doesn't exist in a satisfactory fashion. But if the premises are there. Even the bottle, in fact, is a great invention. In any case, it is not the same thing to speak of one, two or three children, as to speak of children churned out one after the other, and of pregnancies inflicted on their mother without her having a chance to have her own say. A man's power over a woman is reduced from the instant that she can decide, and not he, the moment and the number of her pregnancies. In my adolescence, a man could inflict a pregnancy in a strategic manner, like forcing her to marry him, or one more pregnancy to force the woman to quit work, for example, and become his servant at home, or to stifle vague desires for divorce. Or a first pregnancy to cut short her studies. The absence of contraception was one of the great bolts enforcing our imprisonment.

CR: You see others?

MLD: The Christian tradition has a lot to answer for, and let me recommend reading Uta Ranke-Heinemann, *Des Eunuques pour le royaume des cieux*,[11] an exposé of the folly of theology on matters of sex and an indictment of the Catholic Church.

CR: Do you think that Beauvoir was affected by her Catholic education, for example, in her view of women's sexuality?

MLD: She certainly didn't need to encounter existentialist philosophy to have a sinister vision of women's bodies and sexuality! Before being Sartre's partner, she grew up with Catholic bourgeoisie and in a confessional school. The ideas inculcated in her about sexuality were certainly as bad as Sartre's when it comes to inspiring disgust with the body. With to boot, during her early days, the locking of the tongue: the difference between the Catholic and existentialist spheres is that in the first one hardly had the right to speak of sexuality, whereas on the existentialist side one had the right, but only to evoke the sinister. It's not much, but for her it could have represented a liberation. In the course of a childhood of holy water, she surely would have interiorized these appalling representations – think that, until very recently, women who had just given birth were regarded as impure by the Catholic Church and could not put a foot in a church before a ceremony of purification! And the law to be silent, and only silent in church ...

Besides, it is obvious that the sadomasochism of the Catholic tradition structured her childhood play. She tells the story herself – how with her sister Hélène they pretended that one was the saint who was martyred, the other, the executioner, until the point when she declared that she was dead. Cast a glance at *The Golden Legend* by Jacques de Voragine: women saints were barely good at being martyred, and a sadistic joy is expressed in the descriptions. And yet being a saint is the only ambition Catholicism had left to women, other than the pains of labour.

What is tragic in Beauvoir's history is that she was trapped between the milieu of her family and her lover, conservatism and transgression, the two sides leading to the same results and the same prohibitions. In the life of Simone, existentialism was an episode, rather than the structuring event par excellence, as I believed at the beginning.

CR: Though the analysis you made of the limits that created existentialism in the thought of Beauvoir in *The Second Sex*, and also the changes that she had to put up with quietly in the existentialism of Sartre, very much helped me to understand *The Second Sex*.

MLD: So much the better, and thank you for telling me! When I wrote *Hipparchia's Choice* I set myself a question which, because of documents, I did not manage to answer with certitude: was the philosophy from which she drew really, as she said, existentialism – one must add, that of Sartre – or wasn't it more a Hegelian vision? Since the publication of his letters to her I have seen this more clearly. In June and July 1940, she read Hegel at the Bibliothèque Nationale. At first sight, it's mind-blowing: the Germans were there, it was defeat, she was without news of Sartre and, in this collapsing universe, she goes to the Bibliothèque Nationale, and reads *The Phenomenology of Spirit*. In fact, this is understandable: in a particularly difficult moment, there is nothing like grappling with a tough philosophical text to keep the chin up – when I feel low I do the same. But what she said of Hegel provided the key I missed for understanding *The Second Sex*. That's why I added a note to the English edition of *Hipparchia's Choice*, and I came back to the question in 'Simone de Beauvoir: the ambiguities of a rallying'. In her correspondence, she inclines towards Hegel more than Sartre, because in Hegel but not in Sartre she had found the theme of conflict between consciousnesses which exist externally, outside each other, and which collide.

In 1943, if someone asked Beauvoir whether she was existentialist, she would have had no idea of what was being asked. And then later, she would give in. She had already capitulated in the Jardin du Luxembourg; she capitulated anew when she said she had accepted existentialist philosophy as an obvious fact. She was forced to accept it, until she wrote *The Second Sex*. But, if she had positioned herself as something other than existentialist, *The Second Sex* would not have had the force it did. If it was necessary to summarize the work in one sentence: when one considers the relations between the sexes, one has to be in a Hegelian universe (in which the protagonists do battle) but, *de facto*, one is in a Sartrean universe (in which one of the protagonists has won at the outset). It is the tension between these two philosophies that supports *The Second Sex*. For the question of the book is: Why therefore have women always/already lost? Why do we not revolt? And why does the dialectic of master and slave never reverse itself in relations between the sexes? Beauvoir went straight to that which, in Hegel, allowed the best way of posing the problem. This woman had great philosophical sensitivity, potentialities I believe superior to those of Sartre.

CR: In *The Second Sex*, she creates a hierarchy of values, with the activity of the warrior at the top, the fact of risking his life, and at the bottom, breeding, the care given to infants, breastfeeding. But inside existentialist philosophy, couldn't the infant be considered a project?

MLD: She says that society has recognized more value in the sex that risks its life than that which gives birth. She supposes therefore that there is a hierarchy of values respective of the two sexes, a hierarchy that society imposes as it is. It's not very existentialist. . . . As for a child being a project, see Simone de Beauvoir's *A Woman Destroyed*, including the short story, 'Age of Discretion'[12] in which the main character's son is, shall we say, making his own projects far away from what his parents had contemplated for him!

CR: But this hierarchy she adopts can be questioned – and it has been.

MLD: She didn't adopt it; she believed that it was a fact of society, which was at the origin of oppression. One can question this hierarchization, and we do this all the more so easily today because, free not to have children, we understand well that society values us when we are reluctant to give birth, but do so all the same. What is more, one must also question the separation that this hierarchy supposes. For a long time, 'to give birth' was also to risk life. It is still true, even in our time, but it is unacceptable. In another sense, it is still to risk life, even if one survives, because it is to risk the framework of her own existence. There are heroic values in maternity.

CR: In the same spirit, she condemns housework because it produces nothing, does nothing but reproduce.

MLD: I would say that Beauvoir describes housework as unappealing and non-creative. On this question, Italian women have proposed a strong, interesting analysis in recent years, which I am going to try to summarize in my own words. Up until the present, social time was seen as divided in three: time for work (viewed as productive time), time for rest and time for leisure. In such a representation, the work accomplished by women as well as what it produces was invisible, and the time dedicated to reproduction completely disappeared. Reproductive work is the making of meals to restore the strength to work from one day to the next, the ironing of blouses and shirts, and of course, the care of the future generation. All of this requires work, and therefore dedication. Time taken from the leisure of women, or from time they could have dedicated to productive work, or even from their sleep, this time necessary for reproduction had to be integrated into the standard day, for one sex and the other. As a result, social time must be recognized as counting four categories, not three. Our Italian friends propose to reduce the so-called productive working time for everyone, in order that reproductive working time can truly be taken into account, and of course, distributed evenly between the two sexes. It is one of the most interesting ideas I have come across in recent years.

CR: It allows the identification, the naming of this work which is often accomplished without recognition.

MLD: Yes. Also, up to the present, the discussion has been phrased in terms of spaces – private space, public space, the right to circulate in the streets, to travel alone. There was little reflection on time.

CR: Beauvoir shrugged these problems off quickly enough; her solution was that responsibility for reproductive work should be taken by society, which did not work well in reality.

MLD: It is an option, all the same.

CR: Nurseries?

MLD: The main thing, the scandal being that there is not the necessary quantity of places in nurseries. But even the kitchen. One of the effects of the social changes that we have brought about is that one part of reproductive work – food – is collectivized, and one can exchange money for it.

CR: Yes, pre-prepared foods.

MLD: And when, in a couple, the cooking is split half and half, the meaning of it changes. When it seems a service that one gives to the other, it is totally alienating. If two equal persons nourish each other alternately or peel the vegetables together, this can become a pleasure and a source of greater quality of life.

CR: What do you think of Beauvoir's rejection of psychoanalysis?

MLD: From the moment when Freud was introduced in France, and became popular, one could not name a single philosopher who appreciated psychoanalysis, even of the Freudian variety. Alain, Sartre, Merleau-Ponty fought it out, every man for himself. This rejection is to be interpreted as a corporate reaction, philosophers against psychoanalysts, two fields emulating each other. All the more so because French philosophy is markedly psychological. Until 1967, it was necessary to pass an exam in psychology to graduate and obtain a *licence* in philosophy. The two disciplines found themselves in rivalry because they shared a common object, the human soul such as it is in itself, and so on. When Sartre assured us that in fact it was philosophy which produces true psychoanalysis, he was standing up for his field, that's all. Beauvoir is part of this tradition. What is more, she understood well that Freud provided a new legitimation of phallocracy. She both retained and held this finding against Freud who indeed was not very progressive. She does not seem to notice the critical spirit which he sometimes showed, nor his wish to explore unknown territories, nor his capacity to question schemas. But it must be recognized that the institutionalization of psychoanalysis often drove it to degenerate into dogmatism.

CR: The dogmatism was made worse with Lacan.

MLD: Certainly! Lacan is the theologian of psychoanalysis and practically God-the-Father! In Lacan's work before the war, one certainly could still find a quest. But the Lacan of the age of his celebrity is completely closed, and disastrous concerning the relation of the sexes. The section of the Movement which annoyed me most were the Lacanians, who held they should place themselves, and we should all place ourselves, under the aegis of a father, in order to redeem ourselves, perhaps?

CR: You don't claim to draw your inspiration from anyone?

MLD: I draw inspiration from numerous readings, but no one in particular. In the 1970s, when I began to write about feminist theory, I was frequently asked: 'Oh? Feminist, but from what point of view? Lacanian, Derridian, Althusserian, Foucauldian?' Recently, someone who believed he was pronouncing my eulogy said that I was 'a John Stuart Mill feminist'. As if it was necessary that I had, that every woman had, a God-the-Father? And as if I should do Patristics? That I upheld that only a man could be the founder, even of feminism? One of the difficulties of Beauvoir is in this, perhaps.

CR: To be viewed, by contrast, as a mother?

MLD: To have been a woman who could have been viewed as a founder. She said that she would not like to be seen as the mother nor the grandmother of feminism. Patriarchy thinks that only a man can be a founder. I think that feminism has a foundation collective and plural, and that it is refounded anew in each of us. Simone found herself, in fact, at the point where these three negations met. Difficult.

CR: Do you agree with the critique Beauvoir made of Freudian psychoanalysis?

MLD: The importance of criticizing Freud's phallocentrism – again and again – is unquestionable. And yet, certain of his ideas seem very interesting to me. The concept of masculine hysteria, which still hasn't made its way into mainstream thought, displaced a traditional division for which we were paying the price: since it is not necessary to have a uterus to be hysterical, one can also have a uterus without necessarily having hysteria. But above all, his discovery of childhood sexuality allowed the disjunction of sexuality from the reproductive end assigned to adult heterosexuality, which had hitherto been viewed as the only form of sexuality. Defining sexuality as an activity of pleasure, instead of categorizing it as reproduction, contributed to unlocking the question of reproductive rights and gave homosexualities recognition as forms equal to heterosexuality. Finally, genital sexuality, even if he considered it as the highest stage of maturation, is never anything more than one stage among others, with the oral and anal also playing a structured role. This permits one to balance the importance it is accorded within the framework of the differentiation of the sexes, including by Freud himself, to one sex over the other.

Besides, psychoanalysis is a practice as much as a theory – a practice that could probably free women from mental blockades, on the condition that this is the goal. When there is oppression, there is also internalization of the said oppression. A form of psychoanalysis which would give itself, as its main project, to helping to dis-internalize these things is conceivable even if now, de facto, self-help groups best fulfil that function.

CR: What do you think of this sentence by Beauvoir, which presents her ideal for the future: 'When it is finally possible for all human beings to place their pride beyond sexual differentiation, in the difficult glory of free existence, only then will woman be able to make her history, her problems, her doubts, her fears, be those of humanity'?[13]

MLD: One can hear it as a recommendation addressed to men as well as women, to place their pride beyond their respective sexual specifications, which would surely be good for everyone. Only, Beauvoir seems to address it to 'woman', as though for men it was a foregone conclusion, which is far from being the case. Consequently, the recommendation can be heard as an invitation to rejoin men. To propose that women and men should rejoin in a common consideration of humanity is superb. On the other hand, the project of assimilating with men, such as they are, is an idea that no one today would consider reviving. One can be delighted that certain aspects of life which have long been the privilege of men are now open to us, and recognized as good for us. The possibility to travel, alone if needs be, the possibility to study and think are great joys. What has always irritated me about those who are blindly keen on *difference* is that they are constantly forbidding women access to that which, traditionally, has been associated with the masculine condition. As though one couldn't handpick – travel, yes, war, no thank you – or as if one couldn't adopt a reputedly 'masculine' activity without *ipso facto* therefore identifying with men.

CR: In *Hipparchia's Choice* you lament the association of the theoretical with masculinity.

MLD: I have suffered from this absurd association, which gives me the following choice: to creep illegally into a masculine community and sit quietly in the corner, hopeful that no one perceives the illegitimacy of my presence, or – which is no better – to define myself by contrast, take the scraps and accept the exchange rate the system offers. For me it was, and I believe that for every woman it would be, much more valuable to make steps towards dismantling the association.

CR: At one time, Beauvoir proposed something like a theory of difference, when she wrote that 'No mathematics can make an equation out of this mystery of a spot of blood that changes into a human being in the mother's womb, no machine can rush it or slow it down; she experiences the resistance of a duration that the most ingenious machine fails to divide or multiply. She experiences in her flesh that which is subjected to the rhythm of the moon'.[14]

MLD: It is a contrast to mathematics and machines. But note in the passage that she borders on lyricism, on vitalism, with a cosmic dimension, which only comes to prove that she was also susceptible to glorifying women's bodies. Personally, I have some reservations about the self-seduction that celebrating sexual difference implies. But it is more urgent to denounce it where it truly prevails, namely on the side of men, than where it emerges on the side of women. It is present in football matches, one of the most clearly phallic institutions of our societies, or in military language. Feminist *différentialisme*, at heart, is an attempt to build a symmetrical celebration.

CR: As in *Parole de femme*.[15]

MLD: For example, and with notably conservative effects. Likewise, differentialists constantly tended to be a bit tyrannical, in that they have aspired to define and determine a model of woman to which all must conform. I never had patience for a man or a woman deciding what I am to be as a woman, and I hope never to have the temptation to decide it for another. Changing circumstances – concrete, socio-political – towards a greater liberty for all (men and women) implies that one ceases to want to mould people.

CR: Beauvoir goes on to explain that since masculine logic doesn't draw from the experience of women, it is understandable that women have rejected masculine logic, and that she adds that she rejects it because she also knows that 'in the hands of men reason becomes a sly form of violence'.[16]

MLD: In the hands of men, reason *becomes*, which implies that logic is not a form of violence before it falls into their hands. But then everything may become a form of violence when associated with tyranny, and this would also apply to unreason. Even madness can become a method of oppression: see how Petruchio, in *The Taming of the Shrew*, manages to quell the unfortunate Katherina through mimicking madness. Let reason be, and leave it alone! It is such a rare commodity in this world![17] Let us rather pose the problem in relation to knowledge, these combinations of consciousness and verbiage which, carried on by institutions, tend to be enclosed. A ritornello as apocryphal as you might imagine, once mocked a very learned Master of Balliol:

> I am Jowett, Master of Balliol College,
> And what I don't know is not knowledge.

Poor Jowett! I am pretty sure he never hinted at such a closure. But this could characterize the problem we are constantly confronted with. There are things we do know, which we learnt outside universities, and which academic knowledge refuses to integrate. As a result it is deemed a non-knowledge, therefore it is grotesque to even mention them.

CR: Could you give an example?

MLD: A course of law, at the end of the 1960s at the University of Geneva. The professor says that universal suffrage was established at such-and-such a date. A student raises her hand and says: 'not universal, sir, *women* still don't vote'. Howling with laughter in the classroom, at the expense of the unhappy girl:

the critique of the false universality of male-only suffrage is not an element of legal or legitimate knowledge. Another example: from the instant that abortion was free and reasonably well reimbursed by social systems in France, the global number of abortions each year fell. The more it is free, and the more humane the conditions, the fewer there are! Moreover, we can explain why. Here is an element of quantified knowledge, seriously established, a joyous knowledge to boot. But demographers carefully fail to integrate it in their studies, studies often marked by some doctoring of data. L'Institut National d'Études Démographiques never ceases to cook its figures, to make them alarmist, while if one counts the actual number of births there is no demographic implosion underway. Feminist groups have become centres of documentation, where they collect nuggets of knowledge and ideas which traditional disciplines refuse to include. There is therefore a collective knowledge that wouldn't exist or be amassed without the Movement. Beauvoir did not envisage that women could form a collective experience, let alone create archives.

CR: In fact, in *The Second Sex* she explains why women do not have a sense of being a community of women.

MLD: Even today this problem exists. Not that women don't have 'a sense of community' but that the deck is stacked against this community. In the 1970s the Movement was almost a historical miracle. A sense of solidarity is not acquired forever, notably between generations of women. Most young women today barely know what my generation had achieved for them and for us: contraception and abortion. But they often wished that the chapter be closed; they hardly like it when we invite them to identify with a global project – contraception and abortion being simply the crucial beginning.

CR: Yes, I have the impression that feminist activity has regressed in France.

MLD: Terribly. There is less and less space for expression, from every point of view. The theoreticians have more and more difficulty finding a publisher. If *Hipparchia's Choice* was published in French, it was because Le Seuil knew of an English-speaking editor or another who would buy the translation rights.[18] Christine Delphy has not succeeded in publishing a book in France, while she has published several in English.[19] At the level of content, as well, sometimes we witness regression. In 1991, a colloquium on women was being organized by the director of Beaubourg, just before her departure. Unfortunately, it was a colloquium of denial: women who had been feminists in the 1970s sacrificed feminism at the altar of Parisian sophistication. With regard to their careers, strategically, no doubt they were right. But most serious is that many among the youngest women imagine that my generation is always firmly there and that we are strong enough in number to continue the fight. I still think, however, that something will click, and that the terrain must be prepared, at least at the intellectual level, for the future wave, which is certainly coming. This is the meaning I give to my work as a researcher and writer.

CR: Feminism has a tendency to forget. One sees this with Beauvoir: she herself 'forgot' the women who came before her.

MLD: She did not know much of the great demonstrations made by English-speaking women from mid-nineteenth century onto the beginning of the twentieth century, although she knew something of it, which was an achievement for a French woman in 1949. She knew of the French movement for the right to vote, which was extremely small by comparison. What's more, even though she did hear about the American and British movements, perhaps there was not in her mind the space to accept and retain the significance of this information. If only we managed to create a tradition, a mode of transmission from one generation to the next, that would be a great step forward.

CR: When Beauvoir reflected on the intellectual achievements of the women of the past, she said: 'If they try to write, they feel crushed by the universe of culture because it is a universe of men: they can only stammer. Inversely, the woman who chooses to reason, to express herself according to masculine techniques, will have to suppress an originality she distrusts; as a student, she will be studious; she will imitate the rigour and the virile vigour. She can become an excellent theoretician and acquire a solid talent; but she will be called to renounce all within her that is "different".[20]

MLD: This is typical and telling about what it was to be a woman in the 1940s! That one currently feels crushed, when writing, by a cultural environment that is massively masculinist is true, and many women have complained of it, before and after Beauvoir. And yet, when one reads Virginia Woolf, Christine de Pizan, Jane Austen, George Sand and Marie de Gournay, one can construct for oneself a mental universe which, far from being crushing, makes it one's duty not to be crushed.

CR: I suppose that she thought rather of philosophy, and that she was making reference to the fact that there are only a few known female philosophers?

MLD: 'Why aren't there any women philosophers?' Hearing such a naïve question is a recurring joke in my life. There have been, and there are, women philosophers. The names of fifty have been preserved in antiquity, among them Hypatia. Nearer to us, one finds Simone Weil, Simone de Beauvoir herself, Hannah Arendt, Jeanne Hersch. . . . The reaction of my interlocutors, when I say this, consists of slicing it up: Hannah Arendt, that's not philosophy, that's political science; Beauvoir, don't speak to me of her, during the war she did nothing for the Resistance (a certain number of her male colleagues either, but that doesn't matter!); Hersch, who is she? Weil – fine, if you think so, but that's nothing much. Every argument is good for challenging the idea that there have been women philosophers, and good ones, while when any magazine does a 'panorama of French philosophy in the last ten years', they will bring you dozens of men, of whatever type, whose work doesn't always merit the title 'philosophy'.[21]

CR: To finish, do you agree with the well-known statement in *The Second Sex*, 'one is not born a woman, but becomes one'?

MLD: Yes, although I would like to give it another meaning. Simone wanted to say that one acquires subservience, that nothing in our birth predestines us to shoulder that burden. What I have been able to see in our collective epics is that nothing destines us to become servants, but at the same time a second birth is possible which opens up to us the possibility of another becoming-women, namely a becoming woman-creators. When one is a woman today, one may discover that everything is to be made anew in this world, and that this is possible for us on the condition that we want it. It is fantastic to plan to transform the world, to make it more human and more humane.

CR: To be a woman is also frustrating. You show very well in your article in *Nouvelles Questions Féministes*, 'Gens de sciences bis: le mauvais genre dans l'éprouvette', all of the obstacles you've encountered, *qua* feminist, in your career.

MLD: Frustrating, assuredly. But to find oneself in a situation where one can act is a rare enough chance. Despite everything that I could have said against auto-seduction, a woman can find today that it is marvellous to be a woman, bearer of as-yet-unseen responsibilities. Perhaps girls who are born in an epoch when all problems are settled – if one day, they really are settled – won't have much interest in the fact of being women.

CR: Do you think the ideal would be to transcend sexual difference?

MLD: In an egalitarian society, men would also, necessarily, have changed, to the point of being unrecognizable.

CR: It is certain that one sex cannot change without the other changing.

MLD: One already sees how, on the women's side in any case, the slim progress that we have made towards greater equality has made the individual differences between us multiply and blossom. The difference of gender, the obligatory 'masculine' for one and the 'feminine' norm for the other, constitutes a factor of dreadful uniformity, which, inside each sex, stifles individual differences for the benefit of a stereotype. One cannot even imagine what such an egalitarian society would be, if left to bloom: not just in terms of the diversification of persons, but also in terms of new ideas and abandoning ugly, old practices. Since we no longer produce children by the dozen, and even less to order, we have made each infant precious; the risk of war, which presupposes the possibility of a frightful squandering of human lives, seems to fade, at least between countries where women are finally mistresses of their own fertility. If world peace is the horizon of our liberation, then it is not an exaggeration to say that we have truly been working towards a change greater than anything I had ever dreamt of. How could this be found frustrating? But I agree with you: it is frustrating, because it does not progress quickly enough!

Notes

1. Michèle Le Dœuff, *L'Étude et le rouet. Des femmes, de la philosophie, etc.* (Paris: Éditions du Seuil, 1989; 2nd (revised) edn 1998). *Hipparchia's Choice: An Essay Concerning Women, Philosophy*, translated by Trista Selous (Oxford: Blackwell, 1991; 2nd (revised) edn, New York: Columbia University Press, 2007).
2. Since giving this interview, Le Dœuff has spent considerable time working on the genesis (or rather polygenesis) of *The Second Sex* and published a number of essays on this question.
3. Le Dœuff, *Hipparchia's Choice*, p. 133.
4. See 'Highly Singular Memories of '68, etc.', this volume.
5. The phrase '*féministe historique*' is an ambiguous one, often used by people who don't like feminism at all. It is often (if not always) pejorative. However, Le Dœuff has occasionally been criticized by other feminists for not being 'historique'. *L'Etude et le rouet* cheered a lot of women up, particularly activists on the brink of discouragement ('If feminist theoreticians still hold up, so can we'), all the more so because the book contains an invitation to value the knowledge one acquires in

being a grass-roots activist, the ideas you may get from reading 'in dialogue' with books, and basically an effort to combine what comes from experience and what comes from libraries.

6   The Women's Strike for Equality, 26 August 1970, was a nationwide strike which used varied tactics to draw attention to ways women are treated unequally. August 26 has since been named Women's Equality Day.

7   A petition signed by 343 women stating that they had undergone abortions and demanding its legalization. It was published by the weekly *Le Nouvel Observateur* on 5 April 1971, and its signatories include Simone de Beauvoir, Catherine Deneuve, Christine Delphy and Delphine Seyrig among others.

8   A *nouvelle vague* star. Le Dœuff says (in correspondence with the translator): 'Delphine Seyrig was one of the sweetest women I ever met – at meetings, when communication became jammed or grating, she was the one who would promptly pour a drop of oil on the blockage, giving the floor back to the shy or the marginalized – she was indeed a charmer but she was also a very charming woman.'

9   A French law of 17 January 1975 which legalized abortion if the woman feels that her pregnancy is a cause of distress (named for Simone Veil, Minister for Public Health, who very bravely and calmly defended the text in front of a not-so-easy-going Parliament).

10 CR is probably hinting at a well-known joke: 'If men could get pregnant, abortion would be a sacrament.'

11 *Eunuchs for the Kingdom of Heaven: Women, Sexuality, and the Church*, translated by Peter Heinegg (New York: Penguin, 1991).

12 Simone de Beauvoir, *A Woman Destroyed*, translated by Patrick O'Brian.

13 Translation amended from *The Second Sex*, translated by Constance Borde and Sheila Malovany-Chevalier (London: Vintage, 2010), p. 845.

14 *Le Deuxième sexe*, Tome II p. 423 translated Constace Borde and Sheila Malovany-Chevallier, New York (Beauvoir, *The Second Sex*, p. 725).

15 A book by Annie Leclerc (Paris: Grasset & Fasquelle, 1974).

16 Beauvoir, *The Second Sex*, p. 738, translation amended.

17 Since giving this interview Le Dœuff has taken up again the question of rationality in her book, *The Sex of Knowing*.

18 As things turned out, *L'Étude et le rouet* was widely read in France and the French-speaking world.

19 This interview took place in 1995 at a time when we were at the trough of the wave. This pessimistic point of view was soon proved exaggerated. Christine Delphy published a book in French: *L'Ennemi principal. I. Économie politique du patriarcat*, Paris: Syllepse, coll. Nouvelles Questions Féministes, 1998. Quite a handful of feminist books appeared including Michèle Le Dœuff's own *Le Sexe du savoir* (1998).

20 Beauvoir, *The Second Sex*, p. 816.

21 Michèle Le Dœuff took up that point in a more developed way in the *Sex of Knowing*.

3

On style and experience
Ulrika Björk in dialogue with Michèle Le Dœuff

Ulrika Björk: In the preface to *Hipparchia's Choice: An Essay Concerning Women, Philosophy, Etc.* (*L'Etude et le rouet: des femmes, de la philosophie, etc.*, 1989; 1991) you write that philosophical thought is not self-contained. And further: 'There is no thinking which does not wander, and any serious work should have etc. in its title and honestly state that it will not stick to the topic' (2007: xii). The context, in *Hipparchia's Choice*, is the question of women and philosophy, which you say requires the discussion of many other issues. My first question will then be about philosophical style. Could this wandering thinking be described in terms of method? Or is it rather opposed to method understood in a systematically philosophical sense (I am thinking, for example, of Descartes)?

Michèle Le Dœuff: Strictly speaking, I would not describe this wandering either in terms of method or as opposed to method. When I say that there is no philosophical thinking that does not live on wandering, I see this first of all as a statement of fact. And such a statement could apply to Descartes's works as well as to Plato's dialogues or to any author you may want to mention. Perhaps because philosophy is research in itself, at least an inquiry or an exploration, it cannot be strictly encompassed in a finite set of methodological rules; on the other hand, it creates methods as it goes and may then try to apply them to its own discourse and to its own style.

A Finnish version of this interview (translated by Virpi Lehtinen and Sara Heinämaa) appeared in *Tiede&Edistys* (Helsinki, 27, no. 4 (2002): 293–303). There is a German translation, Michèle le Dœuff im Interview mit Ulrika Björk: 'Was bedeutet es, eine Philosophin zu sein? Michèle le Dœuff über die vielfältigen Ursprünge des Denkens und die Rolle persönlicher Erfahrung für die Philosophie'. Übersetzt von Anne Reichold. *Freiburger FrauenStudien. Zeitschrift für interdisziplinäre Frauenforschung*. In: 'Screening gender', FFS Band 14. Hrsg.: Meike Penkwitt. Freiburg: jos fritz verlag. Voraussichtlich Automne 2003. There is also a Swedish version. Michèle Le Dœuff rewrote the piece in French for the *Australian Journal of French Studies* (XL, no. 3 (2003)). The present version is based on the French version, translated and revised by Kate Kirkpatrick, Pamela Sue Anderson, and Michèle Le Dœuff.

Now, without forgetting that your question is about feminism and philosophy, perhaps I may already make a little detour myself about 'history of philosophy' as a field or a discipline, and explain how some points of view about the nature of what is philosophical may determine our approaches to works considered as such, and why therefore my 'statement of fact' may not be as self-evident as it should be. As a young student, I was lucky enough to follow Martial Gueroult's last lectures at the École Normale Supérieure de Fontenay. His approach to Aristotle's philosophy, or Hegel's, was architectural – he focused on an architectonic reading of their works. In a sense, what mattered chiefly for him was to bring to light and describe the framework of a given philosophy, the structure of it, even if what he saw as the core – or main beam – could be a problem, or a question, rather than a proposition or a dogma. Such a perspective, however remarkable and however helpful to memorize the gist of an author, may well tend at the same time to turn any philosophy into a system. As a result, the historian's method itself had an effect on the object or more precisely on what we consider as the object. However, you could also read Henri Gouhier, who rather saw a philosophical thought as something which develops, like a living being so to speak, from the early works of such or such a philosopher to more mature works; such a point of view could turn any philosophy into a genesis which could be recounted. It was also possible to follow Michel Serres's seminars, who at the time was a Leibnizian, I mean a specialist of Leibniz and a believer. His method was based on close reading and he really taught that art to his audience; we would take one page by Leibniz, assume that it had a beginning and an end, and that something important took place in between. After a seminar, you walked out with the idea that every single page of philosophy is full of meaning, full of food for thought, in a sense self-contained insofar as you were not supposed to refer to other works by the author in order to understand it (we could call this '*une fiction régulatrice*': a fiction that is among the working conditions of a technique). But not self-contained at all because you had to know about seventeenth-century mathematics for this bit, or about astronomy for that one, or about some Ancient Greek debate for the next paragraph, and about philology all the time. . . . In fact, you were supposed to be a well-read person, but not *blasé*, constantly able to read one page with a fresh eye. That approach determined the person you had to be as a good reader: be that fresh eye, intelligent and well informed, so that this page by Leibniz may exist for good, as it truly is, and gets its due!

I should also like to mention Vladimir Jankélévitch, who was a moral philosopher (and by the way my supervisor). It took some courage to be a moral philosopher in Paris in the structuralist 1960s and 1970s, because at the time, the field of ethics was utterly despised; philosophy of science was fashionable and highly thought of, perhaps allowing some space to Marxism and psychoanalysis, particularly when these fields of studies could be seen as pursuing structuralist explorations further, thus bearing the mark of good Frenchness and male monopoly (poor Melanie Klein's works hardly got a chance in such a context). I had to brave my friends' mockery to register as a graduate student with 'Janké' as we called him, just as he himself had to stand loneliness and marginalization at the Sorbonne for years, along with a sense of being neglected as an author; this changed overnight when the handful of people we were around him launched into a positive conspiracy: we had decided to make a star of him and we succeeded. Yes, if you (who live in Scandinavia, in Australia, in Chicago or in Saint-Ouen) have heard of him, and read some of his books, this is because our conspiracy worked. At any rate, his use of past texts was most original: he would take up two lines by an old author and then take off, unfolding his own views and refining them, in a somewhat fusional rapport with them. Two lines, sometimes less, for it could be just a phrase, like Plotinus's idea of 'the lazy, or amorph, beautiful' [*kallos argon*].[1] I never saw anyone who could be so kindled by a mere fragment of an old piece of work. And he would never make the historical distance between the text and us be felt. It was as if Plotinus was our contemporary, since what he wrote was still full of meaning for Janké hence potentially for his audience. But then, he chose to quote only those lines that he could see as nuggets of delight. As a supervisor, he gently warned me against getting too much immersed in history of philosophy pure and simple, advising me never to forget moral philosophy and the discussion of values, but rather to rub shoulders with texts of the past from the point of view of values.[2]

All in all, and even if we limit the question to my younger days, there never was a unified French school of history of philosophy, certainly not a school unified by a doctrine. You could already get the idea that a given philosophy may be seen this way or that different way, hence that you – say, a young woman – may feel free to find out your own way of looking at texts. If you were independent enough from a 'mentor', that is. And within the limits of some rules, of course. For do not mistake me: this didn't imply that texts are utterly flexible! The field was not unified but all people concerned had a few norms in common. Texts matter, first of all; they exist and you may refer to them; as a matter of course, texts themselves take precedence over commentaries, which come second and are occasionally quite secondary: as a result, you'd better be precise and exact!

And all would agree that the practice of philosophy ought to keep a connection with philosophy's past. What we call 'general philosophy' has to be nourished by ideas you acquired through reading history of philosophy, meaning the works themselves. When developing your own way of thinking, you must allow some space for our 'oldies but goodies', old works which may still have something to say to people or which will help you find your way thanks to a contrast with what you want to mean (solipsism is not an option; being a *tabula rasa* from your early days onward won't do either). Reciprocally, the practice of history of philosophy should include some philosophical angle. If you read old works, think with them, think against them, think half with and half against them, as you wish! But always pause to consider if they provide food for thought and never hurry up to simply memorize what is just necessary to become a specialist of a given author.

This is at least what I believe I grasped. Perhaps it was not as clear as that, in the community at the time; perhaps I am reconstructing with hindsight. The most important aspect of it, however, is that I perceived a diversity within the field and truly enjoyed rethinking at one remove or two what was taught to us. I was lucky enough to assume that my freedom could be found in such a context, provided I had the strength to seek this very freedom with determination. For I had already understood that a young woman has to keep a little away from any 'mentor' if she wants to find her personal lane or way, even in doing history of philosophy. A *master* is always *one, and only one*, master. Plurality helps undoing any mastery, a crucial step when it comes to create a feminist emancipation of thinking. Jankélévitch was a dearest friend and a liberal supervisor, never a mentor. And even before I became a feminist philosopher, I began finding my own perspective when I wrote 'Red ink in the margins', for then I understood that there is a history of history of philosophy;[3] I mean that the 'object' we may call Descartes has not constantly been 'carved' in the same way. Fair enough, this is a Platonic metaphor: pay attention to the way you carve a chicken! Years later I was happy to make such an idea bear upon (or: apply to?) John Stuart Mill's works, and, thanks to it, I managed to disentangle a bit the relations between Harriet Taylor Mill and the works that go under his name.[4]

And I had understood somehow that the question of 'who am I when I read this or that?' is relevant in many respects, which may well be the beginning of an answer to your question. 'Know thouself when you read' could be in fact a good scholarly principle for everyone. Know yourself in order to mix yourself as little as possible with the text and to resist as much as possible the temptation of projection. Particularly when reading an author close to you (like Beauvoir or Gabrielle Suchon for me), it is important to keep yourself at bay and know that you are one person and the author another one. It is important as well to 'know yourself' when reading something you do not like at all. I always felt that there is something wrong in Rousseau's *Emile*, book V. Something very, very wrong. And of course I could refer that feeling to my political persuasion, except that it also left me with a vague question of a more intellectual kind: there is something bizarre, philosophically bizarre, in the discrepancy between the values put forth in the first four books (where education for the boy Emile is described) and the appalling education arranged for Sophie in this fifth book. I certainly object to double standards, and when I read Mary Wollstonecraft, who basically protests that Rousseau is a bastard, I could agree but still had the feeling that this was not the end of the story. For many years, I had that puzzle in mind: 'there is something really wrong here, and it is not just because I'm a twentieth century feminist'. An enigma – a mystery, if you like! Then I read Gabrielle Suchon and began to understand. In *Le Sexe du savoir*, I explained that young Rousseau probably read Gabrielle Suchon and later in life made a perverse use of her ideas; she values self-training and autonomy and she saw that as the right lane for girls (but this did not exclude boys), for women (and it could also be such for men), because basically it ought to have been the lane for Adam as well as for Eve. A feminist reading a piece of patriarchal philosophy should know that, if she disagrees, it may not be just because there is a political discrepancy between the author and herself, but also because there may be an internal discrepancy in the text itself, something intellectually unacceptable, except that patriarchal consensus has hidden the problem to many, many readers so far!

More to return to your initial question concerning the topic of feminism and philosophy, in relation to philosophical style and particularly wandering thinking, I would not separate the question from our responsibilities as younger women's and men's teachers. I believe it is important to help them perceive that there is a lot of wandering in canonical texts, just as there is lot of imagery and imaginary and also conceptual tensions everywhere. Let us make them understand that this is normal or legitimate, unavoidable or fruitful, so that the day they start writing philosophy themselves, they should not be embarrassed to go into detours and meanderings. Basically, I think that the first issue is for us to provide a less intimidating vision of what philosophical work is, to show it as it is and as it always was. Forget for a minute about Descartes's 'system', which may or may not be an artifact invented by commentators anyway. Read at leisure! Feel free to perceive a piece of work as it is offered to you, the reader; pay attention to the way it unfolds itself, which is far more complex and interesting than anything you may hear about it. And perhaps we could bet that a more direct and realistic contact with the text will prove also more enjoyable. Allow yourself from time to time to casually spend an evening with your nose in a book ['*bouquiner de la philo*'], or a rainy Sunday, or when life is going wrong. This will amount to reading without an immediate goal, just in order to read, at will and peacefully. You will then discover that classical works will tell you what they seldom reveal when you read them with a piece of work (always urgent of course) to complete in mind. Look: my notion of *epikleros*, which readers of *The Sex of Knowing* liked so much, I owe it in fact to this habit; you while away a boring Sunday pecking at some Aristotle, laid-back and with no particular intention, hence also giving involuntary memory a free rein. Years later, you realize it could be a useful concept for some analysis of yours.

No method, no codified procedure, can work without a good dose of informal thinking. Moreover, no methodology can renew itself if there is no free exercise of mind, if life is absent, and imagination too. Philosophical feminism, which is as a matter of course engaged in changing and renewing the subject, and could indeed even be the mightiest effort philosophy ever agreed to do in order to change, cannot do without all possible modes of exploration, including detours and meanders. And by the way, it is for the time being the only way we have to insert as many concrete points as possible in our enterprise. Hence, never mind if we appear to be dawdling! The fact is that we must constantly confront what we understand through our political life, which is 'lived experience' in itself too, with what we started thinking, say when reading a book of philosophy or whatever. At least, this is my way of looking at the question. A philosophical thought does not have just a genesis, but a polygenesis, or so I claimed in *Hipparchia's Choice* and I have not changed my mind since then. You have to insert or, if you prefer, to see what happens when you try to rub one against the other several aspects of your cognitive life. They may be illuminating one to another, thus helping you to think further; they may upset one another, thus forcing you to think further. Anyway, even in logic, when you start creating a formal system – an axiomatic – you first need to use your ordinary language, however ambiguous, ill defined or vague it might be. Having understood that, you may realize that wanting to start and stay at the level of formal procedures, methods, systems, pure concepts (etc.) is simply condemning oneself to be blocked at the very start and remain in speechlessness. An inquiry is a process, something dynamic, and you never know what accidental finding will help you sort out a problem.

UB: What, in your view, is the meaning of personal experience in philosophical work, that is, in philosophical reflections and investigations? How central is it and what is its role? Let me specify my question by giving an example from your writing. One of your articles, 'Feminism is Back in France – Or Is It?',[5] takes its point of departure at a lunch you had with a friend who chaired the French Movement of Family Planning. The topic of the lunch meeting was state-sponsored feminism's focus on parity in government as opposed to (and to the detriment of) women's rights such as access to abortion, contraception. Your friend's frustration over having no public space to debate such issues actualizes a general problem: the possibilities, or rather, impossibilities of free debate within political institutions and with politicians. The article studies this problem by introducing, in contrast, a kind of active citizenship through writing, suggested by the French seventeenth-century philosopher Gabrielle Suchon. So, while discussing public debate on a general level, the article is structured around a particular experience from your own dining room. Virginia Woolf's essay *A Room of One's Own* comes to my mind, where the general question on women and the novel is told through the fictive experiences of Mary Beaton (as we might call her). But is the friendly lunch in your article only a fictive example? Or is there a connection between personal experience and philosophical thinking?

MLD: In *Hipparchia's Choice*, I offered a cut-and-dried answer to this: if we cannot fit any personal experience in our philosophical thinking, this is a bad omen. And yes, the lunch with my friend Danielle took place in the way I described. Danielle herself didn't find anything amiss in the printed narrative (although later on she mentioned that the French Movement for Family Planning is more collectively 'chaired' than what appears on official paper). But we must take into account that, when writing an account of an event, one may be unconsciously influenced by something previously read, and in the case Virginia Woolf's essay, something read several times. . . . Hence, we may want to qualify our notion of 'personal experience', at least as soon as this experience gets written down: intertextuality may influence the form in which we give an account even of a meal which was eaten for good. Moreover, you may consider that Virginia Woolf, in this case as so frequently, gives us all permission to consider that a homely discussion in a kitchen or dining room is worthy of going into print. However, you may want to notice that Danielle and I were discussing the government policy about women's rights, just after I had heard a minister give a formal talk about her agenda (to summarize: 'we are heartily determined to get equal numbers of women and men in the Cabinet and Parliament; as for reproductive rights, well, we do have a project too which will be announced in a year's time'). This is not exactly the discussion Woolf places between two women friends in a kitchen. It was an inspiring, personal–political experience of dialogue, hopefully as much for Danielle as for me. About how women who are not within the government or the State apparatus should be able to put forth propositions, should get a hearing, should freely discuss what our priorities are, but, more often than not, are prevented from doing so.

Free debate, free speech, independent points of view . . . all these most desirable political goods are, I fear, difficult to find and this sometimes even in person-to-person communication. Not difficult to find in this case, which makes the memory of the lunch precious, also as an exceptional event. Because a sort of inter-individual tyranny has developed these last years and could be sketched like this: 'if you do not agree a hundred per cent with me, this is evidence of the fact that you are against democracy, clean air, young people and the future!', this is at least how my friend Liliane Kandel quipped! A calm dialogue, like the one with Danielle, is a rare experience, perhaps made possible by the fact that we are friends speaking from two different 'sites'. She is in charge of an organization; I'm a pen and a voice, I occasionally help the cause we have in common this way. We are trying to pool together what we know, in order to understand and analyse a political situation. She represents a women's organization; I'm just an individual. None of us is trying to persuade the other to share a 'line' or whatever; actually, at the very beginning, we discovered that we both were equally fed up with the then government. For both of us, it is a personal experience of a fruitful dialogue, an event which is already of an intellectual nature. I could of course simply say: 'and what would be my philosophical thinking, were I not interested in other women's political experience and knowledge?' My feminist writings always have an angle open to practical issues; I certainly must learn from the real activists and I would recommend to younger women academics to become closer to activist movements and to engage a dialogue with them from time to time. But it is not just that. The beginning of what we call 'thinking' takes place when there are two or more minds. And a real encounter between two minds (or more) is always personal. There is the space where they meet, the concrete circumstances. . . . Your encounter with this or that person at the right time is never granted, it is often a piece of luck. And you may well be there with all your life story. After all, reading has once been defined as 'a conversation with decent people of the past'. I agree, but in this case as well, it is a real encounter – the author is real and speaks her or his mind, and may have plenty to tell you which perhaps was not exactly what you wanted on that day, just like with living friends, but never mind: reading is not like accessing an electronic encyclopaedia. As far as thinking is concerned, I would put intersubjectivity at the same level as subjectivity – philosophy is not a Robinson Crusoe story, though the 'model' of Defoe's novel was a philosophical tale about a parentless child born on a desert island, growing up all on his own and discovering all levels of knowledge as an autodidact. Ibn Tufayl's tale is lovely but I can't see philosophy originating and developing this way.

UB: Recognizing that your personal experience is political has been an important theme in the women's movement of the 1960s and the 1970s. However, in *Hipparchia's Choice*, as well as in the above-mentioned article, you stress the consciousness-raising effect not of a group of people but of a written work, since it offers 'the possibility of meeting the particular voice, an intelligence and a particular kind of generosity'.[6] The book you refer to is Simone de Beauvoir's *The Second Sex*, and you even call it 'the movement before the movement' (ibid.). As I understand this, Beauvoir's book had political effect not because it expressed a 'feminine experience' or way of thinking. Rather, what explains its feminist significance is the ethical authenticity that enabled Beauvoir to distance herself from her situation as a woman, and describe it. Would you agree on this? Would you say that she is the first of women philosophers in the past to do this systematically?

MLD: In a sense, my very first encounter with feminist thinking took place some years before I read *The Second Sex*. But you are right nonetheless, for it was also a story of distanciation! In my early teens, bedridden with flu and listening to the radio, I heard Andrée Michel speak on a programme and say that, in all societies, women take care of activities or forms of work men do not want for themselves. Now, if we look at the partition of occupations in that light (as a rule, we are offered leftovers, whatever they are), a theoretical and therefore mental distance is thus created between occupations allotted to us and the idea of 'womanhood': there is not such a thing as 'feminine occupations', naturally feminine; there is a social distribution of roles, and it is possible to reach an abstract formulation of it or a theoretical view on that. This remark, heard on the radio, made me think – think what? Probably nothing on the spot! I just had the idea that I would give some thought to it eventually, although I can remember feeling rebellious and determined not to allow this to happen to me.

As for Beauvoir, you are right to put the emphasis on distance, ethical authenticity, but *The Second Sex* is written on various levels. (Or is it that every time a general view of Beauvoir is put forth, including by myself, I then remember aspects somehow at variance with this view?) She certainly tries to think out how a woman, and herself in the first place, can distance herself from all the mythical rubbish poured out about women, from the destiny imposed on us (matrimony, motherhood, housecleaning) but also from what I would call 'emblems' for lack of a better word. What she writes about puberty and menstruation is mostly an 'emblem': it is 'bodily lived experience', appearing as part of the situation, in fact her own memory of her bodily life. Intertwined with minuscule remarks which had a political influence on my generation. Like this one: 'Whether the girl has been told in advance or not about puberty . . .'; none of my friends in the 1960s had been really told in advance! This brief remark by Beauvoir could help each of us to acknowledge that not-having-been-told-in-advance was a common feature of girlhood, along with a questionable deprivation. A book may thus reveal to a woman reader something which has been for her a personal experience and a serious one. And it may start a questioning. What is the meaning of this denial of knowledge about ourselves which had been our lot? Yes, *The Sex of Knowing* is in this respect a 'Beauvoirian' work. My own 'lived experience' of my body may well be quite different from what Beauvoir wrote about her experience. But to be denied access to important portions of knowledge, I do know what it is.

There are many aspects or facets to *The Second Sex*, and occasionally there is also perhaps an attempted but repressed discourse. Something like a wish to get reconciled with herself. Or say, a question, lurking here and there: What is it to be a modern woman? No, that would be too crude a formulation! Perhaps: What can I make of myself? Or, to put it in a more philosophical wording, what forms of life is our freedom, my freedom, able to create? Here and there, you'll find a good word about birth control, a brief image of women in trousers on a beach, a little remark about sensuality and eroticism. . . . It is always furtive but it is there. Surely not a reconciliation with 'feminine experience' in any traditional way; rather, something to look forward to, perhaps. Except that she cannot quite envision it. But even if the answer is not really given, at any rate Simone knew what to do with her freedom: to write and in particular to write *The Second Sex*. Perhaps this was her answer. Do reread the beginning of volume two: it took an enormous amount of mental freedom to be able to write that. Simone de

Beauvoir has set her freedom to work, as, for example, by putting a name on what was still considered as unspeakable.

UB: Especially after the fiftieth anniversary of the publishing of *The Second Sex*, there has been a growing interest in the philosophical implications not only of Beauvoir's critical texts but also of her literary and autobiographical writing. Moreover, her work is studied from different philosophical contexts. One approach is to read her work in relation to phenomenology. Being a French Beauvoir scholar, and given your earlier critical remarks on Edmund Husserl's phenomenology (e.g. 1991: 99–100, 108), what is your opinion on Beauvoir's philosophical relation to this hardly feminist movement?

MLD: Hardly indeed! Philosophically speaking, I believe she is closer to Hegel's phenomenology than to the Husserlian school. The movement we just described, of a subject distanciating itself, painstakingly re-creating its own freedom through separation, but also through accepting 'the austere necessity of a discipline', and so on, and then perhaps – but it is only on the horizon – creating concrete forms of living . . . such a movement may be seen as Hegelian, whereas with writers like Husserl or Sartre, you usually have a big 'ego' at the centre, to which everything is subordinated. Besides, she does not limit herself to 'things as they appear to consciousness'. Consider the passage about women workers' exploitation and how in Lyon in the nineteenth century, half of the young women contracted TB before the end of their first year of apprenticeship.[7] You could not find a description of facts like that in Husserl or any of his immediate followers! Not just because they were men and bourgeois, but also for a question of philosophical 'method'. Beauvoir's thinking here is documented on surveys, empirical inquiries about workers' way of life and state of health. In Hegelian 'methodology', you can certainly find a space for the knowledge of 'something which is not me' and which does not 'appear' to me as a phenomenon of the Ego. Knowing something given as 'exterior' to the subject can exist, at least as a 'moment' in the huge Hegelian framework. See what Hegel writes on Bacon and on the idea that knowledge is work, an effort to know something which is exterior. It was not taxing for Marx to adapt Hegelian dialectics to a materialistic understanding of the world, the consideration of exploitation and oppression and to demand as scientific as possible a knowledge of exploitation, its sides-effects, and so on. Husserlian phenomenology is certainly a disavowal of sciences when they are emancipated from philosophy, and, by the same token, a disavowal of any empirical enquiry, leading or not, eventually, to theories about society. Beauvoir's does not repudiate any mode of exploration; she wants to know all that can be known about women's lives, she wants to analyse all she can of the situations imposed to women.

UB: Reading your writing is an intellectual journey between the present and the past in the history of philosophy, politics and philosophy; in contemporary life; and on the level of expression, also, philosophy and literature. In your latest book, *Le Sexe de savoir* (1998), you discuss science and its methods. From the perspective of a philosopher who wants to think for herself, critically and creatively, you argue against the idea that science is inherently masculine. Instead, you distinguish scientific method from men's masculinization of science and hold that women as well as men can do critical research. The masculinization of science manifests itself in academic institutions and discourse. What is the role of the departments for women's or gender studies, established as a result of activist feminism, in the work for institutional and discursive change?

MLD: What a difficult question! On the one hand, some teaching of women's or gender studies, when inserted in the regular courses of departments, helps women students to feel better at ease. Moreover, it is also clear that, in the arts, in sociology or politics, a degree without any bit of gender studies would simply be behind the international standards of the subject. Most PhDs have or ought to have gender studies as a component...

UB: So you would agree with the Swedish journal for women's studies which claims, in a special issue on the academy, that gender research is no longer a movement in the margin of the academic world, but has a position in its centre?[8]

MLD: I would. On the other hand, up to now, there is no evidence that the introduction of gender studies in academia has produced much change in the institutional structures in sciences, nor at the level of appointments of professors in many fields, including philosophy.

What I have tried to do, in *Le Sexe du savoir*, was indeed to offer a discursive change, which may empower (at least at the level of morale) young women who enter this world, to give them ideas that should help them resist the negative perception of themselves which the academy may impose on them. I challenged the idea that science is inherently masculine, in the hope that women scientists will read my work and thus feel less challenged by the crazy opinions still floating around their labs. In the hope too to persuade the few women who have decisional power, and some decent men too, that they could feel it is their responsibility to bring about some change. In France, my book has had many readers, even some at high institutional level but something strange happened. Back to personal experience again! One day, in September 1999, someone [*une chargée de mission*] in the Ministry of Education approached me and asked if there had been any woman philosopher in the past; I replied 'plenty' and elaborated. 'Really? Here in the ministry, someone told me on oath that there was only Olympes de Gouges and that her work does not stand up to scrutiny'. Then she asked if we could alter the syllabus in philosophy for secondary schools so that women philosophers of the past would be more present in it, and so on. All in all, I improvised a two-hour-long seminar to that person over the phone about characters and ideas of women philosophers. 'Would you be enthusiastic to defend a revision of the syllabus?' I would. And then, nothing. Whenever I tried to phone her at the ministry, she was unavailable. I had agreed to work with l'Inspection Générale to introduce this change, but was mysteriously disembarked, and so was André Pessel, the Inspecteur Général I had suggested as someone with whom it was possible to work. The project had been cancelled. Another day, I gave the keynote address at a conference organized by the Ministry of Research; the minister himself invited us all to work and then meet a year later. A year later, the assessment conference took place; I was not even invited to attend. This didn't come as a surprise: a year before, my keynote had been immediately challenged by the (male, of course) representative of a major trade union, who had explained that in order to bring about real change, we should alter the sciences themselves, put more intuition in them and less reasoning, since women are intuitive, and so on. Nicole Mosconi excellently retorted: 'Sir, had you read *Le Sexe du savoir*, you would not be talking nonsense like that!' There is a sort of institutional regulation which exists also at discursive level, apparently. The views I had offered were not institutionally acceptable! I pointed out that there is such a thing as a 'scientific sociability'; that (mostly male) heads of labs do not relate to women budding scientists in the same way they relate to male beginners, and so forth. Unacceptable, apparently. From 1998 to 2002, it was a repetitive story for me. Some innocent soul, who had read my books or met someone who had, would approach me for this or that. I always said yes, and then would not hear about it again.

'How not to do it?' In Dickens's novel *Little Dorrit*, there is a mysterious ministry, called the Circumlocution Office, where the motto is said to be 'How not to do it?' This office in fact sits over 'all the public departments'.[9] In France, during the last years of a century and the first years of a new one, I have had the feeling that the line was 'how to pretend to do something while in fact not doing a thing at all'. With European recommendations to promote women, this is probably taking place in more than one country. At an institution which will be left unnamed, some colleagues started a women's lobby, on the strength of these European recommendations, later to discover that all their good work had been beneficial only to important men's wives. . . . Don't call this personal experience – I have the feeling of witnessing an experiment in progress, with the experimenters discovering with astonishment the end result of it.

UB: Do you welcome the idea of state-sponsored gender research?

MLD: I would! Particularly if this research didn't exclude at once from its programmes an attention to women's real lives (What about women and poverty? What about women and part-time employment? What about violence within intellectual institutions?). If it was conceived as a huge lab, trying to analyse 'experiments' like the one I just mentioned, and to invent new strategies, all this in perfect freedom, meaning free from the regulation at discursive level like what we just described.

Which state on the earth will have the courage to create this large lab? Perhaps Sweden, but should it not exist in all countries and at international level? Anyhow, even if it were not created as amply as that by a state or international agencies, nor as free as that, perhaps (and this will be a last curtsy to Virginia Woolf), perhaps we could all contribute to create it, perhaps we are already all contributing to the existence of such a lab.

Notes

1 Plotinus, *Enneads*, VI, 7, XX.
2 See also 'Jankélévitch: sous le souffle du signe', in *Critique*, mai 1980.
3 That piece was first written in 1975 with a Spanish publication in view and appeared in an abridged version as 'En torno en a la moral de Descartes', in *Conocer Descartes y su obra*, sous la direction de Victor Gomez-Pin (Barcelona, 1979). It was first published in French in *Qui a peur de la philosophie?* Greph/collectif (Paris: Flammarion, 1977). See now *L'Imaginaire philosophique* (Paris: Payot, 1980) or *The Philosophical Imaginary*.
4 See *Le Sexe du savoir*, *The Sex of Knowing* (part III).
5 *Hypatia: A Journal of Feminist Philosophy*, special issue Contemporary French Women Philosophers, ed. by Penelope Deutscher, 15, no. 4 (2000), pp. 236–242.

6 Hipparchia's Choice, Basil Blackwell, 1991, p. 57.
7 Book 1, part 2, section 4.
8 Lund, Sweden, Kvinnovetenskaplig tidskrift 1/2001:4.
9 Charles Dickens, *Little Dorrit*, 1857, chapter X; reissued in World's Classics (Oxford University Press, 1979), pp. 87 sq.

4

On a twentieth-century French woman philosopher

Penelope Deutscher in dialogue with Michèle Le Dœuff

Interview

MICHÈLE LE DOEUFF, *interviewed by Penelope Deutscher*

Michèle Le Dœuff speculates about why the parity movement enjoyed attention and sympathy in France over recent years. She discusses recent developments in 'state-handled' feminism, and the resurgence of interest in feminist debate in France. Perhaps patriarchy is an institution more fundamental than the state?

Penelope Deutscher: Some readers might be surprised to hear that you have not been a strong supporter of the movement for an enforced quota of equal numbers of women in Parliament in France. You have laid out your position on this matter in 'Problemes d'investiture (De la parité, etc)' (1995). The important issues include those of whether public health, contraception and abortion are adequately funded. You point out, 'despite 40% of local shire representatives being women, Oxfordshire has not inundated itself with creches and kindergartens' (Le Dœuff 1995: 44). You emphasize that women politicians are not automatically in social and political solidarity with other women. Why do you think the parity movement has suddenly enjoyed so much attention and sympathy in your country, given how much opposition there is in France to those affirmative action policies which are considered very 'American', 'politically correct', and so on?

Michèle Le Dœuff: I reacted not so much to the idea of 'parity' in itself as to the lines of argument put forth by its supporters. With their claims that the aim was not that women MPs represent women,[1] surely someone had to raise a few questions. The sympathy this movement enjoyed in France is not to be overrated. It made the headlines of newspapers; this does not mean it has ever been vast, popular and solid. It did find an echo in the frustration of women members of political parties. At the grass-roots level these women do a lot of work but when it comes to being a candidate, their colleagues do not consider them eligible. Another thing is at stake. Forty-eight per cent of the current mayors (mostly male) in France don't want to serve a second term. The position is thankless because these days people readily take local authorities to court. Of course, it is just the right time for women to take over and in fact rescue a position which lacks inheritors (*qui tombe en déshérence*)! Nonetheless, male members of political parties remain reluctant to give away to women what they don't want to keep for themselves. With such a discrepancy, one might want to say something in favour of parity. It is a way to encourage male politicians to do the unavoidable. As for the government, what has been mainly at stake in parity is, I believe, to see politics (i.e. elections) be based on identification rather than programmes. As if women electors would vote for MPs who are women for that reason alone. In any case, the present situation speaks volumes. Here is a newspaper cutting from *Libération*, 2 March 2000, as tiny as a postage stamp, you will notice, entitled 'Chevènement defends parity'. And it reads that during a debate in the Senate about parity at the municipal level, M. Chevènement, minister for the interior, declared: 'It is a matter of conjoining firm principles with suppleness in their application.' After all the fuss they made!

PD: Your position seems related to an approach you have long taken in your work, which you refer to in *Hipparchia's Choice* as 'institutional analysis' (Le Dœuff 1991: 236). You call on us to cultivate complex readings of the interconnections between overall institutional forces. You suggest we should never assume that an apparent gain really is a gain. For example, rather than being pro or contra parity, we should engage in an institutional analysis of the social circumstances and forces accompanying, and consolidated by, the argument for parity. Is it accompanied by, and does it reinforce, lesser or greater government support for publicly funded childcare, abortion and contraception, for example? Is it because 'the rights for which we fought are being progressively eroded' (as you argue in 'Problèmes d'investiture' [Le Dœuff 1995: 8]), that you are particularly suspicious of the parity movement? Why do you think we need to cultivate our skills in institutional analysis, in particular? Is it your view that we too easily accept and are duped by apparent progresses?

MLD: My position is that citizens (intellectuals among them, of course) should not be passive respondents to questions devised by the powers that be. We have a right to intervene into the very terms of any question. Australian Republicans recently gave a good example of that. About to have a referendum asking them whether they wanted a Republic, they first inquired what sort of a Republic it would be. Many felt they were not being offered the real thing, not what they hoped for a Republic. Similarly, I felt it was my responsibility to draw feminist attention to the implications of the parity movement: there has been an ostentatious absence of solidarity of women politicians with ordinary women. There is not a word on practical issues which matter to vast numbers of us, and therefore to all. Parity was a displacement, a distraction, if not a deception, shifting the attention from domestic violence or clitoridectomy to a more dainty topic. As a legerdemain, it failed, I'm glad to say. I don't think we are too easily duped by apparent progress. But our goals, issues and topics can easily be swept away and silenced – for example, by the institutionalization of one topic as *the* only topic against all others, or the rendering fashionable of this one topic, whether one's position is pro or contra.

PD: A similar caution informs the present piece, which begins in an optimistic spirit, in the light of an apparent resurgence of interest in feminism in France.[2] But the time of concern about parity in political representation is a time of indifference to the rights of immigrant women in France. State-handled feminism might seem to be a good, but it is stifling debate, you also argue. It seems the fundamental question is not whether an initiative is intrinsically 'positive', but, how does it function institutionally? Does it work to foster or stifle rights, initiatives, debate? As your essay progresses, we are asked to reflect on exactly which women are being heard today, under what circumstances and at whose expense? In particular, you provoke women intellectuals, politicians and philosophers (who, perhaps, are doing better these days?) to consider the situation of activists, teenagers, immigrants. I am reminded of an early piece (translated as 'Long Hair, Short Ideas') in which you point out that permissiveness can be a sly form of prohibition (Le Dœuff 1989: 103).

MLD: There is a real resurgence of interest in debate, whether feminist or not, in France. I should know: since *Le Sexe du savoir* (1998b)[3] was published, I have driven myself literally to the point of collapse in trying to meet all the invitations received. People ask you to come and talk with them, and not just to them. Sexism in textbooks, the position of women in philosophy, or of girls in the schooling system, peace and women, reproductive rights today and before or abroad ... are topics in which my fellow citizens of both sexes are interested. They demand a theoretical approach to these topics and a debate with an intellectual component. They want to talk and they want to learn something. I certainly believe that women intellectuals should (and can, in this way) help activists whose voices are stifled. Of course, the first thing to do is respect activist groups' knowledge and understanding of a question. For example, an article I wrote for *Libération* (Le Dœuff 1999b) was in part based on documentation available at Family Planning headquarters, as was a more developed talk I gave in Lyon on contraception and abortion.

In some cases, state-handled feminism is a genuine effort to introduce a new form of social justice. In Switzerland, maternity leave is not necessarily paid. Actually, it is seldom paid. In 1998, the government tried to introduce public funding for it. This was defeated by a referendum, though no one opposed the proposed reduction of military expenditure which was to have funded the reform. In this case, the state (just about to have its first woman president, by the way, Ruth Dreifuss) tried to take up an idea which groups of women had promoted for years. The government was no more successful than feminist activists had been. How is it that sometimes the state itself seems powerless when addressing patriarchy? And, granted that it is at times powerless, what is it we should understand about patriarchy itself? I have begun to ask myself if patriarchy is not an institution more fundamental than the state? The defenders of patriarchy think the state (along with other institutions such as religious institutions, l'Académie Française, etc.) should be patriarchy's instrument. And it so often is. But not necessarily, not always. We, who are in favour of women's emancipation, don't we also think that the state should play its part? But perhaps it goes against the grain for it to do so. In this case, state permissiveness as a sly form of prohibition is pretty much unavoidable. They must appear to do something for us while in fact marginalizing our demands. With the parity theme, this became clearer after the Socialists took over in 1997. From then on, the campaign for parity was led by the prime minister's press attachés and his wife.[4]

PD: You favour (in your reading of Gabrielle Suchon) a concept of liberty, and active citizenship, in terms of the fostering of conditions for debate – a qualitative practice of changing one's own views as well as those of others. You have often criticized feminists (and others) over the years for 'hearsay' references to the history of philosophy – imprecise, generalizing, conventional or inaccurate references to the Presocratics, rationalism, humanism, and so on. Must feminists bring an institutional analysis to feminism? It might be one way to understand your concern about these 'hearsay' references, since the present essay seems to clarify that your concern is with fostering the conditions for debate. Do you think that the detail, specificity and the letter of Francis Bacon's writings (for example) needs to be heard, just as Hipparchia, Hypatia, Suchon, Christine de Pisan (etc.) need to be heard?

MLD: I retain a right to be critical, even when reading essays which are rightly or wrongly considered feminist. All the same, pointing out mistakes in feminist writings could never become a central issue for me! It is just a step that I find necessary whenever pure fiction is built out of misinterpretations of the history of philosophy. Particularly when this fiction itself proves to be very impure, because tainted with conservative values. Evelyn Fox Keller hardly invents mistakes about Bacon:[5] they all come from male translators or commentators. Feminism does not contribute to a limiting of the quality of debate (as some of our conservative colleagues are prone to say) except when it blindly follows previous misinterpretations. In any case, I believe that younger women (who often discover feminism through books) deserve to be given the best scholarship we can offer to them, the best food for thought. Respect for accuracy or textual facts is respect for your readers and for the sort of feminism we want.

PD: You remark in 'Feminism is Back in France – Or Is It?' that we might want to adopt Gabrielle Suchon as our grandmother. In *Le Sexe du savoir* you argue that feminist epistemologists tend to leave out important figures such as Marie and Irène Curie (Le Dœuff 1998: 353n). Why do you consider it particularly important to engage in the strong interpretation (and presumably, location, republication and translation) of those women philosophers who have been present in history? Do women need to take up a more positive relationship to women thinkers of the past in order to philosophize effectively?

MLD: Gabrielle Suchon existed, though some seem to think (or wish it?) otherwise, and *pace* all the editors of Encyclopaedias who ignore her, probably the better to reinforce the false idea that philosophy is a male activity.[6] A mere respect for facts should be enough to burst this fiction. What is more, I find her philosophy inspiring and solid. Women do need to have a better knowledge of women philosophers of the past and more consideration for them. But each of us can choose and elect. We are under no obligation to love them all. Such an obligation would bring our philosophical vocation to an end, really. But we should realize how lucky we are not to have to be the first generation of women in philosophy. How great it is to feel grateful to some women of the past who prepared something for us, a better understanding of our freedom and dignity, for example. How splendid to be able to engage in conversation with Suchon and others. Republication, translation and, most important of all, intelligent interpretation are certainly needed (and are in some cases already being undertaken[7]) for everyone to be able to talk with them. For I believe that to read a philosophy book properly is to have a sort of dialogue or debate with the author (and you are right: there is a connection between accuracy and an idea of philosophy as debate). After such a debate, your views may be different, you may even be a slightly different person. Not because of some 'influence' of the book on you: this would imply you are a passive being when you read. But because, through the debate with the author, you will have grown ideas of your own. And you do not relate to an author who passionately wanted you to be free, active, sharp and joyful in the way you relate to someone who saw you as a lesser being who could rightly expect nothing better than a pathetic life.

Notes

1. Le Dœuff makes reference to a formulation from Françoise Gaspard: 'the objective of the parity movement is not to ensure that women in parliament represent women' ('la mobilisation qui est à l'oeuvre n'a pas pour objectif de faire que des femmes, dans les assemblées élues, representent les femmes') (Gaspard 1994: 42) and discussed in Le Dœuff (1995: 63). *Ed.*
2. Penelope Deutscher refers here to "Feminism is back in France – or is it?", *Hypatia, A Journal of Feminist Philosophy* no. 4 (2000).
3. Now in its third print run since its first publication in 1998, republished in 2000 in a pocket paperback edition (Champs Flammarion), and forthcoming in English translation with Routledge. *Ed.*
4. Syviane Agacinski, author of *Politique des Sexes* (Agacinski 1998).
5. Fox Keller's interpretation of Bacon is discussed in Le Dœuff (1998b: 237–47). *Ed.*
6. However, thanks to Michael Ayers, one of the editors of the *Routledge Encyclopedia of Philosophy*, Gabrielle Suchon has an entry in it (Le Dœuff 1998a).
7. See, for example, the translation and publication of Sor Juana de la Cruz's 1691 *La Respuesta*, edited by Electa Arenal and Amanda Powell (1994).

References

Agacinski, Sylviane (1998) *Politique des sexes*, Paris: Editions du Seuil.
De la Cruz, Sor Juana (1994) *The answer/la respuesta*, ed. and trans. Electa Arenal and Amanda Powell, New York: The Feminist Press, CUNY.

Gaspard, Françoise (1994) 'De la parité: Genèse d'un concept, naissance d'un mouvement', *Nouvelles questions féministes* 15 (4): 29–44.

Le Dœuff, Michèle (1989) 'Long Hair, Short Ideas', in *The Philosophical Imaginary*, trans. Colin Gordon, London: Athlone.

——— (1991) *Hipparchia's Choice: An Essay Concerning Women, Philosophy, Etc.*, trans. Trista Selous, Oxford: Blackwell.

——— (1995) 'Problèmes d'investiture (De la parité, etc.)', *Nouvelles questions féministes* 16 (2): 5–80.

——— (1998a) 'Gabrielle Suchon 1631–1703', in Edward Craig (ed.), *Routledge Encyclopedia of Philosophy*, vol. 8, London: Routledge.

——— (1998b) *Le Sexe du savoir*, Paris: Aubier.

——— (1999) 'IVG, l'état d'urgence', *Libération*, Mardi, 30 novembre, 5.

'Bringing us into twenty-first century feminism with joy and wit'

Pamela Sue Anderson and Meena Dhanda with Michèle Le Dœuff

Independence for a start

PA: Michèle, I see you as a philosopher who has always had a serious commitment to politics. Can you tell me something about your political commitment? Did you join a political party at a young age? If so, which party, and have you changed at all in this commitment?

MLD: In fact, I never joined any political party nor indeed any '*groupuscule*', a word the French use to describe small leftist parties. In the 1960s, many of my fellow students were involved in that type of activism. It was the normal thing to do, for young people with a commitment to politics, to join one of these groups, mostly Maoist or Trotskyist or, if you were already a cut on the conservative side, the Youth Branch of the Communist Party. Most of these people are now slightly left of centre or perfectly right of centre.

To me, at the time, it was obvious that to join that sort of politics, one had to take oneself seriously, and I couldn't! Leftist groups' members behaved as if they could teach you a thing or two; they tended to be on the pompous side, come to that. I couldn't identify with such an attitude. Pamela, you have read my work; you know that for me philosophers should take philosophy seriously, not themselves!

The interviewers would like to thank Tanya Singh for her help with the transcription and preparation of this interview for publication.

PA: An important distinction – with a nice twist! A touch of your 'witticism', as well?!

MLD: Some sense of humour, some irony and modesty, that's what we must hope for and that's what should accompany our work, whether it is hard work or not.

Besides, I already was – we are talking of the 1960s – I already was an independent mind. Perhaps without being aware of it, I was protecting this independence. The only groups I ever joined in my life were groups where a certain amount of free speech was allowed. I have found that possibility of free speech occasionally in trade unions or in the French Movement for Family Planning and I always maintained it in my involvement in feminism.

True, I was involved in the movement against the Vietnam War. This mostly meant going to demos quite frequently – in stilettos, by the way, because no one ever thought, before 1968, that a demo could again be dangerous; older people had experienced police violence during the Algerian war, but we thought that was past history. I was convinced that a demo, although involving legs and vocal cords, was just citizen activity that would be respected as such by both government and constabulary. Sometimes, a demo was also an occasion for intelligent views to be circulated. I remember hearing an impressive speech by the famous mathematician Laurent Schwartz in 1966 or 1967, on some Parisian boulevard, out of a loudspeaker.

As soon as I could vote, I did vote, of course and, when I discovered the historical American and British women's struggle which launched the demand for all women to have the vote in the nineteenth century, I began to think that voting is also a way to pay tribute to them. It added some colour to visits to the voting station. And today, I really think that it is an issue to vote and encourage others to vote.

My memory of the first women's demos in Paris tallies with my first experience. By the way, the very first I ever went to was November 1971, which I think was the second Women's Liberation Movement demo in France; the first one had taken place in August 1970. There were nine women there, in August 1970, but in November 1971, we were, I can't remember . . . perhaps 50,000. . . . I mean, a huge number.

PA: Could it have been much more than 50,000?

MLD: Perhaps! I cannot say that on oath, but it was a huge demo, that is all I can say. On the streets, you discovered a whole new world and way of thinking, sometimes through slogans and songs, sometimes through pamphlets or leaflets. From 1971 to 1973, as far as feminism was concerned, I was simply a 'demogoer', if you like, getting new ideas or new perspectives – enjoying myself a lot when the language of political protest was propped up with witticism![1]

The issue in which I was most interested was access to contraception and abortion. In 1973, a movement called MLAC ('Movement for Liberty of Abortion and Contraception') was created. I immediately joined it. With a friend who taught classics, I created a branch in Colombes, a suburban town. Very soon, women working at the local hospital came and then took over, which was a good thing. Let classicists or philosophers start something and let nurses continue! Women have talents, talents which are diverse and which, when pooled together, may prove creative indeed.

Later on I joined an MLAC group in my own area in Paris, in which I discovered at the same time the most distressing aspects of life and wonderful acts of solidarity. I understood how being the beneficiary of an act of respect or kindness may transform a woman's life. A Spanish *concierge* in her early forties endowed me with this true nugget of understanding. The group had sorted her out, which means that everyone had taken the risk (at least on paper) of charges and imprisonment to help her, free of charge of course. I saw her blossom and open up. For a while, she joined the group, radiant. Perhaps it was the first time in her life that she was treated as 'an end in itself', someone who had rights and needs that others would bother to meet.

PA: How has your political commitment made a difference to your feminism? Or is it impossible to say, because your politics and feminism are inseparable, perhaps emerging and developing together? And then, what about their relation to your work in philosophy?

MLD: I believe that social questions should be seen as a beacon from which we may get an orientation in thought. We need to know about how things are for ordinary women; your ordinary feminist philosopher ought to know what is suggested by those who do good work to try and change the position of women in society. I do believe in being involved, let us say from time to time, in practical issues and in debates about practical issues. Activist associations in France occasionally ask just for that. You have to be patient sometimes, you may develop an idea which will not be accepted straightaway. An intellectual's responsibility is simply to explain an idea to the best of her own understanding, in as well-reasoned and well-documented a way as possible, and no more. It is certainly not our job to persuade. I believe I have acquired this attitude through doing philosophy and with the idea that philosophy does not coincide with rhetoric nor indeed with propaganda of any kind. Philosophy exists by taking into account the fact that we address other people as free minds, able to engage in a critical dialogue with their own beliefs.

In 2000, the Lyon group for Family Planning invited a GP and myself to a public debate. They were campaigning to extend the time limit for getting an abortion. My view (documented in England, by the way) was that asking for no time limit might well lead to hospitals lingering more (even more than they do!) in providing an abortion, and therefore to longer waiting lists, which is not what we want. I suggested that we also devised strategies to reduce the delay between the moment a woman decides she wants an abortion and the moment it is provided. Perhaps such a perspective was not adopted straightaway by my activist friends in the audience. It sounded a little awkward to their ears, I think. Well, that was the year 2000; I'm now reading exactly that here and there, and I'm very pleased! Everyone must be entitled to take their time to change their minds. I don't believe in being brusque or, you know, in ordering people's minds; let them think it out at leisure for themselves. So, if everyone must be entitled to take their time to change their minds, conversely, an intellectual should know that it will take time for some views to be accepted.

In my feminist writings, you may have noticed that I'm not seeking, nor indeed courting, immediate success. Otherwise, I would never have written what I did. In feminist studies, just as in any given field, there is a matter of consensus, or group ideology, or falling into line with accepted wisdom or the wisdom of a group, you know what I mean. My first piece ('Women and Philosophy', now reprinted as 'Long Hair, Short Ideas'[2]) was initially seen as singular partly because it was critical. It was not in agreement with 'the line', which at the time was about female difference; it still is, of course. It was not 'sisterly enough', because it was critical. And – this came as a surprise for many in the English-speaking world – it involved a knowledge of the history of philosophical texts in the discussion about women and philosophy. My second piece, about Beauvoir, was written in 1979 and promptly rejected by a British journal, the editors claiming that Beauvoir was *'passée'*, Irigaray having become the name of the game! In the United States, it was also met, though not by everybody, with explicit disbelief. De Beauvoir, a philosopher? These two pieces have since then been reprinted a number of times and re-xeroxed in a way which could make any publisher feel miserable.

It is hardly the duty of a thinker to look out for a crowd she could follow nor, come to that, to write books that will help promote her own career, which may always involve some kind of compromise with dominant, hence, patriarchal ideology.

PA: Yes; I like this idea that you have to allow people time to change their minds.

MLD: It has to do with the idea of freedom – their own freedom, and my wanting them to find their own freedom. And this is something I've learned partly through activism about contraception and abortion, because my role was to talk with women who were demanding an abortion – at the time it was illegal in France – within an activist group. The atmosphere, all that struggle, was about helping each individual woman to find her own way to her own freedom. It was important to discuss with her why she was not using contraception and therefore was in need of an abortion. It was crucial to make sure it was her, not the husband or the parents, who wanted the pregnancy to be terminated. Our message was: 'It is you, it is your opinion, that counts.' A woman who is in trouble may find an opportunity in it to discover her own liberty. Well, that sort of experience has shaped my work in philosophy or reinforced a tendency I already had. I find deep pleasure in respecting my readers' intellectual freedom; I write in the hope of helping them to be freer and to find a true intellectual liberty.

Women, feminism and food for thought

PA: Michèle, do you sometimes despair of women today, who do not seem to be aware of the need to engage in contemporary politics (as feminists)? Is it ever enough to be a strictly academic feminist? In fact, the latter might be impossible.

MLD: Hmm, I'm now in two minds about that! Or rather, my brief time teaching feminist studies at Geneva has made me change my views. Most of my students, particularly the young ones, were not at all ready to engage in practical politics. They wanted intellectual food, they enjoyed reading the books suggested to them, and enjoyed discussing topics at the level of principles. It was feminism considered as a fine art, almost.

Only some mature students who already had experience as activists were, as a matter of course, carrying on with practical politics. To start with, I was slightly surprised that the younger ones would not engage in discussion with the mature students about also being a practical activist – I was surprised, and then I understood. There is such a thing as intellectual hunger, a pure need for ideas or for a renewed intellectual life. This hunger brought to my seminars an amazing mix of women and some men. Both the mature activists and the young students came for the same reason: they wanted some intellectual food. All seemed to describe my teaching in food metaphors to the point of licking their lips when they had particularly enjoyed the meal! Little bear cubs around a pot of honey! And yes, a right-wing woman magistrate a bit older than myself, just like an undergraduate with no politics at all, could find food for thought, say, in my discussion of John Locke.

At the time, I wondered if teaching feminist studies was not just about intellectual fulfilment, which is an issue in itself. My own political persuasion – namely, that things do not happen if women themselves do not stand up for them – was, for some of my students, like stating the obvious, for others like, well, a personal view of mine to which they didn't need to pay much attention. Moreover, those who also had connections with the Department of Politics were taught exactly the opposite as truth pure and simple, namely, that feminist movements never achieve anything, because they always are and were too weak; that progress for women comes only through international agencies! This was the creed, subject of exams, and of course, when I would hint at the opposite, well, it would be seen by some students as just an idea of mine. The mature students already knew that women themselves have to conquer and defend their hard-won liberties.

Anyway, since then, many of the younger students have understood what I meant. Again, time is relevant in debates. They really understood at the time when the question of paid maternity leave came under discussion in Switzerland. Many women had thought that the federal government would win that issue without their help. When the reform aimed at giving compensation for maternity leave was defeated by referendum, they realized that even when something makes sense, even when the Head of State is a lovely woman, utterly dedicated to the reform (and Ruth Dreifuss, the aforesaid lovely woman, had put all her heart into it), all the same, it is necessary for ordinary women citizens to devote time and energy to the debate as well. To go around and explain why compensation for maternity leave is a just and good thing, to attend meetings on the topic, in order to show a keen collective interest, to distribute leaflets on the streets, and so on.

MD: In a paper you gave to a philosophy seminar at Oxford, you've quoted Louise Weiss with some relish when she wrote in 1936 while campaigning for the vote that it would be necessary 'to kick feminism out of the few drawing-rooms where it shows off'. Are you engaged in a similar exercise with respect to certain types of intellectual currents in feminism?

MLD: Meena, you are right to put the emphasis on 'certain types'! There are some types of feminism or women's studies which do not seem to lead anywhere or which seem to aim at creating apathy. All the same, I would not consider 'kicking out' any intellectual current. I would rather be critical and a little caustic as I always was, and then let my readers think it out for themselves. As long as there is an intellectual debate, it is fine by me. Being polemical has nothing to do with an attempt to exclude from the arena, nor indeed with forcing anyone to get some fresh air outside the walls of the academy. But nonetheless, from time to time, I would recommend fresh air, remembering that life is a long process anyway – there is no need to rush.

Keeping in touch with practical social issues and with the activists who stand up for them is meaningful in many respects. Intellectual women have many means to circulate information, and it is crucial to help information to circulate. To take an example: Martha Nussbaum's book, *Sex and Social Justice* (Oxford University Press, 1999), is the book I would recommend on these grounds. All women considering themselves as feminists, and students in women's studies, should be better informed about the position of women in developing countries. I take my hat off to Martha Nussbaum for having collected so much material.

In the case of Safiya Husseini during the winter 2001–2, it was also crucial to circulate information about her, to get people to email the Nigerian Embassy and the UN Office for Human Rights. I put all my heart and soul into Safiya's defence and I was very glad to see that Amnesty International and some groups of the French Human Rights League took it up. It is our responsibility to help movements as important as Amnesty to understand that they should be involved in the defence of women. This also took a long time. Twenty years ago, it was difficult to get movements which were not 'women's movements' involved in any campaign for women's rights.

Occasionally, we may provide to activists' movements a reflection, a shift of emphasis, new lines of argument. At any rate, when connected with them, or when working on real issues, we take up a social responsibility and become different from what we were. In a sense, this is the reward: to become different from what we were by increasing our social responsibility. Every time I have the opportunity to have a dialogue with activists or to attend a court hearing on the most difficult issues (incestuous rape, clitoridectomy, etc.), I have the feeling that I'm changing, intellectually (because I discover aspects of life I had no idea of) and also personally. However disturbing it is to find out about the worst effects of patriarchy, one may have the feeling that there is a 'duty to know', and that one becomes more human by allowing oneself to know about what is most painful in human life. Besides, it is educated women's responsibility to organize into some theoretical construction empirical material and findings about oppression. A PhD about single motherhood in the United States today may put your future as an academic a bit at risk. It is all the same a most respectable and extremely valuable endeavour.

And, if we return to the question: 'is it possible to be strictly an academic feminist', on paper, it might be possible. Except that, within the aforesaid walls of the academy, one is confronted with a masculinist tradition, which has despised women and women's contribution to the historical development of liberties or to the history of ideas. Therefore, if the better part of the community holds opinions slightly or heavily biased by contempt, it is very hard to remain loyal even to intellectual rigour without touching base from time to time with the knowledge, discourse and values of activists working on practical issues.

Besides, I'm sorry to say, opinions which are questionable, not to say simply untrue, may get propagated within the academic context. See how many colleagues will credit Michel Foucault for the French women's liberation movement, or for having introduced the idea that sex is political. As if Mary Wollstonecraft, Simone de Beauvoir, Kate Millett and a few others had not broached the topic before, nor even existed! See how many claim that John Locke's or John Rawls' philosophy is just what we always needed. Ideas always come from men, you see – that's very well-known, isn't it? – feminism is derived. You may even hear women academics claim that we did spend ten years with Lacan, but Heidegger is our mentor now...

But after all, were we to have a look into the works of geographers, we may well find aspects there which are biased as well by, say, nationalistic beliefs or by the last government's policy concerning regional development! At a certain time, a given set of ideas may be rewarded or may be punished. A grown-up person should never allow that structure to influence her production of ideas. We should know there is a 'tempo' for intellectual life. And if you produce ideas in accordance with what is rewarded or punished, well in that case, twenty years later things will have changed and your work will no longer have any relevance. It is, anyway, unworthy of any thinker to do that. But let us take a more optimistic view: life is a long process. Sometimes, you come across women who first started thinking about themselves within a 'current' you consider as leading nowhere and as inviting us to stay in the drawing room, but who eventually freed themselves from the limitation imposed on them.

MD: Michèle, what you said just now about Locke and Heidegger reminds me of your continuing aversion to intellectual mentorship by men. You've always rejected an uncritical acceptance of ready-made frameworks. But you've also said that a search for a philosophical framework, which could prove appropriate to the theorization of women's freedom, is a search that you have been engaged with. My question is: Do you think such a framework is possible, and do you see yourself as constructing such a framework?

MLD: I'm constantly trying to open up vistas and to push questions further. This might not be what could in the end produce a framework, particularly because I see thought as a dynamics, as something on the move, and myself as trying to remove obstacles on the way or to challenge fixations. What I offer may well be 'unfinished' in nature and I feel at ease with that. I often think that someone who has read me will perhaps produce a more complete theory eventually, I often think of my work as preparing other works.

All the same, I have some beliefs. I do see feminism as a yet-missing, or often-missing, face of humanism; women's rights are human rights. Besides, if we take up the Renaissance idea according to which the human being does not have any 'essence' but becomes human or more human by embracing the interests of humankind as a whole, I believe that this is true of feminism. By challenging patriarchy – not in order to put any kind of matriarchy in its place, nor to seek any sort of juxtaposition of patriarchy and matriarchy, but gradually to undo the power of one sex over the other – we may hope to achieve more than just what we are doing. For patriarchy may be responsible for more than sex oppression. It is clearly at the core of all sorts of fundamentalism, from Televangelists to the Taliban. Nazism was a reinforcement of the power of both men and the state over women, transforming them, as Rita Thalmann put it, into reproductive mares and beasts of burden.[3]

Conversely, resisting male power is resisting fundamentalism. I'm also convinced that, if her reproductive life was everywhere in the hands of each individual woman, families would be more balanced, children less numerous, not produced one after the other or by the dozen, until the woman collapses, which is unacceptable in itself. It is believed that in developing countries, hyper-production of children counteracts attempts to redress the economy. The fact that many of these children will die before adulthood is heartbreaking and, again, economically speaking, a disaster. Women free to choose how many children they really want: this would probably lead to their having less numerous children, but better fed, vaccinated and schooled . . . which is in itself a good vision to contemplate. It may also help promote peace. Societies that assume that there will always be new children to replace those that get killed at war take sending their members to be butchered too lightly.

All in all, I believe that there is a lot of hope, for everybody, for the planet itself, in the dismantling of patriarchy.

Philosophy as detection

MD: You seem to take a peculiar joy in detection – a bit like a Miss Marple of philosophy, if I may say so – in laying bare little known, and often overlooked connections in the reconstruction of intellectual lineage. I mean 'detection' in the archaeological sense. Are you mainly concerned with paying homage where it is due, or are there deeper purposes at work in the laborious digging and exploration that you so often do?

MLD: 'Peculiar joy' . . .! Of Meena, it must be said: 'this woman knows me!' Yes, it is a joy and one must suspect that this tendency to archaeological diggings is a personal trait of character, hence something I could not account for. In *Le Sexe du savoir* (1998, 2000), I obliquely acknowledged that such a tendency may come to you early in life. It is linked to the habit of sensing that there is something the matter in an event or in a passage from a book, something one is not able to understand straightaway; you must be wise enough to know that you do not understand it all on the spot. I must admit that I always was in the habit of somehow stowing away a fact in a corner of my memory, as a question, and with the vague idea that one day perhaps I would decipher what it meant. Perhaps reading Agatha Christie to teach myself more English when at school developed that sort of habit. Miss Marple collects bits of facts or conversations and, in the last chapter, the puzzle falls into place.

Let me try and explain how it may work from a cognitive point of view. We were taught that there is a basic opposition between analysis and synthesis. Analysis separates components one from another, synthesis puts them together. Analysis goes from things conditioned to what conditions them; synthetic order would go from what conditions something to what is conditioned. Please forgive this simplistic outline. Now, in usual thinking (as opposed to ways of reasoning which are more formalized), there may not be such a cut and dried difference between synthesis and analysis. In ordinary life, we often put two and two together and suddenly understand or decipher the meaning of this or that. If intellectual '*rapprochements*' are illuminating, it is because a synthesis (however summary or cursory) may produce an analysis.

It is not just to reconstructions of intellectual lineage that this may apply. Take Bachelard's books on the poetry of fire, water, space, earth, and so on. He accumulates fragments of literature, and the more numerous these fragments become, the deeper understanding you get of the image of fire, of daydreaming, of water or of spatial organization. But it's true to say that this may also apply to the history of ideas, in the sense of reconstructions of lineage. It may be actual or probably actual lineage: say, Y had read X. For instance, I am pretty sure that the young Rousseau had read Gabrielle Suchon. It may be something a little different, namely, the reconstruction of shifts in a long evolution. This is, at least, what I have tried to do concerning the emergence of so-called female intuition. You take the period of time when intuition is God's mode of knowing (or the wonderful human mode of knowing first principles); you take the period in time when intuition has become 'feminine'. What happened between these two historical times? What does it mean for a mode of knowledge to undergo such a change? The question is already a '*rapprochement*', demanding an explanation. In forming the question, we already have a humble synthesis. Except that there is a huge gap between the two moments and it is this gap which has to be filled as much as possible. What will fill the gap is a work combining analysis and synthesis.

And let me add this. On paper, or in principle, the analysis of a concept can be carried out quite easily (supposedly, all you need is to be sharp and endowed with methods of analysis), whereas synthesis implies collecting all sorts of odd bits and pieces, and a good dose of luck to get hold of the necessary findings. Except that lucky findings will produce '*rapprochements*' which in their turn will help unfold a more relevant analysis. This could be the biggest lesson in modesty which research may teach us, namely, that you have to be lucky. What would have become of my attempt to reconstruct the complex shift from intuition as God's mode of knowing to female intuition, had I not been lucky enough to have read Gabrielle Suchon and to have got hold, by accident really, of a rightly forgotten book by a Scottish Reverend?

We analyse concepts with our already acquired knowledge of many things; our reading of dusty documents is informed by questions which were lingering in our minds. And luck is crucial, even when you try to be methodical. One day, I was wondering how to find out more about the connection between Bacon and Galileo. I got the idea of looking in the papers of someone who had been an English ambassador in Italy (diplomats were good go-betweens). It so happened that he had also been an ambassador in Vienna, and on his way had made a detour to meet Kepler and... what I found in the Bodleian Library was material, not about Bacon and Galileo, but about Bacon and Kepler. What I had 'scented' for some time, against the received wisdom of Baconian studies – namely, that there had been some kind of connection between Bacon and Kepler – was suddenly substantiated.

PA: As a feminist, you have important things to say about other feminists who fail to read past philosophers correctly. I find this really important. In an interview with Penelope Deutscher (2000), you suggest that these mistakes (often) come from misinterpretations originally done by men. But are there also problems with how women are taught philosophy today by other feminists?

MLD: There are always problems with how anybody is taught anything by anybody. This is why we should advise young people to add as much self-teaching as possible to the curriculum. As for what you are referring to: yes, nineteenth- and twentieth-century translations of Bacon's Latin works, by male translators, contain mistakes which in fact insert into the texts the sexist ideology of their time, as if these texts were not full enough already of sexism, early seventeenth-century sexism. How is it that some feminists accepted these translations, which basically claim that science is a male knowledge of a female Nature? If we consider that the dominant ideology of the twentieth century has it that women and men are different, or rather that women are different from men, and if we see this ideology as shared and upheld by both the majority of men and by 'differentialist' feminists, then it is no wonder that they will agree on the so-called fact that science is for the males of the species, and research is a male and fairly violent attempt to know a poor lady Nature so as to enslave her. The problem is that it is not like that in Bacon, for one thing. There *is* blatant sexism in his writings, but it is a different sexism, based on the idea that a group of people who have scientific knowledge will have as much power over a group deprived of science as a God would have over a human being.

Besides, if you take Bacon's sexism as it is, the conclusion will be that sex equality will not be achieved without women having as much access to science as men. If you focus on the twentieth-century form of sexism inserted by male translators and commentators, then the conclusion is bound to be that women should keep away from science, for they would put their souls or identities at risk by doing physics or biology!

MD: You have said many inspiring things about teaching philosophy. One simple comment that struck me was about why the continued teaching of a text can be fascinating. You explain that with successive generations of students the teacher has to explain different things, fill in different gaps. It is indeed good advice for the teacher to bear in mind the receptivity of the students when teaching the 'same' text again. To take this further, what criteria should govern the choice of a text in teaching philosophy?

MLD: Meena, you should keep the question of my views about teaching philosophy for yourself; you probably understand them better than I do myself. So why not keep the topic for an essay by yourself!

MD: If you did a seminar on 'Women and Philosophy' now, what text would you choose?

MLD: Right now, I would gladly teach Gabrielle Suchon.

A critical philosophy of parity?

MD: In the parity debate in France, you have seemed to defend the idea of genderless citizenship. Given the nature of the debate's reliance on the philosophy of radical difference, your support for the demand for parity seems to have been conditional. Further, you have argued that parity must not mean simply what Parliament looks like, but what it is able to do. What is your response to the direction that the pro-parity movement has taken?

MLD: The story is more complex than that. First in an article published in *Les Temps Modernes* in 1981, and then in *Hipparchia's Choice* (1991), I had pleaded for equal numbers of women and men sitting on decision-making committees. Although I may have mentioned *en passant* in that book, and also in a paper given at a Beauvoir conference, that it would be a good thing if Parliament became a fifty-fifty group, my real focus was on committees appointed from above. Particularly boards of electors for civil service positions – you know that in France, teachers, post-office employees, and so on are all state-employed. I saw that as the real means to achieving equal opportunity in public appointments and employment. I really believe that we should make a sharp distinction between councils, commissions and panels nominated 'from above', and hence acting on the behalf of public institutions, and elected bodies, elected from below by the people. The latter, at least in principle, are elected on the basis of a programme, to defend certain ideas in Parliament.

When the parity movement started in France, first launched by Françoise Gaspard, Claude Servan-Schreiber and Anne Le Gall, I had the feeling that my beautiful idea had been taken up, but in a distorted way. They utterly forgot about councils and panels which are nominated by the highest agencies. (By the way, in 2000, Evelyne Pisier carried out a survey showing that in recent years no progress at all had been made regarding sex balance as far as appointments from above were concerned.) Parity activists have put the emphasis only on 'the' elected body, namely Parliament. With no reference at all to a political programme, even suggesting that 'women MPs would not represent women'. Their followers took it a step further by describing parity as the last and only goal of feminism. It was not parity as a means to achieving better laws or regulations for ordinary women, it was parity instead of political issues and to the detriment of all practical issues. It was as if a shift in language was taking place. As if talking of battered women, of lack of education about contraception for what were still large groups of women, were no longer acceptable topics in the public sphere, not fit for polite conversation, evoking dirty aspects of life perhaps, hence to be pushed out by a new topic. It was as if only the 'posher' topic of parity could still be discussed.

My criticism of the parity movement also involved a discussion about what 'representation' means. Taking the idea more or less from Hobbes, I explained that there is a theatrical meaning of the word and another one which is quite different. The latter is based on delegation of authority. When I give a mandate to my ground floor neighbour and friend to represent me at the general meeting of the building, he or she is not there to 'represent' me in any theatrical sense of the word. She or he will kindly vote on my behalf about repairing the gutter or redecorating the stairway according to what I said I thought best. I choose to give a mandate to Martha or Thomas, rather than to Philippe or Christine, because Martha or Thomas is more likely to defend my views than the latter. In politics, bodies supposed to be 'representative' should be elected like that: a programme, first of all, and then the choice of people who are likely to defend it sincerely. If parity were discussed from that perspective, we would first of all have to discuss, at grass-roots level, what our programme could be, and then to discuss with women politicians to what extent they – this woman politician, or that other one – could identify with it.

Unfortunately, we have all noticed that candidates in general elections or presidential elections talk less and less about a programme. Elections are more and more a matter of 'showbiz' and theatrical performance. I saw the parity movement as a new aspect of this shift, a shift which in itself is anti-democratic – you elect people without being told what they are going to do. . . . And more often than not, they will do things you may not like.

All the same, this criticism does not amount to a defence of the idea of genderless citizenship. Quite the opposite, actually, and when anti-parity activists tried to make me sign petitions against that law, they were disappointed at my firmly declining to sign. They advocated a 'universal', and in this case it meant genderless citizenship. I'm a woman and a feminist, I have ideas about the necessary progress of sex equality, which France should support. I want these ideas to be represented in political programmes and discussed in the public sphere. Discussed with everybody, men and women alike. In fact, I want an insertion of feminist ideas into the collective discourse and onto the agenda, which should be one held in common. If the parity movement had held this as its political end, and drafted a programme, however summary, I would have been with them enthusiastically.

Unfortunately, the opposite is taking place; we experienced a severe shock in February, when the government (which had prided itself on having introduced parity in the Constitution) submitted to Parliament a reform of parental authority. This reform was aimed at giving more rights (though not more duties) to divorced fathers and didn't even take into account the fact that some divorces are pronounced because the man had been violent to his wife or his children. A violent man, divorced because of that, may demand shared custody of the children, and half of any child benefits. This law will make the life of many divorced women more of a misery than it may be already, and it will impoverish many of them. As if there was not already a large enough discrepancy between the incomes of male and female divorcees.

MD: In the Fourth Notebook in *Hipparchia's Choice*, you wrote that the state must 'take as its prime aim to create a space where all can live together with their differences, which will probably be multiple and not planned by anyone' (1991: 313). Would you like to elaborate on that?

MLD: I always believed that if there were more equality between persons, equal freedom of consciousness – equal freedom full stop – and equal protection from the community, the outcome of this would be the emergence of multiple differences and not, as some claim, uniformity. And these would be differences to treasure because they would not be the end result of coercion. When I first discovered Harriet Taylor, I had the feeling that I had met a bosom friend.

Her idea of 'good' differences was certainly not that Chinese women's feet are cramped whereas in the West it is the waist and chest of women which are compressed by corsets. With her, I would hold that absence of coercion allows nonconformity which in its turn produces true individualities – not two human beings alike.

With such a view, you may and must adopt an ethics: when no one is predictable any longer, we need an ethics of sympathy for this very unpredictability of other people. But I think this is not enough. Nothing will happen without a clear definition of individuals' basic rights, from birth onward. Had we in France a positive law stating that bodily integrity is part of children's rights, and schooling a fundamental right for children of both sexes; had we the idea that the Republic must protect all children equally, it would be easier to stand up for little girls who are at risk of undergoing clitoridectomy and to stand up for Muslim teenagers who want to attend school with a scarf on their heads. Don't misunderstand me: I'm not a fan of this scarf, but I believe that a girl's right to schooling must prevail. As for clitoridectomy, I believe parents should be forbidden to carry out this ablation on their babies. On the other hand, if an adult woman were to decide to have this ablation carried out on her own body, I don't think the law should interfere, though I would feel very sorry for her. As for the scarf, you may have noticed that on the streets, on trains, one may come across Muslim adult women who clearly have rights, education, employment, the possibility of walking or travelling on their own . . . on them, the very aspect of the scarf changes.

From politics of sex to politics of race

MD: Just as there was an urgency about the politics of sex in the 1960s, in the current climate in Europe, it seems to me that the politics of race needs to be seriously addressed. What in your view should feminists be doing about the rise of the Far Right in France?

MLD: Anti-racism is constantly urgent, as is a politics of sex, or perhaps I should say that in both cases, we should remember that only sustained action, and thinking in the long term, may achieve a better society. We usually advise battered wives to plan their steps; associations working to give them support often say that acting only in 'urgency', giving them help only when there is an acute crisis, is not what might really help. I feel tempted to say the same for many other political problems.

Now, to take a feminist angle on racism, I would first of all want to turn to a phenomenon which is not taken into account enough, namely xenophobia, which may well be a global platform for racism or interwoven with racism. I understood that when I lived in Geneva. In a tram, I was chatting with an elderly lady and trying to comfort her (she was distressed because she had found a public phone broken). At a certain stage, I gave away the fact that I was French. Her face reflected deep horror; she exclaimed 'You are French?' and then turned her back on me.

I have sometimes been the witness, sometimes on the receiving end, of incidents of that kind in other European countries, and in retrospect, I began to understand what I had witnessed or experienced. Xenophobia is a negative attitude towards people who in some way or another do not belong to the community, because they are not nationals or, when a nation is defined by one religion, because they are not members of that faith. Xenophobia may be hatred pure and simple, or distrust, or a wish to humiliate you, or systematically to take advantage of you and exploit you. It may take up many forms, so let us say it is about making a difference between people who belong and people who do not belong. And I think that in many cases it is the hidden platform of racism. 'These foreigners, you know'; a global hostility to foreigners except that, once this is set down, then a given community may think of introducing degrees of foreignness. The Swiss law about immigration is clear; it is called 'the three-circles principle'. The first circle defines first-class potential immigrants, namely European citizens, considered as, and I quote, 'almost like us'. The second circle is for Americans, Australians and Canadians (almost like the 'almost'). The third circle is for the rest of the world – with an occasional exception for the Vietnamese and Cambodians who fled from Communism; 'the enemies of our main enemy being more or less perhaps our friends'.

If you take a close look at Le Pen's position, you will notice that it is xenophobia he is explicitly propagating. Jobs and housing should be given to French nationals, not to foreigners. 'French mothers' should have child benefits and even be paid to stay at home (but nothing is said of mothers who are not French). He does often let slip racist attitudes as well; his anti-Semitic remarks are particularly repulsive. But his explicit and real line, I think, is xenophobia. He occasionally tries to remind himself that there are a lot of French citizens who are black; he might even remember that many French citizens are of Maghreb descent. These attempts clearly go against the grain with him, but perhaps some among his think tank insist that he should try – try to limit himself to xenophobia, that is. Xenophobia which is not punished by law and which is aimed at migrant workers and migrant families.

If, from this description, we now turn to women's attitudes, we shall have to describe an old political gap among women themselves. In Germany, at the beginning of the twentieth century, women who were real feminists in my view, who had campaigned for the vote and contraception, were among the first victims of Nazism along with other political opponents, namely the Communists and the Socialists. A third of them (if my memory of Claudia Koonz's book is good) were assassinated in jail before the end of 1934, another third were in exile by then and a third underground.[4] We must never forget that fascism first gets rid of political opponents, feminists included, before attacking people who, according to a fascistic definition of conformity, should not belong. Before organizing mass deportation and the extermination of Jews, tziganes and gay men, the Nazis assassinated those who would have stood up for them.

On the other hand, many associations of conservative women (mostly religious groupings, like women's institutes) joined the Nazis. We must never forget that. As my friend Liliane Kandel would put it, 'Being born a woman does not grant you any political grace'. Even if statistics show that today women vote less than men for Le Pen in France (except housewives who vote exactly like the men), even if a law against racist statements was approved by referendum in the Republic of Geneva only thanks to women voters, we must never forget that a portion of the women in any given country may turn out to be supporters of the worst politics. And the more traditional their lifestyle, the higher the risk of their identifying with a politics of exclusion, discrimination and extermination.

There may be an archaic factor in that attitude. In many traditional societies, women are allotted the role of being, in the words of Nira Yuval-Davis, 'the bearers of the collective'. They are in charge of maintaining traditions and are supposed to identify wholly with the community; to be the 'belongings' and instruments of this community and of its closure. This may well be an unconscious mechanism; the point of anchorage of the community in the people is probably under the surface.

PA: Michèle, here I am reminded of the passage in *Le Sexe du savoir*, where you query the significance of the idea of a 'gender gap' (1998, 2000: 335). Taking as your example the French election of 1988, you note that the gap between the sexes is most apparent in votes for the extreme right. Certain women – those who are educated and have had the opportunity to learn to think freely – diverge most strongly from the male supporters of the right's racism and xenophobia. These women are much less likely to follow men who vote for Le Pen and his like. However, it is women who work at home (e.g. housewives) and are under the thumb of patriarchy who still tend to follow 'their men'. This is a good example of equality and divergence among women.

I find this example an important challenge to twentieth-century 'difference feminism', that is, those who replace(d) 'equal' with 'different'. Moreover, this is a highly significant marker for your own divergence from the so-called French feminism of 'difference'. While twentieth-century feminists tended to reduce the debate to difference or equality, that is, either following the so-called French feminism or not, you – Michèle – were waiting for women to take hold of their political freedom to change their own minds. The patience of your wisdom, treating each woman as autonomous in her thinking, would seem to be bringing us into the twenty-first century with your distinctive approach to feminist philosophy. In this particular case, women are to work for change by seizing the reality of their equal rights to vote, and their possible divergence from patriarchal men, as well as possibly from other women. I am excited by this third way to read women, philosophy and the significance of their political commitments. You also anticipated – uncannily – the crucial role of voting by women (against the extreme right, but also patriarchy) in this new century: it's their power for/to change! Michèle, I hope that I am not putting words in your mouth with these comments . . .

MLD: You are not! And it is true that, if I had the means to campaign to encourage women to develop the habit of voting, in Europe or in America, I would! But, speaking of the Far Right in France, there is something I would like to tell my feminist friends and many other citizens. It had been known since the late 1980s that, as soon as a politician drops a remark about migrants' right to vote, this kindles xenophobia and displaces 3, 4 or 5 per cent of voters from the classical Right to the Far Right. It was François Mitterrand who experimented with that, in order to defeat Chirac for the 1988 Presidential elections. The Socialist candidate this year, Lionel Jospin, mentioned this 'migrants' right to vote' on his official leaflet sent with other candidates' leaflets to all electors just before the first round. Without doubt, this again took some voters from Chirac to Le Pen, or some potential abstentionists to the voting station, with the result that Le Pen did better than Jospin in that preliminary 'round'.

I believe that an idea first introduced by the MODEFEN, the Movement for the Rights of Black Women, and called 'autonomous status for immigrant women', should supersede the topic of a migrant's right to vote. Most immigrant women in France are there on the grounds of 'family *rapprochement*'; basically, they are in France *qua* wives of their husbands, not as autonomous persons. It means that if any kind of separation takes place, they lose every right, including the right to stay in France. If in their country of origin, the repudiation of the marriage is accepted, this may happen in five minutes. If the man is violent to them, they can't even leave the home. The same applies to any children: the father has every power to send them back to the country of origin. All in all, our legislation concerning migrant families gives to the husband and father more power over the wive(s) and offspring than these men had in their old country. No wonder teenagers have a tendency to be more submissive or more rebellious than they would in the old country.

The MODEFEN claims that 'autonomous status' for all women immigrants should come first, and I am with them. It should be put at the forefront of any political agenda concerning immigration. A migrant's right to vote would in fact benefit mostly male heads of families, anyway. Let us work to give immigrant women equal rights with their French counterparts, to give them literacy and to create a solidarity between women of all origins. And let us have the courage, because it will take some, to tell the Left that we do not want to hear about a migrant's right to vote for the time being, not before autonomous status is achieved.

PA: Yes, 'autonomous status for immigrant women' is clearly the correct priority.

Tell me all your secrets . . .

MD: How does philosophy get produced? And what gets you writing?

MLD: I believe we should make a distinction between desire, the desire to do philosophy, and the production of philosophy. Of the desire to do philosophy, I would say I don't quite know where it comes from, but such a desire may lead you to read philosophical works, or to discuss philosophical topics, or to produce pieces, or to teach, or all these forms of philosophical activity at the same time. This desire does not have a pre-established destiny.

When it leads to production, I think it is because you perceive that something has not been said yet, which ought to be said. In my experience, there is often more to it, because the energy you have to put into completing a book is not a small matter. I have occasionally managed to have intense days of writing because life was bleak. Every morning, I would walk to my desk, thinking: 'when Pascal had a toothache, he did maths'. To resist intense suffering, an intense concentration of the mind is known to help or indeed to be necessary.

Occasionally, and this is what *Hipparchia's Choice* is, I have been led to produce philosophy as a pure act of joy. I started writing this book as a convalescent. It is no secret that I had a severe form of cancer in the 1980s, one which does not leave much hope. As a result, doctors have to take the risk of trying to treat it by prescribing heavy chemotherapy, and so on. It was an experience in a way beyond the limits of normal human experience. When, in the end, I recovered, I thought of Nietzsche and his *Gay Science*, a book written as convalescence work, he claimed. I wanted to say 'thank you' to the friends who had taken care of me and to life for having kept me. Naomi Schor, when we first met, explained to me that she had been reading the book with constant amazement. She saw it as '*osé*', foolhardy, ignoring all sorts of conventions except intellectual rigour, indeed sacrificing conventions to intellectual rigour. She couldn't believe that an academic could take so much risk. And then, when she reached the passage where I allude to chemotherapy, she suddenly understood, she said: 'After such an experience, one can say to hell with trivial considerations.'

Had I not lived at death's door for a year, I would not have dared write *Hipparchia's Choice*. Nor had I not experienced the bliss of convalescence. It is amazing how persistent your body is; as soon as it is left in peace, it starts repairing itself as much as it can and resumes its old ways. I wanted *Hipparchia's Choice* to be a message of hope addressed to women who are diagnosed with breast cancer: there is a life after that tough experience. Moreover, you will not be mentally bound to the memory of it, you will find again the diversity of your previous centres of interest.

But if you want to know it all, what usually sends me to writing is that I am asked for a piece or a book. The dialogue we are just having together may well prove responsible for some project later on. Occasionally, I have first written 'pieces' on demand, as it were, because I had been asked, then got some feedback and eventually merged various pieces into a larger project. The 'origin' of a piece of work is not to be sought entirely in the subjectivity of the person, taken as a separate entity, but rather in the interaction between that person and her environment. Sometimes also, a little fit of anger may send someone to research and writing. One day, I told Sarah Kofman that I had the feeling that there was some anger or impatience, of course tamed and kept under control, at the origin of all her books. She agreed!

Notes

1 Examples of such witticism are mentioned in *Hipparchia's Choice* (1991: 223).
2 'Women and Philosophy' appeared in *Radical Philosophy* 17 (Summer 1977) and in French Feminist Thought (Moi 1987). It is reprinted as 'Long Hair, Short Ideas', in *The Philosophical Imaginary* (Le Dœuff, 1989, 2002).

3 See Rita Thalmann, *Etre Femme sous le IIIe Reich* (1982).
4 See Claudia Koonz, *Mothers in the Fatherland: Women, the Family and Nazi Politics* (London: Routledge, 1986).

Select Bibliography

Works by Michèle Le Dœuff

Books

(1980) *L'Imaginaire Philosophique*, Paris: Les Éditions Payot.
(1989) *L'Étude et le rouet Des femmes, de la philosophie, etc*, Paris: Éditions du Seuil; trans. into English as *Hipparchia's Choice* (1991).
(1989, 2002) *The Philosophical Imaginary*, trans. C. Gordon, London: Athlone; Continuum.
(1991) *Hipparchia's Choice, an Essay Concerning Women, Philosophy, Etc.*, trans. T. Selous, Oxford: Blackwell.
(1998, 2000) *Le Sexe du savoir*, Paris: Aubier; Champs Flammarion.

Articles in English

(1977) 'Women and Philosophy', in *Radical Philosophy* 17; reprinted in 1987 in *French Feminist Thought*, ed. T. Moi, Oxford: Blackwell; and also as 'Long Hair, Short Ideas', in *The Philosophical Imaginary* (1989, 2002).
(1979) 'Simone de Beauvoir and Existentialism', in *The Second Sex Thirty Years Later*, Proceedings of a conference hosted by Institute for Humanities, New York University.
(1982) 'Utopias: Scholarly', in *Social Research*, Special Issue: *Current French Philosophy*, New York.
(1987) 'Ants and Women, or Philosophy Without Borders', in *Contemporary French Philosophy*, ed. A. Phillips Griffiths, Royal Institute of Philosophy Lecture Series, Cambridge University Press.
(1990) 'Women, Reason, etc.', in *Differences – A Journal of Feminist Cultural Studies*, Providence: Brown University Press.
(1993) 'On Some Philosophical Pacts', in *Journal of the Institute of Romance Studies*, London, Autumn 1993.
(1994) 'Mastering a Woman: The Imaginary Foundation of a Certain Metaphysical Order', Conference Proceedings of the Society for Phenomenology and Existential Philosophy, in *Transitions in Continental Philosophy* (selected studies in Phenomenology and Existential Philosophy, 18), ed. A. Dallery and S. Watson, New York.
(1998) 'Gabrielle Suchon', entry in the *Routledge Encyclopaedia of Philosophy*, Routledge.

(1999) 'Each Man in His Cave', in *Women's Voices, Women's Rights*, the Oxford Amnesty Lectures 1996, ed. A. Jeffries, Boulder (USA) and Oxford: Westview Press.
(2000) 'A Little Learning: Women and (Intellectual) Work', in *Gender and Society*, ed. The Herbert Spencer Lectures, C. Blakemore and S. Iversen, Oxford University Press.
(2000) 'Feminism Is Back in France, or Is It?', in *Hypatia* 15 (4), Special Issue: *Contemporary French Women Philosophers*, ed., P. Deutscher.

For a fuller bibliography of Michèle Le Dœuff's writing including works in French and references to selected secondary literature, see: http://www.ac-toulouse.fr/philosophie/phpes/micheleledoeuff.htm

Other works cited

Koonz, C. (1986) *Mothers in the Fatherland: Women, the Family and Nazi Politics*, London: Jonathan Cape.
Nussbaum, M. (1999) *Sex and Social Justice*, Oxford University Press.
Thalmann, R. (1982) *Etre Femme sous le IIIe Reich*, Paris: Laffont.

6

Women in dialogue and in solitude

Michèle Le Dœuff

'C'est très difficile de "s'expliquer" – une interview, un dialogue, un entretien. La plupart du temps, quand on me pose une question, même qui me touche, je m'aperçois que je n'ai strictement rien à dire. [. . .] Les objections, c'est encore pire [. . .]. Les objections n'ont jamais rien apporté' (Deleuze and Parnet 1996: 7) ['It is very hard to "explain oneself" – an interview, a dialogue, a conversation. Most of the time, when someone asks me a question, even one which moves me, I see that, strictly, I don't have anything to say. [. . .] Objections are even worse. [. . .] Objections never brought about anything'].

Oh dear! Gilles Deleuze expresses these pessimistic views on the very possibility of dialogue at the beginning of *Dialogues*, a book he and Claire Parnet co-authored; perhaps after the fashion of Hegel's preface to *The Phenomenology of Mind* – in which he states that a preface is unsuitable to philosophical work: just begin by saying that things are hopeless and then you will feel better. Or perhaps there is more than mere self-irony here, more than an Antonioni-like mood or verbal exorcism of stage fright. This is what I would like somehow to explore.

Dialogues was first published in 1977, a year which may not have received the attention it deserved, at least as far as French philosophy is concerned. At the same time and not very far away, Vladimir Jankélévitch and Béatrice Berlowitz were completing *Quelque part dans l'inachevé*, to be published early in 1978. The two volumes have something in common, since in both – at least apparently – a man and a woman are talking to one another. These volumes have contributed a lot to enhance the reputation of both Deleuze and Jankélévitch – much to my dismay, I have been unable to find out what has become of Claire Parnet and Béatrice Berlowitz.

Other events marked that year 1977, of course, some of them receiving more attention than *Dialogues* and *Quelque part*, and some hatched a little while before.

In 1976, books by young men calling themselves the 'nouveaux philosophes' had begun flooding in, and then, during the summer of 1977, 'French philosophers say: Marxism is monstrous' made the headline in *The New York Times*. Moreover, the Socialist Party and the Communist Party fell out, with the result that left-wingers had to face the fact that, unbelievable as it might seem, the 1978 general election would not go their way. And because the personal and the political are frequently interwoven, the inhabitants of the Latin Quarter, who are always so interested in philosophical sociability, were discussing the fact that Michel Foucault and Gilles Deleuze had fallen out, which was a pity considering how much they had meant to each other. The so-called new philosophers were at the heart of this estrangement of the two friends who had been as close as Montaigne and La Boétie. Foucault lent his support to these young men while Deleuze published a pamphlet against them – a pamphlet distributed free of charge by Minuit bookshop: clearly, Deleuze tried to mobilize the philosophical community against what he saw as an alarming trend towards crass modishness. With hindsight, we may also consider that the 'new philosophers' had played a part in the split between the Socialists and the Communists. Perhaps the Communists already knew that they reflected, as it were, one of the hidden faces of François Mitterrand, something that ordinary and candid people were to grasp only some years later. Now, the Communist Party was in the throes of relinquishing the concept of dictatorship of the proletariat – could they go even further and consider running for the general election as the allies of a party which was itself connected to a group of media types claiming that Marxism is monstrous . . .? The Communists might have feared that they would lose their identity, significance or *raison d'être* in such an alliance, hence considered it would be better to postpone the victory. Eventually, in 1981, the Presidential and General elections were won – and the rest is history, some aspects of which are perhaps still to be written.

The genesis of *Dialogues* by, though not between, Claire Parnet and Gilles Deleuze may be deemed to be found in the context of those strange times. Deleuze had lost his philosophical interlocutor. True, he still had Félix Guattari as a friend and cooperator, but he never described their relation as 'interlocution': rather he described it as 'travailler à deux', 'travailler entre les deux' (Deleuze and Parnet 1996: 23), two people working and writing together in an in-between zone, between two fields. Besides, for him, a real disaster had taken place, namely the experience of being deserted or rejected. Not that Claire Parnet was some sort of substitute for Foucault. The shock went much deeper than that, I think. Betrayal, indeed treason, is an important theme of the book. In it, Richard III is said to be, more than a cheat, a real traitor. He wanted not only power – state power – but treason for its own sake, and Lady Anne was desired as the figure of this eroticization of treason (Deleuze and Parnet 1996: 53). At the time, Deleuze, and people who identified with his critical stance against the Nouvelle Philosophie, certainly felt cheated or let down from a political point of view, and the word 'treason' certainly came up. According to some, these angry young men were betraying the philosophical ideals of rigour and subtlety, ideals which were, of course, to be put at the service of good left-wing causes. Betraying the standards and refined questioning of philosophy was seen as plotting the end of a role or character, namely the 'intellectuel de gauche'. Some, particularly feminists I suppose, saw these young men as would-be oppressors claiming to be the oppressed – or did they, did we all? Was it so clear that feminists, all feminists, saw this new production of discourse as a new form of oppression? No, it was not so clear, in spite of the fact that two of these young men, namely Guy Lardreau and Christian Jambet, had inserted in their book some wacky development about Woman who, according to them, was, like the child and the slave, lacking Reason (Jambet and Lardreau 1976: 37). We had had that one before!

For the sake of historiography, I must mention that my 'Cheveux longs, idées courtes' ['women in/and philosophy'] was written during the summer of 1976. Some photocopies were circulated straightaway; perhaps not increasing the goodwill of some male colleagues towards me; perhaps the text made more than one of them nervous. Nonetheless, it appeared in the Spring of 1977, first in English and then in French (Le Dœuff 1977 and now 1980: 135–66, 2002: 100–28). It was certainly my reaction to what I then understood of the problems both of women (in the field of philosophy or otherwise) and of philosophy – at the time and long, long before. In the 1970s, I did not compare nor indeed connect my own endeavour with the two books published soon afterwards, *Dialogues* and *Quelque part dans l'inachevé*. But my essay is a sort of dialogue too, in this case a half-imaginary one, between myself and my students. During the summer of 1976, I was preparing my seminar for the following year at an all-women institution, and thought it useful to write down a sort of theoretical contract; a minimalistic basis to offer my students, with the idea that people need to have a handful of assumptions in common in order to begin to talk to one another. A woman philosopher who talks and wants to talk with other women? Perhaps some men thought it urgent to restate their own existence and their (brand new, not to say still to come) ability to talk with women too.

For ... *Dialogues* and *Quelque part dans l'inachevé* ... 1977 and 1978 ... when was it that a French male philosopher had last spoken with a woman? As far as I know, these two books were a 'first'. Diderot's *D'Alembert's Dream*, in which d'Alembert, Mlle de L'Espinasse and Bordeu talked, is a work of fiction, not a piece of work to which Julie de L'Espinasse herself would have contributed. As a result, the two books I want to discuss mark – whatever their limitations – an important change. In a sense, you may see these attempted conversations as 'first steps, by toddlers', as clumsy, which is only to be expected, and the difficulty is marked by downright pessimism concerning the endeavour itself. The opening of *Quelque part* too signals the uneasiness of both Vladimir Jankélévitch and Béatrice Berlowitz towards their project. It is true that, at a certain stage, they experienced a togetherness, through an explicit and shared rejection of a bad object, namely the tape recorder. The preface, by Berlowitz, states that they both felt 'contempt' for the machine, then invested some kind of hope in it, a hope which was (of course) disappointed. Moreover, *Quelque part* expresses 'a fundamental mistrust' in the interview *genre*. And Berlowitz's first question to Jankélévitch is: 'Que vous dire, et comment vous parler? Vous refusez tant de choses. Les facilités propres à l'entretien nous sont dérobées par l'interlocuteur intransigeant et imprévisible que vous êtes. Comprenez mon embarras' (Jankélévitch and Berlowitz 1978: 11) ['What is there to tell you, and how is one to talk to you? You refuse so many things. The facile aspects of interviews are not an option for us since you are such an intransigeant and unpredictable interlocutor. Please understand how embarrassed I am']. And Jankélévitch replies that one never has 'une oeuvre' in one's own eyes; a man who would discuss his own books as we commentate Plato's dialogues would be 'un singe' (Jankélévitch and Berlowitz 1978: p. 12 and p.13) ['like a performing chimp']. At times, come to that, there is something of the 'zoo' [*sic*] about the Republic of Letters. There is a 'guignol philosophique' (*guignol* translates as Punch; only, in the French tongue it's all Punch and no Judy), and there is a risk, for any writer, of becoming a clown through too much self-awareness. Oh dear! If the very idea of the project induced such a melancholy mood, the book promises to give us all, authors and readers, a miserable time. The first chapter is entitled '*Ce Je haïssable*', the hateful I. An awful drama seems about to break out, and there are three main components to this drama: (i) when you are a writer, an interview is probably doomed to be about your work; (ii) Plato wrote dialogues, which perhaps should be the true model, but 'we', whoever 'we' may be, we commentate these dialogues; (iii) *Conscience* [self-awareness] makes fools of us all; this is no small matter, it is as if Socrates were being shown the door, his 'know thyself' being indirectly rejected and Pascal's point of view, '*le moi est haïssable*', adopted instead.

The book is wonderful all the same, like many books written out of despair, and it contains views which are not to be found in Jankélévitch's other works, which in my eyes just goes to show that Berlowitz was a remarkable midwife. She succeeded in extracting from him points, or sometimes fragments of imaginary, which he had not expressed before. And we can see how stable in its fluidity his philosophical imaginary was. He begins daydreaming about Ulysses, the errant Odysseus, entering his own house as a beggar. And then, when Odysseus triumphs, he loses interest in the character and switches to Charlie Chaplin, sympathizing with the inconclusive endings of many of Chaplin's films. At the level of values the text is stable; it is as if Jankélévitch were saying: 'I don't like triumphant positions.' But at the level of identifications, it is fluid – you may feel an affinity to Odysseus and then go over to Chaplin.

A clear rejection of might, under any form, always appeared in Jankélévitch's post-war work. Long before Deleuze launched the idea of 'becoming minoritarian', he had started writing philosophy in a minor key, as if there were a lethal risk in identifying, even for a minute, with any mighty discourse, stance or character. The explanation for this may be historical. Before the war, Jankélévitch had been a great connoisseur of German philosophy. Then came the trauma of the war. He turned back to Bergson, rejected German culture *en bloc*, was to call Heidegger 'the philosopher of the Wehrmacht', since he had sided with the Nazi regime, and turned away from any form of thought that might appear too sure of itself. As if the beginning of evil could be found there; as if, when you adopt a dogmatic stance in philosophy, you are already setting yourself up as the accomplice of tyrants and of the most abominable forms of state power.

I would indeed feel tempted to call Béatrice Berlowitz a wonderful midwife, but this is not how she describes herself and her part in the process of writing the book: 'Mes questions furent en quelque sorte contemplatives, et si j'observai une règle, ce fut plutôt celle de l'accompagnement, respectueux du rythme et du souffle, qui soutient la mélodie' (Jankélévitch and Berlowitz 1978: 10) ['My questions were in a way contemplative and, if I followed a rule, it was rather the rule of accompaniment, which, making respectful allowance for both the rhythm and the breathing, supports the melody']. Meeting her once, and congratulating her ('you made Vladimir write a wonderful book'), I got the reply that he had not been pleased with the endeavour. Having known him for years, I shall venture an explanation: he needed solitude and utter responsibility for his writings. Producing a book with someone else must have given him the feeling that this precious solitude was somehow under threat or being stolen from him. Or to elaborate: I have always acknowledged a special debt to him; as my supervisor he gave me my head, and I would have found it impossible to produce a line of philosophy without this utterly respected freedom. The first time I spoke with him and mentioned the subject I had in mind, he said: 'I don't know a thing about it, which is great; I shall then learn something when reading it.' He certainly gave me just the solitude I needed, respected it up until the last, and I must say that Deleuze, later on, did the same, simply dropping me a note when he had read a piece. 'Sort it out for yourself', which suited me down to the ground. On the other hand, my students were constantly putting questions my way. Jankélévitch's attitude towards me certainly tallies with views expressed at the end of his book on Bergson: 'La liberté n'est pas seulement libre, elle est libératrice'; 'La liberté fait don aux autres de la liberté' (Jankélévitch 1959, 2nd Edn 1999: 295, 294) ['Freedom is not just free; it is liberating'; 'Freedom makes the gift of freedom to others']. . . . I can testify that he meant every word of it. All the same, what does it imply, if it implies anything at all, regarding the insertion of women, or of a woman, in philosophical debate?

I have already quoted Deleuze's opinion that dialogue is something that does not exist. The back cover of the French edition is even clearer: 'Il faudrait que le dialogue se fasse, non pas entre des personnes, mais entre les lignes, entre des chapitres ou des parties de chapitre. Ce seraient les vrais personnages' ['Dialogue should take place, not between persons, but between lines or chapters or paragraphs. They would thus become the true characters or protagonists']. Such a view of course tallies with the paths some French philosophers have taken and reads like the ultimate result of the subject's self-effacement. It certainly has to do as well with the assumption that 'les questions se fabriquent' (Deleuze and Parnet 1996: 7), a philosophical question, is in itself made or constructed. Apparently an interlocutor is not helpful on a building site. Interlocutors put forth questions or, worse still, objections. Let Claire Parnet have her say, in her own chapter, separately, as it were and why not? A philosophical question is certainly something you need to produce – you assemble things and doubts; hence solitude, as a moment, is required. But does it need to be more than a moment? And, if solitude is so necessary, why embark on a dialogue, especially after deeming dialogue to be impossible? And will the book itself provide an answer to this problem?

We may want to take the event of Deleuze's and Foucault's estrangement together with remarks made in *Dialogues* itself. If I am right in assuming that Richard III, in *Dialogues*, represents the character Foucault had become in Deleuze's view, if treason is central to the production of the book, then I would say that this did not call for a substitute but for an agent who could equal or double the event, by (hopefully) bringing in an upheaval that would square the upheaval created by Foucault's betrayal. And who could have embodied such a hope better than a woman? There is a quest for what Deleuze calls 'destabilisation' [destabilization], ironically after Giscard d'Estaing (Deleuze and Parnet 1996: p.159). Amazons, as the ultimate figures of disruption, as women who do not side either with the Greeks or the Trojans or with any male group, are first introduced by Claire Parnet, referring to Kleist, and then mentioned several times by Deleuze (Deleuze and Parnet 1996: p.40, p.54, p.159, p.171). True, Deleuze in retrospect had no difficulty in finding from his past other figures of what he calls a 'secousse' [jolt]. Bergson is described as one, Sartre (at the time Deleuze was a student) as 'un peu d'air pur, un courant d'air (Deleuze and Parnet 1996: p.19), 'a little fresh air – a gust of air' (Deleuze and Parnet 1987: p.12); Spinoza gave him the feeling 'd'un courant d'air qui vous pousse dans le dos chaque fois que vous le lisez, d'un balai de sorcière qu'il vous fait enfourcher' (Deleuze and Parnet 1996: p.22) ['of a gust of air from behind each time you read him, of a [female] witch's broomstick which he makes you mount', Deleuze and Parnet 1987: p.15]. Disruption always-already exists; factors of disruption can be found, even in the old male world of philosophy. But the philosophical imaginary here seems to hint, through the valorization of Amazons, that after all, if what you are looking for is disruption, the real thing will be brought about by independent women, that is, Amazons and Claire Parnet perhaps as a representative of such a figure; or more likely by Claire Parnet as the person who could reclaim that segment of mythology (from Kleist) and speak as someone with some connection to the Amazons, thus endowing Deleuze's imaginary with a new dimension. He was trying to deepen the negative or to find a productive negative. At a time when he was bitterly disappointed to see that the philosophical community *en bloc* would not resist the New Philosophers. . . . At a time when he had lost his twin.

Eventually, Deleuze was to take an interest in the 'Héloïse complex', a concept I had coined to describe the traditional position of women in philosophy;[1] and then, he and Guattari were even to attribute to me the creation of the *persona* of the woman philosopher (Deleuze and Guattari 1991: 69). I have already expressed my objections to such a view (Le Dœuff 2003: 364). All the same, I would like to tackle the question again and to comment on the choice of the Amazons as an emblem borrowed from Heinrich von Kleist's *Penthesilea* (1808). At the beginning of Kleist's play, Odysseus assumes that the 'centauress' must be fighting for either one side or the other. Considering she is attacking the Trojans, he is certain that she is on the side of the Greeks! We have here, apparently a use (in fact a misguided one) of the '*tertium non datur*' principle: either ... or ... But Odysseus is wrong, for Kleist's *Penthesilea*, who is clearly an irruption or an eruption, will not side with the Greeks either. On the other hand (*tertium datur*), she will fall in love with one warrior, Achilles, and will take her own life at the end of the play. Not siding with any group of men but having a passion for one, and only one, man: this, transposed into the field of philosophy, is again a version (and a sad one) of what I described as the 'Héloïse complex', a woman who limits herself to understanding the work of one male philosopher and is in love with this one man. This is exactly the opposite of what I tried to recommend and of what I still wish all women to find: a non-limited access to the whole world of philosophical works and a free use of their own minds. And it is tragic that the figure of the Amazon, who seems to be summoned up in *Dialogues* as 'disruption in the flesh', may in fact refer to a 'taming' story.

According to *Dialogues*, Richard III chose treason both in the hope of winning state power and for the sake of treason (Deleuze and Parnet 1996: 53). It can be argued that Foucault had hoped for some state power from the Socialists cleansed of any association with Marxism: witness his annoyance when, instead of being offered a position as an advisor on the penal system, he was to hear in 1981 that the Socialists would gladly send him to New York as 'cultural attaché'! It came as something of a shock to us all in any case, to discover that our left-wing government wanted to govern with as little interference as possible from our fountain pens. Deleuze had certainly been prepared for this. Jankélévitch had stated in *Quelque part* that he felt apprehensive about what 'our political friends' would do to philosophy and the teaching of it. I am still talking of the year 1977 – you can see a Deleuze feeling betrayed and guessing that there may be more of it to come, and transforming this unhappiness by looking out for more destabilization and a real upheaval (Amazons and Claire Parnet) while Jankélévitch, for his part, expressed his concern as follows: 'Nos amis politiques ne sont pas tous nécessairement des amis de la philosophie'; 'Nous aimerions tellement n'avoir des ennemis qu'à droite, parmi les caïds du textile et du béton' (Jankélévitch and Berlowitz 1978: 102) ['Our political friends are not necessarily all good friends of philosophy'; 'it would be so nice if we had enemies only among right-wingers and among magnates of the textile or concrete industries']. One can sense the ghost of Paul Nizan here, Nizan who, as a young man, had attacked Bergson and philosophy teachers generally, seeing them all as watchdogs of the bourgeois order – the same Nizan who was eventually to die resisting the German invasion in 1940. To this renewed scare – perhaps a left-wing government will do what Nizan put in writing? – Jankélévitch opposed the fact that philosophy, in order to exist, needs to be transmitted from one person to another and therefore needs 'des hommes et des femmes en chair et en os' (Jankélévitch and Berlowitz 1978: 101) ['real-life men and women'] – as agents of this transmission; philosophy teachers in schools, with a stable number of teaching hours. An arrow also targets l'Inspection Générale, which is found guilty of not wanting moral philosophy or Bergson on some syllabus. At the time, it is true, l'Inspection Générale for philosophy was run by a fervent admirer of Auguste Comte. I am sure that occasionally good old Jankélévitch could see Marxism too as a form of positivism, and positivism as a political project that would suppress any form of critical thinking.

If, in the mid-1970s, havoc broke out in the French philosophical community, it was not entirely our doing – we feminists, or we women. Perhaps 'Cheveux longs, idées courtes' can bear witness to this: the project, at least for me, was to broaden philosophical possibilities, which implied challenging the limits of the field, and the limits imposed on women in the field, not disavowing the field itself. But conflicts between men had brought about a serious malaise, leading the aforesaid community to discover that perhaps it had never been one. So is this how two women in the late 1970s managed to find their way into the time-honoured philosophical form or *genre* known as dialogue or debate? Both *Dialogues* and *Quelque part* may certainly be read as if each was based on a fit of anger which could be summarized thus: 'if some men betray philosophy, then the sacrosanct male contract making it compulsory for us all somehow to marginalize women is broken; so, let us talk with women now'. Anyone tempted to read these two books with such an interpretation in mind could certainly find some grounds. Deleuze takes up the image of the Amazons just as Claire Parnet had presented it, without questioning it. To me the image of Amazons not siding with the Trojans or the Greeks, whether or not it is borrowed from Kleist's *Penthesilea*, is at any rate Homer seriously rewritten, a point Deleuze certainly knew. For, according to Homer, the Trojans and the Greeks had been allies against the Amazons in the past. Homer's very brief note refers to a male contract between the two armies against the women in previous times, two armies unfortunately at war with each other in the present time of *The Iliad*. What was taking place in Paris in the late 1970s somehow echoed all this. In the good old days, 'in illo tempore', there was an alliance between male philosophers against women.... This no longer seemed possible so . . . , well, as a result, some men were experimenting with a new sociability.

A crack in the fraternal contract can also be detected in Lévinas's book *Noms propres*, first published in 1976. For there is a chapter in it about a woman, Jeanne Delhomme, a professor of philosophy at Nanterre, the author of several books, including one on Bergson and one entitled *La Pensée et le réel* (1967). Lévinas's foreword to *Noms propres* also expresses a malaise which is clearly a malaise vis-à-vis the male community, not associated with Paul Nizan or the Inspection Générale but rather to 'bavardage à la mode' (Lévinas 1987: 8) [modish idle-talk]. According to Lévinas, contemporary minds were deserting what is meaningful, with some arrows aimed particularly at the Lacanians, a small one at Jankélévitch, I am sorry to say, one (probably) at Foucault and Deleuze (before the estrangement), and maybe another at *Révoltes Logiques*, a leftist journal which borrowed its title from the Rimbaud line that announces an intention to strangle 'logical rebellions'. Lévinas does not mention any names, and he leaves the reader to guess who is being accused of destroying meaningfulness: those who are in the know will guess that Lévinas's indictment of the ineffable refers to Jankélévitch and that his contemptuous shaft shot at the 'non-dit' and 'signifiants sans signifiés' [signifiers without signifieds'] points to the Lacanians, and so on. But the scare is plainly expressed: Lévinas writes that all this drifting may well announce 'the end of the world' (Lévinas 1987: 8), no less. It is in this context that he includes as a chapter a piece (first published in 1967) on Jeanne Delhomme, to whom he gives the nickname 'Penelope', thus making it clear that what he values in her work is a deep – and most intelligent – faithfulness to certain canonical authors. When everything is falling apart at the seams, proper names are the only beacons left, and Jeanne Delhomme is to be one of them. Penelope as the (probably only) acceptable woman in philosophy? Perhaps we do not want to comment at all.

It is hard to believe that it took so much in the 1970s, to give some women a little space in the philosophical Republic. And this when women had been teaching philosophy for decades, and at university level? One may feel tempted to express some discomfort here or indeed utter disbelief. But, in order to take it more philosophically, I should like to invite you on a detour through the seventeenth century and the amazing work of Gabrielle Suchon. Or perhaps we needed to take a detour through twentieth-century essays in order to avoid a purely antiquarian point of view on her work and to understand a special feature thereof.

Gabrielle Suchon was born in 1631 in Semur-en-Auxois in Burgundy and she died in 1703 in Dijon. First pressed into a convent by her family, she managed to leave, in circumstances which are now better known thanks to Sonia Bertolini's research (2000: 289ff.). In 1670, apparently after a crisis, her convent decided to banish her to another. It is unclear whether she ever reached the other convent, for the next we hear of her she is living as a lay person in her small home town of Semur, reading and writing philosophy. She published two important books, *Le Traité de la morale et de la politique* (1693) and *Du célibat volontaire* (1700).

Solitude – which she explicitly mentions – runs through all her writings. Indeed, she advocated solitary reflection as the proper starting point of intellectual development. One must first be self-taught, though, as a matter of course, the value of intellectual conversations is to be acknowledged, particularly conversations between women, since schools and universities were closed to us. For Suchon, women should form small societies for the purpose of thinking, arguing and debating with one another, and teach one another what they have learned by reading books in the privacy of their homes. This will help them to develop their reason further and more precisely logic and dialectics, for the art of definition and argumentation is connected to this mode of conversing with others. Since I have already developed that point in *Le Sexe du savoir* [*The Sex of Knowing*], I will not broach it again here, but rather I would like to tackle something new: in both her books Suchon *herself* produces objections to her theories and then refutes these very objections.

Of course, one may deal with this feature of her philosophical style simply by considering that she was alone. There was no one around to discuss things with her nor, by questioning her views, to help her take them a step further. As a result, the poor woman had to be her own discussant, a tragic position if there ever was one. And it must be said to her credit that she was able, all the same, to have the somehow utopic vision of these small societies in which women could help each other and have intellectual conversations among themselves. She was able to think beyond her own experience. Such an interpretation can be seriously argued, I believe, and particularly through a comparison with Descartes, because she was not at all in his position. Quite the opposite, in fact. Descartes was able to send his *Meditations* to an assortment of theologians and philosophers, then receive objections from them, offer his reply to these objections and then have the whole set published as a volume. This was not an option open to Gabrielle Suchon.

However, even if such a line of interpretation could seem highly plausible, I should like to argue that it misses the real point: when one is alone, one can still have a conversation with oneself and Suchon's practice of philosophical reasoning in fact fits with what Plato called 'thinking'. There are three well-known passages in *Philebus* (38c–39b), *Theaetetus* (189e–190a) and the *Sophist* (263e) in which it is argued that 'thinking' is a conversation the mind holds with itself about the object it is examining. The mind asks itself questions and then answers them. Such a definition of what thinking is leaves us, I think, with a view on what a philosophical endeavour may be, a view broad enough to encompass both dialogue with other people and solitary work. The comment I should like to offer is as follows: if the mind were not able to divide itself so as to have inner discussions (say, in solitude), it would not be possible to have philosophical dialogues with other people. Each of us would simply express firm beliefs and stand for them, possibly championing them, digging in our heels if needs be, as barristers occasionally do in court. If what is hoped for in a philosophical dialogue with others is some kind of progress in enlightenment or towards the truth, then, even though it is a dialogue with others, every step must also be examined in each protagonist's mind, in a sort of dialogue with itself. Is the remark X just made more illuminating than what I had said? On the other hand, if the mind is able to put questions to itself and have a dialogue with itself, why should anyone talk with other people?

There is not just one answer to this problem; your choice of answer will probably determine your mode of philosophizing: Deleuze's remarks, which I have quoted above, are in fact one option; if chapters and paragraphs are the true protagonists, this means that he favoured an inner dialogue, enhanced, I hasten to add, by what he had read and to which he gladly and generously refers. With Gabrielle Suchon's notion of autodidacticism, as connected – first of all – to reading books, we can say that her solitary dialogue with herself also included a conversation with both past and contemporary authors. The objections she presents to herself are drawn from her readings – meaning exactly this: in her readings, she had found commonly held opinions, a cultural background, to which she wants to 'reply'. In a sense, the many volumes a good library may contain were to her like Socrates' many interlocutors, all having a dialogue, that is to say being confronted, with a mind which could also talk with itself. Books here stand in a role previously held by handsome Meno, promising Theaetetus, pompous Protagoras and all the others. Books from which one can learn a lot, but in a critical mode, meaning that one can also take issue with some of their contents. For this was the post-Gutenberg era, a time which brought about a most significant change. With books having become more affordable, a lower-middle-class woman could invite herself to discussions held in the field without anyone's permission. She could even have a book printed at her expense. In this sense, Aristotle's remark about natural right – which derives its force from within itself alone – had become true and powerful.[2] Every woman had always had a natural right to learning and philosophizing. But this right remained dormant until the concrete means (affordable books) came along.

As I have already remarked in *The Sex of Knowing*, living women do not appear in the long list of Socrates' interlocutors, though he occasionally refers to some women figures of the past, such as Diotima or the Thracian girl. After reading Gabrielle Suchon, it becomes clear that it is not enough for women to try to add their names to any list of male philosophers' interlocutors. For Suchon puts herself at the centre of the endeavour, on speaking terms with the books she has read, and in a sense in the place of Socrates or 'divine Plato', not one of the interlocutors, but the one who brings about the interlocution. I have no idea (yet) whether she knew about Descartes's relation to Elizabeth of Bohemia. If she got hold of a copy of Descartes's *Principles*, she would at least have known of a woman correspondent he had. On the other hand, I am convinced she had read an edition of Descartes's *Meditations*, complete with objections and replies to objections. This particularly shows in the tables of contents of her *Traité de la morale et de la politique*. Some chapters are entitled 'première objection', 'seconde objection', 'troisième objection'; she gives a number to each after the manner of *Meditations*. Then she answers the objections, thus making her points stronger. This play with objections and replies to objections, although we could be tempted to term it Cartesian, can itself be traced back to Bacon's *Advancement of Learning* (Book One). For Bacon gives the floor to people who are not in favour of learning and then replies to them, the better to clear the way, and make his points stronger, the better to convince his king that there is nothing wrong with an increase in learning, quite the opposite. It is not everyday that a philosophical form emerges *ex nihilo*. And do we even have an adequate theory of what it exactly means, to borrow a form from a predecessor?

At any rate, with Descartes, objections and replies to objections come into play within an all-male circle of interlocutors. Elizabeth of Bohemia had a different status, and I quote from the author's Epistle dedicating *The Principles* to her: '... je n'ai jamais rencontré personne qui ait si généralement et si bien entendu tout ce qui est contenu dans mes écrits' (Descartes 1953: 555) ['I have never met anyone who had understood as widely and well all that is contained in my writings']. In his eyes, she was not at all the sort of interlocutor who had been invited to present objections on an equal footing with him! He praises that difference, by stating that 'Votre Altesse' is not 'quelque vieux docteur qui ait employé beaucoup d'années à s'instruire, mais une princesse encore jeune et dont le visage représente mieux celui que les poètes attribuent aux Grâces que celui qu'ils attribuent aux Muses ou à la savante Minerve' (Descartes 1953: 555) ['Your Highness is not an old Doctor (meaning in theology or philosophy), but a still-young princess whose face represents the way poets depict the Graces rather than the Muses or learned Minerva']. My comment: in the Cartesian play, there was no prearranged category or space that could have accommodated a Gabrielle Suchon. She had to create her own space, her mental space, for what she called 'l'entretien de ma solitude, l'emploi de mon temps, le travail de mon esprit, les sentiments de mon âme et les affections de mon coeur' (Suchon 1693, dedication to the Trinity) ['the conversation of my solitude, the use of my time, the work of my mind, the feelings of my soul and the affections of my heart'], with all this dedicated to the Holy Trinity, but with a clearly acknowledged ambition: to wake women from their slumber, to invite them to read and become self-taught and establish small societies to argue with one another, and exercise their own free minds this way. For the joy of developing their minds and also of becoming politically creative. For Suchon imagined her readers practising their ability to philosophize sufficiently for them to become able to put forth propositions about how life in society could be better arranged – particularly regarding the relations between the sexes.

The major discontinuity she introduced – she who was the reader of a large library which included Descartes's *Meditations* and maybe some Bacon too, along with 'divine Plato', Aristotle and Church Fathers – is to be found in the fact that she focused on solitary work, but with a not-yet-existing community in view, women readers, whom she invited to liberate themselves. It is, in itself, a remarkable discontinuity, however much she borrowed from the tradition she claimed as her heritage. A *discontinuity*: I may be myself a follower of Jeanne Delhomme here, when insisting on what an individual may bring about while sympathetically reading the works left by a long tradition. For I truly believe that, instead of reasoning in terms of 'difference', when we commentate philosophical work by women, we could well be better off with that very notion of discontinuity, meaning that when past philosophical texts are reread by a mind which can think, in dialogue with itself, which can work and include the feelings and affections of the heart in the work, then of course a discontinuity will take place, perhaps as small as the deviation Lucretius called '*clinamen*', but sufficient to create, in the end, a brand new world; in Suchon's case a new decipherment of the world as it was, a new set of ethical values or rather a new art of deciphering the existing world from a point of view determined by these values.

And, by understanding how this worked for Suchon, we may produce a fresh and less canonical perception of Descartes too. For we may now give more importance to the fact that he sought objections from other people. The purpose of this interplay was not purely intellectual nor indeed philosophical. Descartes was seeking approval through being put to the test or on a sort of trial. He wanted to be approved by theologians and doctors in philosophy, and then perhaps by the Sorbonne. Hence the fact that the 1641 edition of his *Meditations* was published with the mention '*cum approbatione doctorum*', a mention swiftly to disappear in the next edition, for it was not quite true. Arnault readily spotted that aspect of the play, 'notre auteur se vient lui-même présenter au tribunal de la théologie' (Quatrièmes Objections, faites par Monsieur Arnaud, in Descartes 1953: 421) ['our author presents himself to the court of theology']. The nature of this interplay is in fact legal: let a court examine, judge and hopefully, after issuing some minor reproaches perhaps, approve. This could be conceived as similar to the way in which one entered a corporation or guild at the time, or one defended (defends) a thesis, in order thereafter to belong to a group.

Gabrielle Suchon was sharp enough simply to seek approbation directly, without first asking for objections from other people. Her *Traité* was printed with a collection of short notes of endorsement, 'approbations des docteurs', approvals from doctors all of whom were in residence in Lyon, the first one signing as 'Docteur en Théologie de la Société de Sorbonne'. Each basically says that there is nothing adverse to the Faith, nor to good mores, in this book which can be read with pleasure and profit. Is this a dialogue with other people here at last? I do not think so. Rather, her definition of her own discursive space was presented by her, and acknowledged and deemed respectable by them. You do not challenge the Faith, nor the good mores, you write good things: you are free! A 'Let her be' is implied here, which at the time meant 'do not censor the book'. These notes read somehow like a '*nihil obstat*'.

Historically speaking, one may be puzzled by the fact that she received approvals of this sort, considering the views her first book contains. I think it would be unfair to assume that the 'docteurs' only read it superficially, not noticing how unusual (not to say unorthodox) her claims were. I would rather suggest that each of them had a good dialogue with himself and decided that, yes, after all, Christianity could be that too, and that, yes, after all, good mores could also include what Suchon described. If this is the case, she really won her field and I am delighted for her. She was right to wait until her work had acquired enough consistency and cogency before allowing anyone to read it, even in manuscript.

To be utterly true and faithful to my field here, namely a History of Philosophy which would try to see its corpus as including works by women and men, I must also mention that, in the seventeenth century too, there was something of a scare, and far more serious than what was to take place for a few years in the late twentieth century in Paris. The name for it would be 'libertinage', or merely the fear that atheism was making progress, notably among 'men of letters'. In the preface to his *Meditations*, Descartes traces the problem, in a most orthodox way, back to the idea that only Faith, and not natural reason, could prove the existence of God and the immortality of the soul; and he recalls that a Lateran Council made it compulsory for 'Christian philosophers' (Catholics) to fight back. There is also a clear allusion to this in the Second Objections: 'Puisque, pour confondre les nouveaux Géants de ce siècle, qui osent attaquer l'Auteur de toutes choses, vous avez entrepris d'en affermir le trône en démontrant son existence' (Second Objections, in Descartes 1953: 359) ['Since, in order to confound the new Giants of this century, who dare attack the Author of all things, you [Descartes] endeavoured to make his throne firmer by proving his existence']. For our purposes, it is enough to note that there were 'Giants' around, a big threat, a dreadful scare, represented by male thinkers as the nickname of 'Giants' hints. 'A crack in the male contract' is too mild a phrase to describe the antagonism – and it is well-known anyway that intellectual conflict in the seventeenth century could put one in jail, at the stake or simply on the Index, as happened to Malebranche, although he never saw himself as a libertine or a heretic! It may well be the case that, when there are deep antagonisms afoot among men, a woman philosopher, showing extremely devout feelings for the Holy Trinity and the Scriptures, can more easily be accepted by (at least) a handful of theologians; accepted and even made welcome by men of letters like those in Bayle's circle and later the Encyclopédistes. I am glad to add that a copy of Suchon's second book, *Du célibat volontaire* [On Volontory Single Life], was housed by le Cloître des Billettes until the French Revolution.[3]

I am not going to conclude – for my intention was simply to explore a problem. Such an exploration leaves me, and probably you too, with several questions – which is only to be expected. As for objections, and Deleuze's opinion that they never brought anything about (n'ont jamais rien apporté): if in fact Deleuze, who was an excellent historian of philosophy, simply meant that *the* objections (to *Meditations*) were not productive, I would agree. But, if he meant objections in general, I want to state that this does not tally with my own experience. *L'Étude et le rouet* [*Hipparchia's Choice*] and *Le Sexe du savoir* [*The Sex of Knowing*] will bear witness to this. While I was preparing these books, objections came from friends, or from participants to my seminar at Geneva, which occasionally sent me back to carry out research in libraries for a whole summer. Such is my experience of philosophical work. And everyone's intellectual experience is certainly the strongest standpoint possible from which to object to any philosophical view, including a view about objections.[4]

Notes

1. See Honderich (1995) 'Héloïse complex': 'Diagnosed by Michèle Le Doeuff, this is the tendency of women in philosophy to idolize either a male colleague or teacher (as did Héloïse and Beauvoir), or a "great" living or dead philosopher whose banner they carry (as do contemporary women seeking the best male exponent of feminism, and becoming "Lacanian", "Foucauldian", even "Nietzschean" feminists). This situation benefits the man, destroys the woman – removing her intellectual independence and need to create philosophy herself. Beauvoir, however, escaped the Héloïse complex sufficiently to produce philosophy "unawares"'.
2. *Rhetoric*, Book I, chapter XIII, 1373b.
3. I am much indebted to Wallace Kirsop, who discovered this copy of *Du célibat volontaire* (along with its history) and generously communicated his finding to me.
4. I should like to thank Judith Still, who invited me to give the 2004 Cassal Lecture; Nicholas Mann, who chaired the occasion; all those who attended and created the warmest of atmospheres; Suzanne Dow for her invaluable help in revising the English of this piece and Gill Rye who polished the final version for the *Journal of Romance Studies* (Volume 5, No. 2, Summer 2005).

Works cited

Aristotle, *Rhetoric* (various editions).
Australian Journal of French Studies XL, no. 3 (September/December 2003), 'Autour de Michèle Le Doeuff'.

Bertolini, Sonia (2000) 'Gabrielle Suchon: Une vie sans engagement?', *Australian Journal of French Studies* XXXVII: 289–308.

Delhomme, Jeanne (1967) *La Pensée et le reel*, Paris: Presses Universitaires de France, collection Epiméthée.

Deleuze, Gilles et Félix Guattari (1991) *Qu'est-ce que la philosophie?*, Paris: les éditions de Minuit. Engl. trans. (1994) *What is Philosophy?*, New York: Columbia University Press.

Deleuze, Gilles and Claire Parnet (1977) *Dialogues*, Paris: Flammarion. I quote from the second edition. Paris: Champs, Flammarion, 1996, which was augmented (a short text by Deleuze was added) and is known to the English-speaking world as *Dialogue II*. Engl. trans. by Hugh Tomlinson and Barbara Habsberjam, London: The Athlone Press, 1987 (reissued in paperback, Continuum 2002).

Descartes (written and sent to docteurs 1640; printed 1641) *Meditationes de prima philosophia*. Various Edn; quoted here from André Bridoux [ed], 1953, *Descartes, Oeuvres et lettres*, Paris: Gallimard, Pléiade.

_____ (1644) *Les Principes de la Philosophie*. Various Edn; quoted here from André Bridoux (1953) *Descartes, Oeuvres et lettres*, Paris: Gallimard, Pléiade.

Honderich, Ted, ed. (1995) *The Oxford Companion to Philosophy*, Oxford: Oxford University Press.

Jambet, Christian et Lardreau (1976), Guy, *L'Ange*, Paris: Grasset.

Jankélévitch, Vladimir (1959) *Henri Bergson*, Paris: Presses Universitaires de France. I quote from 2nd edn, Paris: Presses Universitaires de France, 1999.

Jankélévitch, Vladimir et Béatrice Berlowitz (1978) *Quelque part dans l'inachevé*, Paris: Gallimard.

Kleist, Henrich von (1808) *Penthesilea*, translated in French by Julien Gracq, 1954; 2nd edn, José Corti, 1966.

Le Dœuff, Michèle (1977) 'Cheveux longs, idées courtes', trans. as 'Women in/and Philosophy', in Radical Philosophy, Oxford; French Le Doctrinal de Sapience, 1977; Various redn, including in Philosophical Imaginary.

_____ (1980) *L'Imaginaire Philosophique*, Paris: Payot; Eng. trans. *The Philosophical Imaginary*, London: Athlone, 1989, 3rd edn, Continuum, 2002.

_____ (1989) *L'Etude et le rouet*, Paris: Seuil; Eng. trans. Hipparchia's Choice. Oxford, 1991. 2nd edn, Columbia University Press, 2007.

_____ (1998) *Le Sexe du savoir*, Paris: Aubier; Eng. trans. *The Sex of Knowing*. Routledge, 2003.

Lévinas, Emmanuel (1967) 'Jeanne Delhomme; Pénélope ou la pensée modale', *Critique*, no. 237.

Lévinas, Emmanuel (1976) *Noms Propres*. Fata Morgana, 2nd edn, Paris: Livre de poche, 1987.

Plato, *Philebus*, *Theaetetus* and the *Sophist*, Numerous edns.

Suchon, Gabrielle (1693) *Traité de la morale et de la politique*, imprimé aux dépens de l'Auteur, Lyon chez B. Vignieu.

_____ (1700) *Du Célibat Volontaire ou La Vie sans engagement*, Paris: Jean et Michel Guignard.

A bonny dialogue – for French studies
Elizabeth Fallaize in dialogue with Michèle Le Dœuff

Elizabeth Fallaize: I'd like us to start with an issue that's in the news at the moment, which is women's membership of the Académie Française. Michèle, in your book *Hipparchia's Choice* you discuss this in response to the election of Marguerite Yourcenar and you refer to George Sand's views on women's

---

This dialogue with Elizabeth Fallaize (University of Oxford) took place at the 47th Annual Conference of the Society for French Studies, held at St Andrew's University, Scotland, in July 2006, at the invitation of Diana Knight (Nottingham University). A long-standing member of the Society, Elizabeth Fallaize had previously published an article in the *Australian Journal of French Studies* XL, no. 3 (2003): 'The Pleasure of Dialogue in *Le Sexe du savoir* [*The Sex of Knowing*]'. The aim was to present 'live' to the conference an experience of the kind of pleasure one can derive from openly discussing issues that are perhaps non-canonical.

membership. What are your views on this now, given that Assia Djebar has just been admitted 'beneath the dome'?

Michèle Le Dœuff: Our good friend Elizabeth is being delightfully tactful in omitting to mention how caustic my initial commentaries were, faced with the public reaction to Marguerite Yourcenar's election. Let's look again at the background to this – though we should stress at the outset that the election of Assia Djebar to the Académie a few weeks ago is potentially an inspiring event, one which might prove a welcome contrast to Marguerite Yourcenar's, especially if our colleagues who work in secondary education really do signal its importance in their own teaching.

The often dire *banlieues* that have developed on the outskirts of French cities, at times (but not always), seem to demonstrate – against a backdrop of extreme poverty and some quite inhuman urban planning – that the integration of second- and even third-generation immigrants has to a certain degree failed. But in fact the situation is far more complex than it would seem, and it would be wrong to take events that make the headlines (the riots of autumn 2005, gang rapes) as the definitive image of these areas. Every day in the Paris region, you come across young men and women – the daughters and sons of immigrants – who've been able to find a job that suits them, and not only are they conscientious, they enjoy their job, too.

As far as I'm concerned, we're not talking about another planet here, one where I would appear to be, at best, an occasional spectator. In the very fabric of my life – my professional life included – there are little threads that link me in a concrete way to the children of immigrants and their lives. Take the cover of *The Sex of Knowing*: a young *Beur*[1] was involved in producing that. Elisabeth Kauffmann took her photographs to be developed at her local photographic studio, which is run by a young *Beur* photographer and, as he was very impressed with the work that she had done, he took great care in his work, developing numerous prints until they had one that they both considered to be just right. That warmed our hearts – both mine and Elisabeth's – and in our delight we agreed: 'they're the ones who are carrying on the values'. We did not need to say very much as we both knew what the other meant by that: the value of a job well done, in which the craftsman or woman can find satisfaction and a sense of pride, something they share with those they're working with. We were taught that ethic at *la communale*: our secular, state primary schools. No doubt this ethic goes back a long way in history and there's nothing specifically 'French' or European about it. You will all have seen examples of it while on holiday in distant lands. But in France, it does indeed seem to be the secular education system that has made it its motto, which has held it up as a significant value. Finding a sense of personal pride in work well done is not a particularly religious value. On the contrary, the Bible and the Gospels seem to propose a sense of humility; the only character who appears to have the right to look over his work and to find it any good is the Heavenly Father!

Going back to Assia Djebar: she's a woman, from Algeria (who did indeed take part in the struggle for independence), and someone who can look to her *oeuvre* with legitimate pride. If teachers in all secondary schools – not just the ones deemed challenging – started to inform pupils about Assia Djebar's election, then kids from the dreary *banlieues* should have even more reason to be hopeful. It might also reinvigorate one of the great Republican myths, one which I myself grew up with before distancing myself from it, though now, as an issue, it's starting to seem significant to me once more. It's the myth which says that, even in situations where poverty may be extreme, school can offer you a lifeline. Jules Ferry and Ferdinand Buisson[2] contributed significantly to this magnificent French myth which has also been 'textualized' in the arts and literature. Just think of Joseph Zobel's novel *La Rue des Cases Nègres* and Euzhan Palcy's film adaptation of it using the same title – they are a narrativization and dramatization of this idea which, over the course of several decades, led to thousands of people seated at school desks, pens to the ready. José, a young boy from Martinique, is 'good at school' as they say and will get out of the cycle of poverty by means of the education system. The West Indian teacher quite explicitly states the rules to his class, leaving no room for interpretation: 'There are those who will work hard at school; as for the others, it's a foregone conclusion, they'll work on the cane [sugar cane].' The reason for my disaffection for this set-up is probably quite obvious: *What about the others*? Is there no hope of offering something to those girls and boys who are not 'good at school'? It's also quite interesting to look at some of the more implicit assumptions here. One of José's best friends is a girl who, like him, manages to pass the Primary School Certificate. Yet this young girl's father decides that her education will end there; her destiny is to go straight into work, helping out the postmistress in the local post office. In contrast, José's grandmother moves to the town with him so that he can live there and go on to secondary school; she earns a crust for both of them by taking in washing. So if the myth is to come true and the formula to work, you'd better be a boy with a totally devoted grandmother. . . . Truth to tell, from a very young age I had suspected as much, and that explains (among other reasons) why I've kept a degree of distance from the official system of beliefs. The film shows something else that I believe to be true: José becomes politicized and gradually develops a critical attitude to the generalized racism, but it's not school that brings about such a significant political understanding, it's intelligent reflection on his personal experience. School counts for a lot but only within certain limits.

And that's why we do indeed need to call this a myth, that's to say a kind of discourse which puts forward a whole set of actions for individuals to realize but which inevitably risks being illusory. We have to analyse the different sides of myths, their gaps and always try to dialectically overcome their limits. All the same, nowadays I'm again more inclined to be open-minded in relation to this myth which France had somewhat lost sight of; at the very least I'd say that the need to look at it critically does not mean rejecting it outright. When Azouz Begag, the son of an immigrant worker, becomes a writer, the narrator of his own experience (and then a government minister) and when Assia Djebar, from a fairly modest background in Algeria, is elected to the Académie, I'm tempted to return to it as an idea we can pitch against despair (might the Republic finally decide to legitimize all of its 'children'?'), provided, of course, that the sense of the event is properly relayed by teachers working in what are often difficult teaching environments. At the same time, when it comes to finding a way to overcome individual and collective alienation, it is important that schooling alone is never depicted as a sufficient and auto-sufficient way of learning.

This is something I learned from women who work in Family Planning and who do magnificent work, especially in poor *banlieues*, in bringing to other women the sort of knowledge that is essential for their emancipation. All the women who deal with rape cases and violence (whether domestic or not), and all the women who bring to the public arena what they've learnt and understood from working on the front line, know that nothing can replace what we call 'éducation populaire': education for the people. Let me explain this historical notion which goes back to Condorcet and the French Revolution. Basically, it emphasizes the importance of teaching outside the formal education system, as well as teaching all classes and all ages. When, in her younger days, Simone de Beauvoir was involved in Robert Garric's 'Equipes' and was teaching French literature to women apprentices in Belleville, she was in fact engaged in 'éducation populaire'.[4] And today the French Family Planning Movement ('Le Mouvement Français pour le Planning Familial') has the legal status of a 'Mouvement d'Education

Populaire' – a People's Education Movement. My personal contribution to this grand idea would be the following: any act of teaching goes both ways, that is, you learn a lot while sharing your knowledge with others. And you learn a lot while *doing* things for other people.[5]

Women activists engaged in feminist issues are also informal teachers. They're aware that getting invited into schools is a good thing, as is showing educational films on violence, informing pupils about contraception, and so on. What's more, the women I come across who are involved in campaigning often say that what they mainly got from school is a particular interest which they've carried through into their adult life. It may be a liking for Stendhal or Balzac, George Sand or Zola, or maybe an interest in history, yet all of them have discovered intellectual pleasure or, rather, discovered discovery, and I'm constantly struck by the fact that in France it is the milieus that produce political activists that are the true supporters of literary culture, whether classical or otherwise. Remember Proust, who stated that he had 'sufficiently frequented high society to know that it is they who are really the illiterate ones, not electricians'. A Proust who found 'the idea of art for the masses' ill-conceived since, if by that is meant an art that sacrifices the refinements of form, then it will be 'aimed at members of the Jockey Club rather than members of the CGT union'.[6] For a long time the Italian Communist Party proved a tremendous support to a superb film and literary culture. And then you know, one day, by chance, you meet a member of the Anarchist Federation, an employee of Gaz de France, who is bemoaning the fact that he's just finished the complete works of Lévi-Strauss but remains hopeful that he'll find another author of a similar calibre to capture his imagination. Another day, you are online and you happen to see Arlette Laguiller's biography on Wikipedia and it says that the young Arlette would sometimes skip school so that she could read to her heart's content!

These are the real heirs of Lefèvre d'Étaples (1450–1537), of the Estiennes and of Gabrielle Suchon:[7] women and men who nourish their mental resources through literary culture in order to feed their passion for freedom. It may seem like the connection I'm making here is outrageously simplistic, and if it had to be fully justified there would be a good deal of work for a large, multidisciplinary team. But, in brief: around Marguerite de Navarre, there was a movement led by scholars, booksellers and printers, whose ambitions were to establish a firmer basis for religious and ancient texts, to translate them (and thus along the way to develop knowledge of classical languages) and to print them in characters that were as legible as it was possible to make them. This was so that any literate person would be able to directly access the thought of good authors – which greatly annoyed the Sorbonne – but it also lent extremely useful support to the ideas that were starting to formulate in the mind of a certain Luther and several others. It is fairly well known that this scholarly movement formed a sort of tributary of the emerging Protestant movement of the time. But what is less well known, and has not been explored in any way, to my knowledge, is the development of this movement over time in France, including among those who did not go on to embrace the Lutheran or Calvinist reforms. I now think that Gabrielle Suchon (1631–1703) was herself an 'heiress' and a spokeswoman for this school of thought: she always put books before university and would have wanted books to work for the emancipation of women as well as for men. Historians of 'culture' might thus trace, over a long period, a truly wonderful intellectual heritage which runs through French history (at times obscured and at other times resurgent) – one which associates the idea of resistance to authority and oppression with a carefully produced book, good translations and works printed as a labour of love. When, in Year Three of the Republic, Lakanal declared to the Convention: 'Citizens, for some time the enlightened part of the nation has been asking for a good translation of Bacon', he was simply reconnecting with the tradition inaugurated by Lefèvre d'Étaples. Étaples was very close to the Marguerite whose brother, François I, at the request of Guillaume Budé, was courageous enough to create in 1530 a certain 'Collège des trois langues' which was independent of the Sorbonne and is nowadays our Collège de France.

You've probably guessed that, although I'm very pleased that Assia Djebar has been elected, I have not changed my opinion of the Académie Française: its dome encases, at best, an empty shell. Marguerite Yourcenar, the first woman to become a member, was given her reception there in January 1981, just before the election of François Mitterrand as president of the Republic. The reception took place, and found a meaning, in an atmosphere of cheerful conservatism and it gave a certain number of reactionaries – including Marguerite Yourcenar herself – an opportunity to unleash a pack of misogynistic abominations to an extent that any woman would be entitled to feel aggressed by the occasion. You may remember Jean d'Ormesson's delightful comment in his reception speech: 'Traditions, just like women, are formed to be both respected and violated.'[8] Marguerite Yourcenar heaped praise upon those who had voted against the principle of admitting women, which really is a bit much. In order to make herself better understood, she went so far as to clarify her thinking in Latin, '*sint ut sunt*': that things should remain and be as they are, a statement no doubt entirely in keeping with the elaborately embroidered robe that she had donned for the ceremony. As for her status, she situated herself very clearly as a man *honoris causa*, which is of course very disturbing when that entails a rejection of the emancipation of other women. There are men who prove themselves to be more free of phallocracy than that, men with a greater desire to live in a world where women are free at last. 'Most men have got an "other-half", well, I've got a whole woman', an ocean-going captain once retorted when asked (yet again) if he were not bothered by the fact that he'd married a feminist.

At least this time, at the reception of Assia Djebar beneath the dome, there was no outpouring of reactionary remarks. That is in itself significant, and let's appreciate the difference! And no, we must not attribute this change to the passage of time, since time never simply moves on all by itself. There have to be people who will speak out against claims which aim to bring back alienation. By using irony it is possible to discuss the scandal without flying into a rage, and to prove to certain people that their discourse will meet with the kind of response that may encourage them to show some reserve. And so it was in 1981 that your humble servant dipped her quill into some rather acidic ink, quite determined to do her utmost to give that world a thorough mocking. Oh, yes! we are not going to let ourselves be oppressed without saying a word, and we're certainly not going to internalize your stupidities. My commentary was published in the 'Everyday sexism' section of *Les Temps Modernes*, under a pseudonym as was the rule for that section; I took up the issue again in *Hipparchia's Choice*, in the meantime having discovered that, on a more theoretical level, George Sand had challenged the Académie Française and academicism in literary output as well, a critique inspired by the same sentiment and which is in fact a more significant matter.[9]

There was the outpouring of sexism in 1981 and then, in 2006, a lack of that kind of scandalous remark; between the two dates much work had taken place, work that was long, slow, varied, patient and impatient, but work that led to legislation. For in December 2004, the government (a Chiracian one) got a bill through Parliament which placed inciting sexist and homophobic discrimination or hatred on the same footing as inciting racist discrimination or hatred. That was Simone de Beauvoir's political programme, in part developed by the team involved in 'Everyday sexism', indeed! It may take twenty-five years, but all the same it is sometimes possible to change certain facts of social life, provided you persevere.

There nevertheless remains much to do, as Assia Djebar's reception ceremony also revealed. Elizabeth, you attended that ceremony and you told me that the gentleman who gave the welcoming speech stressed quite strongly the apparent fact that she is a Muslim. It is up to her to say whether or not she believes herself to have such an allegiance, which may well be totally untrue. For my part, I see her as a freethinker, some way from all the constraints that any form of religious allegiance entails. If that is the case, if she is a secular person, as I'm very much inclined to believe (though her new colleague wasn't even able to pronounce the French word meaning secular: *laïque*), a good deal of work remains to be done. Honestly! In France, Church and State have in fact been separate for a century. And also, the law forbids discrimination against someone for reasons of belonging, or not belonging, to a religious group. Nevertheless, as far as I know, nowhere is it stated that a person has a right not to adhere to any religion whatsoever and to state that fact. . . . It is high time that a notion of this kind appeared explicitly in the French Constitution and in European law, where it is also sadly lacking. Given that various jurisdictions recognize religious freedom, as well as the right to change religion if one wishes, it would be consistent if they also recognized the right to atheism. It is often said, with tongue-in-cheek, that anticlericalism is the second major religion in France. No doubt that is statistically true but that's not what I'm defending. Anticlericalism challenges religion in a fairly vigorous way, even when it comes from people as religious as Rabelais, and is very often politically justified considering how things turn out. Yet it is secularism, as the bearer of new values, that must be defended, and at the very least the right to declare oneself an atheist *urbi et orbi*: 'in town and with gown'!

EF: Thanks very much, Michèle. Let's move on to another question: since the publication of *The Philosophical Imaginary*, you have undertaken an analysis of myths and images, especially those which abound in philosophical discourse.[10] Could you tell us what led you to consider this question and how significant it is for you?

MLD: You are right in saying that 'from start to finish' this has been a preoccupation for me, not that I can really envisage my interests finishing! There are probably several reasons for my interest in the imaginary:[11] from a 'genetic' point of view, you could say that I read Gaston Bachelard very early on, when I was a student, and that was the initial trigger. Bachelard, who worked on the pre-scientific imaginary, clearly distinguishes between that which belongs to the domain of concept, method and correct science, and that belonging to the imaginary domain, which is therefore deemed pre-scientific and, according to him, exists in the initial stages of science and persists in its teaching. For example, rightly or wrongly, he points out that in a chemistry class, you can't stop half your students thinking that acids are masculine and alkalines are feminine.

I thoroughly enjoyed reading Bachelard's work, yet afterwards it struck me that he was putting himself in a situation of exteriority – beyond the territory of his object. He positions himself as a philosopher (and of course, one who first studied physics and chemistry), a philosopher who is looking at what happens in the scientific world and finds that, in concrete terms, scientific life is suffused with pre-scientific and non-scientific attitudes, and so on. He doesn't question philosophy itself, except when he mocks his colleagues who are 'merely philosophers', with some superiority here given his aforementioned studies. At the beginning, my thinking was quite simple: when one does that, philosophy is once again positioned in the role of a supposedly neutral ultimate arbiter, one that dominates its object and is exterior to that object. But that does not hold up, because in philosophical discourse, too, and in fact in Bachelard's particularly, there are images and myths! If you then decide to apply a Bachelardian form of questioning to philosophical discourse, it leads to an autocritique or an autoreflection, and then to an understanding that it might well be necessary to craft new conceptual frameworks.

What's more, if it's accepted that you are no longer in a position to act as ultimate arbiter or to offer a wonderful neutrality, it is indeed important to be aware that you yourself are caught in the interlacing of fable, myth, the imaginary . . . and that no one is automatically (or effortlessly) an agency providing perfect elucidation. What happens to philosophy if you begin to accept that? And in a more general sense, what happens when you start to think that it's not only others who dream? Along the way, one could invite literary critics, historians, sociologists, and so on, to ask themselves the same kinds of questions. I believe I started that work by writing *The Sex of Knowing*, in dialogue with certain texts – and with myself, as you would say, Elizabeth![12] But it's an issue that opens up lots of work for many other scholars.

After having somewhat shifted Bachelardian views, I said to myself that, if that fact is accepted – that everyone dreams when thinking, and 'I' along with everyone else – then you also have to ask yourself if you couldn't dream in a different way from time to time. Indeed, ask yourself if you couldn't try to modify your own dream world, to find myths which, instead of being burdens or blocks, might be vectors indicating a way forward. And also, ask whether it might be possible to create images that help us in thinking any new experiences, such as, for example (!), the experiences of women who are working for the liberation of other women, or what women philosophers experience when they seek to affirm their own and others' freedom to think. Ultimately, it's about renewing our acquaintance with creative fiction within philosophy; it's about creating reveries, finding pleasure in that and hoping for a greater liberation . . . that's basically what I'm doing. I say 'renewing our acquaintance' because, after all, quite a few male predecessors have enjoyed intermingling fiction and theoretical endeavours. Think of Diderot's *Le Rêve d'Alembert* and his other essays – Diderot to whom I owe, by the way, my discovery of Bacon. Think of Bacon himself, etc.

With hindsight, it could be added that I had a lot of luck professionally; I came across some tolerant and open characters. With such a project, I might very well have never got going in the academic world as my concerns were so beyond the norms of university philosophy. Fortunately, Vladimir Jankélévitch liked things beyond the norms, in both philosophy and music. Occasionally, I felt tempted to laugh: one of the examiners who wrote a report on my work stated that they liked the idea that a (female) philosopher might also be a poet . . . well, I did have to smile at that ('and what about Plato, eh?' 'and Bacon, with his *New Atlantis*?') and then I realized that it did, in fact, come in handy because it dealt with my main breach of alleged protocol. It's not simply that I'm actually interested in something like a poetics within philosophy, it's more that I do not feel particularly obliged to stage a so-called pure philosophy, which in any case has never existed, but which a good number of our male colleagues desperately try to establish, to the point of sometimes reducing a discipline so dear to us to an ascetic skeleton, lost in echoing inanities. Nevertheless, you do have to accept the (troubling) idea that my interest in thinkers' reveries has maybe contributed to making me acceptable, as a woman, in philosophy. Or it's the other way round: I'm less dangerous as a woman in philosophy because I'm also a poet. It's a hypothesis that is certainly worth considering.

Sometimes, however, I had no choice but to cross swords. In the 1970s, the Ministry of Education brought in a system of interviewing candidates aspiring to academic tenure in front of a national exam panel comprised of the entire body of examiners. A young woman who had just left the arena looking rather drawn whispered to me as I was heading towards it: 'it's horrible, and there are only men in there!' That was not entirely true: if you searched thoroughly among the fifty or so highly qualified colleagues who graced the lecture theatre, you could spot two women. In terms of experiences relevant to the archaeology of my ideas on parity (parity in government bodies with delegated authority), this brutal test can certainly be counted as something of a spur.[13]

First, I had to get that grand jury to admit that there are images in the most classic philosophical texts. Because, naturally, they'd never noticed them. Then, having won the first 'round', the real, truly real, question came from the last row, right at the back of the lecture theatre: 'All the great philosophers have argued that the imagination is incapable of thought. Who do you think you are, *Mademoiselle*, in coming here to tell us that imagination does produce thought?' Let's bequeath this outburst to future generations, who will be able to sharpen their analytical capacities on that stone, if they wish – by asking whether the notion of 'great philosophers' is not itself a desperately vacuous idea, and whether vacuous ideas are not be rather harmful to the life of the mind, and so on. As for me, the question gave me a surge of adrenalin which had a marvellous effect on my memory, and supplied me (I don't know how) with a little grain of light capable of jamming the infernal machine of the question and the extremely regrettable group dynamic developing in the room because of it. We were on the verge of a psychodrama, at the point of descending into a quarrel that was not, in essence, intellectual, as can happen in a school classroom or in various university contexts and when it is least expected.[14]

– 'If I may, Sir, I refer you to the passage of the *Critique of Pure Reason* dedicated to monograms of the imagination.'[15]

The learned assembly relaxed; a few of them even smiled, as if with relief. Oh yes, of course, the French philosophical community at that time was rather conservative, especially as far as 'roles' were concerned – as you've just heard – but the rules of engagement provided a degree of stability, and it was that reasonable element that, in the end, I had addressed: the history of philosophy does exist, as does logic, and a counter-example suffices in order to refute a poorly made induction. When it comes to examining a fact in the history of philosophy, which is our guiding reference for all of us in our mental universe, it is surely the texts that arbitrate, not the *dramatis personae*: 'great philosophers', '*Mademoiselle*'. . . . If I might whisper a word of advice to budding women philosophers who could themselves one day be confronted with such awkward aggression: in a tense situation, don't give an immediate, 'tit for tat' response, or be lured into a game of 'Gather thistles – expect prickles', but always seek the reasoned elements of the cultural milieu to which you belong, so as to establish a minimal dialogue that will encourage each woman and man to enter into a dialogue with themselves, which means asking themselves a few questions, and indeed realizing, before it's too late, that they're on the verge of taking themselves down a path that is not right for anyone.

In short, life was not always easy for me but survival was possible. And then, in the 1960s and 1970s in France, people were reading Jean-Pierre Vernant. His way of working on the Greek myths and their relation to thought and rationality had impressed a lot of people and certainly helped me to defend – in the field of philosophy from which he came, incidentally – the idea that there can be a relation between fantasy and invention, and the work of philosophy. And let's not be too hasty in saying that work such as his, focusing on Classical Greece, also enabled its author to stand in a relation of exteriority to the object studied. Things are certainly not that simple.

At the moment, while I still analyse and unpick myths that are alienating and block or shatter our understanding, I'm usually more interested in looking at fragments of legends that are likely to support more appealing perspectives. You heard me in Oxford, Elizabeth, speaking about Ariadne and her encounter with Bluebeard's wives, a theme created by Maurice Maeterlinck and taken up by Vladimir Jankélévitch, who endeavoured to change its meaning, and it's one that I'm prepared to extend in a sort of critical reverie. Colleagues who attended the Adeffi conference in Limerick in 2004 also heard me speak of Brec'het, the woman born without arms and hands but who found they started to grow when she tried to help another woman. It's an image (coming from somewhere in my Breton childhood) I've had in my mind ever since the period when I spent my spare time helping women who needed abortions or information on contraception. A feminist image, of course, but it can be presented as simply a humanist image: Isn't it part of the adult human condition in general to acquire hands, know-how and ideas, when seeking to help those who really are in need of it? And together, couldn't we find legendary themes that might create a more positive imaginary for women, and not only for women? A mixed universe is what I've always dreamt of: let's all seek an imaginary that might solicit within us the desire for a world that is at last mixed and egalitarian.

EF: Thank you, Michèle. As you know, I first came to your work through your writings on Simone de Beauvoir . . .

MLD: Really? Well, there's a surprise!

EF: Your commentary on the passage that you rendered a focus for discussion, by baptizing it 'the Luxembourg scene', has made such an impression on Beauvoir studies! And then you knew her personally and I've noticed that you continue to offer reflections on her and her work in your own work. I would like to take this opportunity to ask you what exactly she represents for you.

MLD: You'll all be deprived of your dinner and there'll be no reception! What does Simone represent for me . . . how can you ask such questions in the late afternoon? OK. First of all, she represents just that: 'Simone', although I can be sufficiently disciplined on occasion to say 'Beauvoir'. Then the encounter with her was really quite something: a written encounter, between a woman writer and a woman reader. I'm not actually talking about the encounter with the person herself, which was to happen quite late on and, to be frank, she and I had no real wish to speak with one another. It's the encounter with *The Second Sex* that counts. I was eighteen years old, I had just arrived in Paris from my native Brittany: no doubt I was looking for some clues to help me understand what it was to be a woman. Who among us, at the start of adult life, has not asked themselves what it is to be a woman or a man? I certainly wanted it explained in some way. The simple fact that I turned to a book proves, moreover, that I had already accepted that I was not the absolute origin of the answer to that question and that I was not expecting it from the many others who would have willingly given me one that suited themselves. I was counting on another woman; I really hoped that she had already accomplished a good deal of the work.

During the course of my reading, I discovered or generated an insight that still seems to hold true today: being a woman means being placed in a situation that is always more *passé* than you might expect. And it's for that reason that an encounter with *The Second Sex* goes well beyond any adolescent attempt to find an identity. We learn that reality is seriously out of step, it lags behind official history which assures you that everything is sorted. . . . Many men and women have led me to understand that this is something they have also found in my own books: there is a serious discrepancy between what people now believe has been achieved for all women and that which, in fact, each woman experiences in her daily or professional life.

In reading *The Second Sex*, no doubt I was also searching for the face of a friendly Parisian woman. And that's because – well, try to picture it: you go to the *lycée* in Quimper; in Brest, you study and then sit the competitive, pre-entry exam for an École Normale Supérieure, then for the first time in your life you take the night train bound for Paris to get to Fontenay for the oral element of the exam. You pass and thus move to the Paris region – but you arrive in Paris as a Breton girl. Oh yes, you've decided to adapt and fit in, but strangely it was always somewhat more difficult than you'd thought. I had been to London and Southend-on-Sea, or rather, Leigh-on-Sea, where I had stayed with a Methodist family during a languages trip. But Paris – I'd never set foot in Paris. It was a complete unknown to me and in a way, quite a worry, even though it was love at first sight when I made my first contact – eating breakfast early in the morning on the terrace at the Café Dôme. I needed to see faces of Parisian women that would not be intimidating, that would not risk snubbing me. Anyone can find such a face, today just like yesterday, in a book: *The Second Sex*. That was what I discovered in that book, more than any theoretical questioning and so much more than knowledge or reflection. The voice of a woman – a Parisian – who was trying to say something to a younger sister. It gave me considerable psychological support.

In retrospect, it would be fair to say that I also discovered my caustic humour through that book. Our dear Simone, ironic remarks were very much her *forte*; a Voltaire in the feminine, a feminist one – I really liked that! It's liberating for everyone to hear a woman taking the mickey out of oppressors, showing that the force of their intimidation sometimes fails to produce its usual effects, that it could well disappear and soon cease to exist. Laughter, the moment of laughter, re-establishes equality, between an ordinary Thracian servant and Thales, say.[16] Laughter marks the beginnings of liberation when, faced with being crushed psychologically or overwhelmed politically, a small grain of good humour can go on to achieve (or not) miracles. Some of us must indeed take it upon ourselves to mock pompous asses of either sex, to mock institutions and especially social norms which are still inculcated in us. I believe in the future of a Voltairean spirit, which comes to us from Beauvoir, in both philosophical questioning and in feminist work. Of course, our women friends who currently deal with extremely serious practical issues, such as supporting women victims of domestic violence, need support that goes far beyond humour; they want historical facts, a theoretical context that still leads to self-understanding – an approach which actually is not as detached as it may seem given that the women theoreticians of my generation nearly all began with an involvement in practical issues; we underwent an experience that was carried over into our thinking. But our friends, women involved in campaigning today, also need to hear a discourse that contains a laugh and a smile – something they usually do have in their daily lives when the situation is not too difficult. Humour and irony are potentially a language we can share, forming a passage between the different women's various kinds of activism.

As for the philosophical world, when it totally rejects the possibility of a humorous outlook, then it automatically lays claim to the heritage of Protagoras and the Scholastics, and each new dawn would gladly poison Socrates again. And by the way, if you feel that Heideggerians, in the name of philosophy, are actually dedicating themselves to a sort of papal cult, it's also worth remembering that a good number of Althusserians were similarly attached to the idea, which has never actually come to anything, that there is a some great Being at the helm. Hence the fact that some were able to pass quite effortlessly, and without having to change in any way, from Althusser to St Paul or Carl Schmitt; others, known to have been Maoists, became high-ranking priests after embracing the most conservative form of Roman Catholicism.

EF: Thank you, Michèle. I have one final question which you slightly anticipated by mentioning Quimper and Brest. In *Hipparchia's Choice*, you write: 'I was born in the clogs of a Breton peasant', and, during the lectures that you have just given in Oxford, I noticed that you often spoke of . . .

MLD: Of 'Bretonitude'?[17]

EF: That's right!

MLD: So allow me to go back to what I specifically said in my 'profession of faith', which is as unwavering as it can be: 'I was born just about everywhere, under the now shattered sky of the Greeks, in a Brittany farmer's clogs, in an Elizabethan theatre, in my grandmother's famines and destitution, and in the secular, compulsory schooling that the state was so good to make available to me, but also in the rebellions that were mine alone, in the slaps that followed or preceded them, in Simone de Beauvoir's lucid distress and in Descartes' stove. And there is more to come.'[18] You appreciate, Elizabeth, that I have never stopped defending the idea of polygenesis. Basically, it's usually thought that individuals are born somewhere, that they are rooted (or suffer the consequences of being uprooted), that they have a genesis that, it's claimed, is well and truly 'one'. In the work of historians of philosophy in France, at least those influenced by Bergson, it is also acknowledged, whether explicitly or not, that a philosophy develops gradually like a living being, and it's better to start by reading a philosopher's early writing, and then move on from there to read the later work, and so read in 'the right chronological order'. This methodological principle has become quite widespread in the history of philosophy, and I think it makes sense. And yet, when I set to work on Simone de Beauvoir, I was one day struck by quite a different (but not contradictory) idea. You see, there are times when ideas are not really produced by you, as such, but they emerge as a result of a labour which is very much your own. And so, when I was writing *Hipparchia's Choice*, I suddenly grasped that Beauvoirian discourse draws together threads that originate in many different places.

And then, while still writing *Hipparchia's Choice*, I also took up this idea in a somewhat autobiographical way (after all, I'm also composite, coming from many a place and who knows where I may be born in the future!), partly in order to explain for my own benefit what I had just understood regarding *The Second Sex*. And partly to translate this idea into a profession of faith, a political one ultimately. In the twentieth century, so many people have spoken of 'my roots', 'my identity' or have asked themselves if they sufficiently match up to what they used to be, because they should do. . . . Such a perspective is never true, and what's more, we inflict violence upon ourselves if we force ourselves into an absolute coincidence with a single identity. Oneness is never true and the same goes for the tormented search for a cultural 'self' in literature, one potentially crushed by colonization and which subsequently engenders a legitimate desire for recuperation – that kind of search can meander widely and require the discovery of far-off horizons. Take the case of Mairtin O Cadhain – admittedly a limit case – the *enfant terrible* of twentieth-century Irish literature: Would we have had his *oeuvre* if he hadn't read Gorki and Freud?[19]

And also: the clogs, between the Greek sky and Elizabethan theatre . . . that was in part a friendly nod to Pierre Vidal-Naquet.[20] We didn't know each other very well, but he was kind enough to read my work, as I, of course, read his. One day, during a rather Parisian social gathering, we treated ourselves to a luxurious feast of shared childhood memories. As a refugee in Beg-Meil at the beginning of the war, Pierre Vidal-Naquet was lucky enough to attend school in Breton clogs, which are worn with felt inner shoes. These are great for children. Outside, you can run in the mud as much as you like, with none of the fuss over damaging them as you have with shoes. But when you go back inside, you leave the clogs by the door, and you find yourself in soft and comforting slippers, and not only that, you can wriggle your feet around as much as you like without being told off because of the noise! We were as jubilant as children, Pierre and I, as we recounted to one another the tremendous benefits of those clogs; we were perhaps secretly acknowledging a deep-rooted hospitality that a certain reserve kept us from naming explicitly.

On the list of my imaginary 'births', there is therefore Brittany as one of them, and the loyalty I have maintained to a people that has suffered so much over the centuries. You know, a 'Breton narrative' is possible, a narrative recounting the vicissitudes experienced after it was annexed to France, in fact. . . . Well, possible perhaps if we keep quiet about how things were before, as it wasn't particularly great then either! But in any case, after it was annexed Brittany clearly acquired the status of a colony, where the people were vanquished, oppressed and despised: mere chattel to serve at whim – a status that unfortunately the fall of the *Ancien Régime* did nothing to change. My first research job – in the regional archives at Quimper when I was a school girl – nevertheless led me to discover that the town supported the Revolution and during that period there was more than a degree of anticlericalism there. (People burned the Cathedral statues – just the sort of anticlericalism I do *not* approve of.) The oppressive connivance between 'Church and Manor' was certainly challenged by the '*sans culottes*' in their *bragou braz*, the breeches typical of the Odet valley. The Brittany that you too often see, the nineteenth-century one, is largely a fabrication of the 1815 Restoration: the people were returned to the harsh and bleak world of the traditional order, made even worse with the Napoleonic Code and all the further problems that represented for women. True, during the Revolution, some families had managed to buy the small farms they'd been running as tenants, but only the men had the legal status to own them. I have seen an inventory from a nineteenth-century farm – the recently widowed woman didn't even own the dress she was wearing, it had become part of her nephew's property.

The status of Brittany as a colony was, for many years, difficult to challenge, particularly as certain Bretons calling for independence unfortunately had dreams of an independence that would enable the people to 'rediscover their natural way of life', meaning total subjection to dim-witted squires and to priests. It was not until the end of the 1960s that a completely different kind of independence movement emerged in the form of the Breton Democratic Union.[21] And shortly after that we saw the opening of Family Planning services in towns and cities across the region. You can't imagine how revolutionary that was! That is the true revolution in my view, and it is still continuing.

In a situation that is colonial in nature, loyalty becomes an obligation; it's something that comes to you quite naturally when an acceptable political discourse, full of positive historical representations, finally manages to escape from the hammer of ethnocide and the anvil of the most unbearable traditionalism. People had thought that it was impossible to get beyond the

1815 Restoration, and then, in the end, it wasn't![22] It seemed obvious to me that I should speak of Brittany from the very first sentence of my inaugural lecture as Weidenfeld Visiting Professor at Oxford. As well as mention Charles Tillon, a member of the Resistance from Rennes, and Joséphine Pencallet, from Douarnenez, the first woman ever to be elected into office in France at a time when the Republic still hadn't recognized women's right to vote. You cannot disown a people who have been wiped out in more ways than one; you still need to find positive things to say about them while refusing to turn a blind eye when it comes to internal social relations – including sexual relations – which may still be oppressive.

Let me give you a few pointers that really characterize this colonization, which left behind it in France one of the most insidious forms of racism as it is rarely recognized as such. During the First World War, although Bretons constituted roughly one-seventeenth of the French population, around one-sixth of the soldiers who died were from Brittany. Historians don't entirely agree over the exact figures, but they all agree that they were dreadfully disproportionate. The Breton regiments were put on the front line because they were looked upon as people who don't count. And of course, the verb *baragouiner*[23] formed from the Breton '*bara*', which means 'bread', and '*gwin*', which means 'wine', is a sarcastic expression deriving from the French armies of the sixteenth century. It alluded to the poor souls who, unable to speak French, had to ask for bread and wine in Breton! For centuries, an entire people was humiliated over its language. It's true that I never experienced the horrible practice known as 'the cow' or 'the infamous clog', as I started school shortly after it had stopped. Any child heard speaking Breton in class or in the playground would find themselves with a clog on a thread around their neck, and they would only be allowed to get rid of it when they in turn came across another child who had done the same; the child thus passed on 'the cow' to another, and so on, the 'game' being that the one who was wearing it at the end of the day would land themselves a punishment. It was assumed that children would think of this as a game! It's also true that with my generation teachers in secondary school, on hearing certain expressions, would speak in a kind voice when they told us: 'Watch what you're saying, that's poorly translated Breton . . .' And it's true, finally, that I only saw the sign which said: 'No spitting on the floor or speaking Breton' in the regional archives, so when it was a museum piece, though for a long time it had graced the interior walls of all public buildings. Yet these various factors still had an appreciable effect in Brittany in the 1960s.

As for Paris, well, rather than repeat the stupid – really stupid – remarks that one sometimes hears in a city that still thinks it's at the top of the pecking order, and whose natives see Brittany as provincial 'twice over', I'd rather focus on how such a situation can find a positive outcome, a dialectical one, which means overcoming it positively by setting the discrepancy to work. All of you here share with me a love of the French language and the multifacetted culture that unfolds in that language; it constitutes a 'common good' which we have received, which we share and together we appreciate; with joy and in good spirits, we feel some responsibility towards it. Thanks to my Breton birth, I will never have a 'Péguyist'[24] relation to the land or to language, which gives me a rather sumptuous freedom and facilitates a better encounter between us. It's such a pleasure for me to represent to you the France that I like; some of my compatriots, even Parisian ones, trust me in that respect and I'm eager to merit their trust. There is indeed a France that I like – that you like – a culture that, for example, appreciates Proust's polemic against Barrès and his support for a patriotic art which Proust rightly regards as 'dangerous' and 'ridiculous'; Barrès who said that 'the artist must, above all, serve the glory of his fatherland'. Serve the glory of one's fatherland? No. But I can bring to life the France that I love, without any illusions, whether that's in my work or in the space of this one hour, maybe.

Brittany also gave me, paradoxically, atheism, or rather a certain attitude to life which comes from atheism. If you grow up in Brittany where your family is to all intents and purposes the only secular and non-practising family, how could that not have an effect on you? When you are non-conformist to that degree, and from birth, it leads to all kinds of experiences which are not necessarily easy. However, it's invaluable to have to learn from an early age that, if necessary and when necessary, you have to stand alone in your views. This was done silently, without ever saying a word, as proselytizing was strictly forbidden by both sides; good manners among children meant that certain things were never discussed. But the fact remains that because of this I learnt to assume my singularity. And as a result of that, as an adult and a traveller, it would so happen that I found my favourite 'others' were very often people from minority religious backgrounds.

When men of the '68 generation started to say that they'd rather 'be wrong with Sartre than be right with Aron' (this was a great war cry among male friends who were or had been involved in the '68 movement), when as a result they started to advocate blind conformity, persuasion, finding a mentor, belonging to a 'following' rather than engaging in personal reflection – I used to tell myself that you can always be right (or wrong!) all alone, if necessary. I knew that such an attitude was tenable and besides, I was damn used to it. When I got involved in the Women's Movement in 1971, I followed no one, and I always separated out what I heard; at times I was enthralled, at others critical and I'd be all the more enthralled given that I reserved the right to be perfectly critical if need be.

So I have no parish, no chapel, and here I am, like so many others, assuming my singularity and my becoming. Yet I cannot conclude this 'Out of Brittany' without referring to an element of the cultural landscape that has been lost, even though it is obscurely close (present maybe because it's lost); in Brittany it is regarded as an alternative to Roman Catholicism. Religious young men and women of my generation drew upon this obscure source when they wished to reformulate their approach to faith. You see, there was a general understanding, based on a sort of local folklore or legend, that in Brittany there had been a different kind of Christianity 'in the past', during some quite vaguely defined time, *in illo tempore*, before a trend for regulation coming from Rome imposed norms and a very regrettable form of centralism. Later, when a fellow Parisian student was quoting with approval and malicious pleasure to some of my friends a vile remark by Cardinal Daniélou ('in Brittany, religion would have long disappeared if it hadn't been supported by superstition', meaning: you are ignorant and barbaric), they were able to connect what a Jesuit from Montmartre had the arrogance to call 'superstition' with that other form of Christianity which may have prospered long ago in Brittany before a clergy linked to *Francilien* rule apparently suppressed it with all the accursed measures they could muster, yet without managing to eradicate it. The sense that official Christianity was not the right one was widespread among my religious men and women friends, which gave them excellent regionalist reasons to take a critical view on it. Some even burst out laughing when the press announced that the said cardinal had been found dead in a house of ill repute.

What we can say of this archaic Christianity without annoying extremely punctilious positivists too much, is this: around the fifth century AD, a wave of immigration came to the Armorican peninsula from across the Channel in the form of the Bretons, who thus gave Brittany its current name.[25] Legend has it that the region's first form of Christianity arrived after them by sea (after all, we weren't going to allow ourselves to be converted via a land route, were we?!), thanks to a nice collection of Irish (or possibly Welsh) saints who, it is claimed, crossed the Channel in stone vessels.[26]

It's quite plausible that the newly installed Bretons in Armorique practised Christianity in a quite different way from what is practised today in the name of Catholicism, especially as there are reasons for assuming a link, for example, with what we know of the congregation of St Cuthbert, who founded Durham, or the struggle led by Canterbury in the Middle Ages against certain practices of the Welsh Church, such as allowing priests to marry. There could have been an ancient Celtic Christianity, one that didn't demand celibacy in priesthood and the outright marginalizing of women. In any case, as far as Brittany is concerned, a historic text dated 510 tells us of practices that were eradicated by forced normalization 'to the Roman way'. The text is a letter full of invectives from the Bishop of Rennes (co-signed by the Bishops of Angers and Tours) and addressed to two unfortunate itinerant Breton priests. They are reproached, in the strongest terms and accompanied by serious threats, for being itinerant, meaning transporting tables to celebrate mass from one cabin hut to another, and for including women in the holy service . . . apparently, the women would serve the wine to the assembly from the chalice. These were two women who, to make matters worse, might well have been the two nomads' partners.[27] Which do you find more acceptable: cohabiting with women who, to add to that, participated in the altar service or, being a Jesuit and ending up a client at a brothel after having insulted an entire people – it's up to you. My Catholic friends would rub their hands in glee every time they discovered a tradition that had been looked down on or barely tolerated by the clergy, one accused of being 'pagan' or a 'local superstition'. They would immediately attribute it to the ancient form of Christianity, of which so little was known, thus playing the arch-archaic off against what was in fact only from the fairly recent past. They would even take it further back: 'Oh, no, the great *Troménie* at Locronan is thought to be a pre-Christian rite, covered with a sprinkling of holy water: yes, even better!' As far as they were concerned, it was 'anything but Saint-Sulpice', and of course, I joined in with them, just as we were all so proud to see the village of Saint-Coulitz elect Kofi Yamgnane and then so pleased to read in an interview that he had no difficulty integrating into the Breton, rural way of life.[28]

The ultimate (and somehow paradoxical) advantage of atheism is that it leaves you with a mental place that's independent of the various religious groups, and from there you can think your own values (independently), even if, in going along with your childhood friends, you may amicably warm to a historic form of religion now lost, hardly known but for the repression it had to suffer and the insulting terms it was to attract: 'heresy, exclusion, excommunication, sullying the holy sacraments', and so on. A form of religion, however, that might well have left in its wake a string of male and female saints who were unofficial yet animated by poetic inspiration and just as capable of transferring from culture to culture as the deities praised by Hesiod. I'll willingly lend them to you. A religious form that has left behind beliefs and practices which, out of necessity, have become concealed to varying extents. A form that might have been less anti-feminist than the one imposed in Latinized Europe and then on the American continent for centuries by Rome, Tours and Canterbury, especially as it is wonderfully malleable, and has no clergy to defend it today as an orthodoxy.

It may also have left behind, and before us if you care to have it that way, some truly original unions between figures that have emerged from a legend we know little about now and some slightly better known characters. You know, the official gospels say nothing about a possible grandmother of Christ; only the masculine lineage counts. Fortunately, the gaps can be filled, as I have heard it said that an Armorican or Gallic goddess was reinterpreted into this role, just as Renaissance artists and poets reinterpreted numerous elements of the Greek dreamworld.[29] Anna was a young woman living in Armorica, perhaps in Auray, or in La Palud. Unfortunately, the poor young lass was married to a violent man: he used to beat her. One day, the angels took pity on her and transported her to Palestine. She met another man there, by the name of Joachim. She made a new life with him and brought into the world a truly brilliant daughter – it would be impolite to point out that this little child was born out of wedlock, the most one can say is that children born out of love, whether illegitimate or not, are more blessed than other children. While still a child, she had a major argument with theologians from the area – I don't know what about – but she very clearly carried the day. Then she and her fiancé Joseph had to marry rather quickly and she gave birth to a little boy who in no time also started to show great promise.

You can continue the story, if you wish – try to ensure, please, that the ending isn't too sad. As far as I'm concerned, I've reason to believe that Anna's grandson first had a passionate affair with a young man by the name of Judas, then another passionate affair with an unfortunate woman by the name of Mary Magdalene, whom he'd taken away from the forced prostitution into which she'd been sold. They are thought to have had at least one son together, whom they also called Judas: make of that what you will. But overall, just try, if you will, to appreciate that the human condition can be found at the heart of this story, too, and that it would be a good thing if simply counting on angels ceased to be a way to resolve the tragedies created by patriarchy.

Notes

1. *The Sex of Knowing* (London/New York: Routledge, 2003), translated from the French by Kathryn Hamer and Lorraine Code (*Le Sexe du savoir* (Paris: Aubier, 1998)). A *Beur* is a second- or third-generation North African living in France [*tr*].
2. Jules Ferry established mandatory and secular State education in France in 1882; Ferdinand Buisson was a Radical-Socialist pacifist and a campaigner for free, secular education who was appointed Director of Primary Education by Ferry [*tr*].
3. '*Enfants*' – a reference to the notion that all citizens are 'children' of the Republic, '*enfants de la Patrie*', as sung in *La Marseillaise*, the French National Anthem (*tr*.).
4. *Mémoires d'une jeune fille rangée* (Paris 1958, reprinted Folio, 1976), pp. 308–9. *Memoirs of a Dutiful Daughter*, translated by James Kirkup (London: Penguin Classics, 2001), pp. 179–181.
5. For the passage about a Spanish concierge, see Pamela Sue Anderson and Meena Dhanda, 5 'On Joy and Wit: Bringing Us into Twentieth-Century Feminism', p. 11
6. *Le Jockey-Club de Paris*: a sporting club for aristocrats and the social elite, particularly prominent in the nineteenth century [*tr*.].
7. Lefèvre d'Étaples was a philosopher and biblical scholar who advocated ecclesiastical reform yet without separation from the Catholic Church; the Estiennes were a distinguished humanist family based in Paris and then Geneva in the sixteenth and seventeenth centuries who supported the Reformation and were dedicated to scholarship and printing; Gabrielle Suchon was a seventeenth-century feminist philosopher, whose notable publications include *Traité de la Morale et de la Politique* (Treatise on Morality and Politics) [tr.].
8. 'Les traditions, comme les femmes, sont faites pour être à la fois respectées et bousculées', published in *Le Monde*, 23 January 1981.
9. See *L'Etude et le rouet, des femmes, de la philosophie, etc.* (Paris: Seuil, 1989), p. 276, translated by Trista Selous, *Hipparchia's Choice: An Essay Concerning Women, Philosophy, Etc.* (New York: Columbia, 2007), p. 252.
10. *L'Imaginaire Philosophique* (Paris: Payot, 1980); translated by Colin Gordon, *The Philosophical Imaginary* (Stanford: Stanford University Press, 1990).
11. Meryl Altman 'Waiting for Lady Reason', Review of the Sex of Knowing by Michèle Le Dœuff, *The Women's Review of Books*, November 2004, vol. 22, no. 2, pp. 14–15.

12 Elizabeth Fallaize, 'The Pleasure of Dialogue in The Sex of Knowing' *Australian Journal of French Studies*, special issue "Autour de Michèle Le Doeuff, vol XL, no. 3, 2003, p. 307.

13 I think I must plead guilty to putting into circulation the term 'parity', owing to my essay *L'Employeur Public [The Public Employer]*, *Les Temps Modernes* (1981), which also appears in *Hipparchia's Choice*.

14 My account of the thesis defence given on p. xi of *Hipparchia's Choice* is a true account, which actually took place at the Sorbonne.

15 In truth, it's not clear that there is such an obvious relation between this page of Kant (*Critique of Pure Reason*, 'Transcendental Doctrine of Judgement', Chapter 1, Schemata of the Pure Concepts of Understanding), and what I had just presented. Kant says of schemata that it is 'an art hidden in the depths of the human soul', which no doubt means he perceived something of which he himself understood nothing, as happens to everyone, but which I myself don't feel able to take up, as I've always tended to leave the human soul out of my considerations.

16 This marvellous anecdote, recounted by Plato in *Theætetus*, is worth considering as a fragment of an affirmative imaginary. See 'Long Hair, Short Ideas', in *The Philosophical Imaginary*.

17 *Sic*. This was our discussion at St. Andrews, which took place several months before all the commotion caused by Ségolène Royal's use of the word '*bravitude*' [brave-ness, *tr.*]. In line with many linguists, it is of course apt to point out that neologisms formed with '-itude' can be traced back to Léopold Senghor (*négritude* – negritude). And yet, before Senghor, French philosophy was familiar with the term 'finitude' (meaning that which is limited), the origin of which was probably phenomenological. Among Beauvoir-inspired feminists, ironic use of the term '*féminitude*' was quite widespread in the 1970s: there was no question of us founding our liberation on the idea of a 'woman-essence' that we allegedly all share and which, given its proximity to philosophical 'finitude', would limit us (or to which we should limit ourselves) and might also create a dreadful misunderstanding: during the 1960s fellow male and female African students in the Cité Universitaire [international student residence in Paris, *tr.*] enlightened us on a certain political use of the notion of negritude, which tended to claim that there are no class relations, and thus no exploitation, within newly independent countries, leading ordinary people to accept the domination of the governing classes.

In December 2006, following a statement from Antoinette Fouque on Ségolène Royal in *Marianne* (that Royal apparently positions herself as a mother which, it would seem, is a reason to get behind her campaign), I do confess to being responsible for the word '*maternitude*'. After all, since Ségolène Royal had ratified this praise, I was quite within my rights to announce that the campaign for the

Elysée would merit 'many an outpouring on maternitude'. Then came her take on '*bravitude*' and a whole raft of neologisms.

18 *Hipparchia's Choice*, Basil Blackwell, 1991, reprinted by Columbia University Press, 2007, p. 172.

19 Cf. *The Road to Brightcity*, short stories translated by Eoghan O Tuairisc, Poolbeg Press, 1981, p. 8.

20 Eminent historian of Ancient Greece and a truth campaigner who exposed the French Government's use of torture in Algeria; his Jewish parents were arrested and eventually murdered in Auschwitz; deceased 4 August 2006 [*tr.*].

21 The *Union Démocratique Bretonne* (UDB) was founded in 1964 by a handful of students, some of whom had been involved in the struggle against torture in Algeria, while others were to become involved in the Anti-Apartheid movement; internationalist themes would always be significant in this movement. Close to the *Parti Socialiste Unifié* [Unified Socialist Party] (which had a considerable number of elected representatives in Brittany), the UDB consistently supported an anti-militarist standpoint, and condemned the terrorism of the *Front de Libération de la Bretagne* [Brittany Liberation Front], etc. Its political success – it still has representatives on the *Conseil Régional* – reveals a side of Brittany that I very much like.

22 I will recount a telling historical incident that I only know from hearsay, but which historians could easily verify as eyewitnesses must still be living. At the beginning of the 1960s, the Ministry of Education had been informed by the University of Rennes that it might not be able to offer the number of places required for the baby-boom generation, especially as the *département* of Finistère had more young people in education than anywhere else in France. Hence the ministry thought it appropriate to create a further campus at Quimper. The mayor was contacted, who then deferred the matter to the bishop, as if there were no separation of politics and religion. The bishop apparently exclaimed: 'What! Students in the good city of Quimper? Never!'. The mayor thus informed the ministry that he would be refusing the offer. And that's why the campus at Brest was set up in 1963, under the name of the Collège Littéraire Universitaire [University College of Literature], which eventually was to become the Université de Bretagne Occidentale.

23 To speak in an incoherent manner; to express oneself poorly in a language [*tr.*].

24 Charles Péguy (1873–1914), from a modest background, was socialist essayist, philosopher and political activist who later converted to Catholicism, expounding in his writings and poetry a mystic nationalism which promoted the spiritual and cultural values of the *Ancien Régime* and idealized the peasantry.

25 At the time of Caesar, *Britannia* was a part of what you call Great Britain, my own peninsula being named *Armorica* or *Aremorica* (the sea country). Then came the

Angle and Saxon invasions, invasions that quite likely forced the ancient inhabitants (the *Britons*) back to the west, the south and to . . . the sea. Stressing this point is perhaps no longer sensitive in geopolitical terms, given the European project of erasing the memory of past conflicts, but it is nevertheless believed to be the case.

26 *Nota bene*: a stone boat is theoretically possible, it does not contradict the laws of physics. Nevertheless, it is generally acknowledged that this belief may have developed following the discovery of Gallo-Roman sarcophaguses in various locations.

27 Joël Cornette, *Histoire de la Bretagne et des Bretons*, tome 1 (Paris: Editions du Seuil, 2005), pp. 147–8.

28 Kofi Yamgnane was born in Togo in 1945, and was a pupil at Kerichen *lycée* in Brest after his baccalauréat, before becoming an engineer. He obtained French citizenship in 1975 and was elected mayor of Saint-Coulitz, near Chateaulin, in 1989. He was probably only the second black person to have ever been elected a mayor in mainland France.

29 See Edgar Wind, *Pagan Mysteries in the Renaissance*, revised edition (Oxford: Oxford University Press, 1980).

8

A jolly panel discussion in Nottingham

Pamela Sue Anderson, Suzanne Dow, Alison Martin and Mark Robson in dialogue with Michèle Le Dœuff

Pamela Sue Anderson, Faculties of Philosophy and of Theology, University of Oxford: In listening to your lecture yesterday I was intrigued once again by your account of myths. Previously your work on the philosophical imaginary and myth influenced my own thinking in *A Feminist Philosophy of Religion: The Rationality and Myths of Religious Belief* (1998), as well as in various journal articles. But in your lecture 'Beauvoir and the Refusal of Myth', you mention 'the dialectic of myths and facts'. This dialectic would seem to have different roles to play depending on whether we are discussing Beauvoir's 'refusal of myth' in the sense of the myth of patriarchal femininity or her unwitting acceptance of *les mythologies de la petite famille*. In *The Second Sex* Beauvoir exposes the fiction of patriarchal thought in the myth of woman 'as the Other', that is, as the inessential. Now, Michèle, I am greatly indebted to you for continuing to expose the myths that inhibit and/or prohibit a woman from being recognized as having ideas of her own. Significant obstacles include the myth of original sin and the damage it has done to women and knowledge as you have demonstrated in *The Sex of Knowing* (2003). Yet in 'Beauvoir and the Refusal of Myth', the myths most resistant to change seem to be the mythologies of everyday life, for example, the values and relations of Sartre and Beauvoir. Often, it seems that the myths in religious belief and 'non-secular' life merely re-enforce the superiority of men, blocking women's access to philosophy and to knowledge more generally. But why do Beauvoir and other women today, too, continue to fail to see that these mythologies obscure facts about life? Women today should be able to avoid the trap Beauvoir herself fell into, partly because she uncovered the myth of femininity in western thought. My question is: How might a better understanding of this 'dialectic of myths and facts' help us extricate ourselves from the damage done to women by falsehoods and pernicious fictions, especially those everyday, and often non-secular, sexist and misogynist myths that are most difficult to unearth?

Michèle Le Dœuff: A dialectic of myths and facts . . . with the existence of myth in religious belief as a background to your question.

Pamela, the first author you may want to read here, could be Freud more than myself! *Der Mann Moses und die Monotheistische Religion*, first published in 1939, certainly tackles the question, because Freud claims that Moses may well have been a historical character, meaning a real live man and an Egyptian, before he acquired the status of a hero through narratives in which historical data were vastly transformed under the influence of powerful drives and also adorned by poetical inventions. No one would feel tempted to call Freud a feminist, no more than a certain Francis Bacon who had broached the topic before him, explaining that, even though Moses was God's first pen, he was also a human being well versed 'in all the learning of the Egyptians'.[1] As a result, in writings attributed to Moses, you will find 'much aspersion of philosophy'. Let me elaborate: and philosophy you may contradict – it is lawful to challenge ideas that are of a human origin.

Feminists may borrow what is at stake in Freud's or Bacon's audacious perspectives, namely the right for human beings' critical minds to scan a cultural heritage and to object to aspects of it. By the way, Freud seems to don the character of a Sherlock Holmes in this last book of his. For he writes that when a narrative has been doctored, there are clues as to the alterations in the text itself; they betray the existence of things which have been suppressed because information about them was not to be conveyed. 'Altering a text is like murder; the difficult part being not to do it but to eliminate the traces.' When we reason about facts, myths (grand or everyday life mythologies), we must take into account that mythologies may also 'kill' facts, the facts of life to start with, and a living being's needs and sexual drives. In *The Sex of Knowing*, I paid tribute to Uta Ranke-Heinemann's work and the way she challenged the notion of Mary's virginity: clearly enough, for her, 'the corpse in the library' is sexuality itself, and as a result birth control as a human right. I should like to mention also Eugen Drewermann, a Catholic priest, a theologian and also a psychotherapist, who gave a long interview to *Der Spiegel* (23 December 1991), after which his bishop pronounced an interdiction against him preaching. For Drewermann, a virgin giving birth is just an image, borrowed from Oriental legends; it was a feature of Oriental kings to be born that way. His reading of many segments of the Gospels, as sheer symbols and not historical facts, seems to be part and parcel with his claim that women can be ordained if they want to, priests have a right to marry if they are so inclined and that the church does not have the right to pass judgement on women who need an abortion. You renounce the borrowed legend of Mary as a virgin mother and then, lo and behold, there is space for sex rights.

As a feminist, I fully sympathize with theoretical endeavours like these; it is great to see that, when misogynist and sexophobic myths are challenged, suddenly theologians, men and women, feel able to agree and to row in the same direction, having found a language and values that can be held in common. Religious mythology does not belong to my own culture but their efforts converge with mine. I also remember hearing at a conference a young woman chaplain give a paper about the story of Sodom in Genesis. She explained that the biblical text is not about or against homosexuality but about and against bad hospitality, a most interesting interpretation. You could feel the wave of relief in the audience. For some reason or other, and apparently by sheer coincidence, she lost her position soon afterwards, just as Uta Ranke-Heinemann was excommunicated because of a book she published and Drewermann was no longer allowed to preach. We must admire those who have the courage to dissent and to question texts or characters considered as 'holy' or sacred, or some of the time-honoured interpretations of these texts. The fact that the scholars who do so are sometimes silenced may well mean that murder is still going on. Or to go back more precisely to your question: How does the dialectic of myths and facts work itself out? The main trace or clue we can get hold of is the silencing of scholars; it seems to prove that the language of myths is necessary to maintain the suppression, like you press a lid on a bubbling saucepan. The next step for us may well be to claim that surely we could do without narratives of martyrdom and without severely paying for our legitimate efforts. I am tired of this structure, which may well be vastly internalized, as a threat or as a source of speculation. When Pope John Paul I died, a few days after he had stated that 'God is equally a Mum and a Dad' (such an innovative and promising view actually), many people were convinced that he had been murdered. This is a side effect of the structure, except that no one will ever be able to disprove that it may well have been a fact too.

Shall I acknowledge that I occasionally hope one day to read works by historians explaining that the Golgotha Crucifixion may be just a legend, made in part of the standard form of capital punishment inflicted upon slaves in Roman times and partly borrowed from Greek philosophy, hence possibly not a historical fact, but an adaptation of Socrates's end of life? I'm hoping some scholars are working on the question because this narrative, in my view, provides half the rooting of Christian anti-Semitism, the other half being probably the standard interpretation of the famous passage in Luke 14:23, 'compel them to come in', understood as 'coerce people to convert'. I believe there are already some Lutheran theologians claiming that this passage does not mean that coercion is at all acceptable. And I have heard Dominicans state that the Golgotha is far less important to them than the moral teaching dispensed by Christ, 'my religion is about life and not so much about death', they claimed, for their reading of Spinoza had done a lot of good to them: 'Wisdom – for a free human being – is a meditation not on death but on life'.[2] Well, I'm not able to challenge the historicity of Socrates's way of death, but I can state that I do not approve of his behaviour: he could have run away and sought political asylum somewhere. By staying and facing capital punishment for his moral teaching, perhaps he thought he was within his rights or even that he was right. In my view, he was simply irresponsible towards the field to which he had contributed. What a legacy, what an emblem, the story of the hemlock! – When he could have left us with a field far more full of *joie de vivre* and from which philosophical lines of argument against the death penalty in general could have blossomed. Have you noticed that philosophers over the centuries have not done their job on this question? That John Locke even gave philosophical status to capital punishment?

When Uta Ranke-Heinemann wrote to me 'I was excommunicated for heresy, which enables me to commune with other heretics', she may well have wanted to point out, in a friendly and tongue-in-cheek way, that surely I was a heretic in philosophy. Now, I am not sure of that – I frequently see myself as quite mainstream; occasionally, I wish I were a late Presocratic – and what would this mean anyway, considering that (in principle, at least) change, along with disagreement with all past colleagues, is supposed to be a most acceptable feature of philosophy? True, since the very beginning of my work, I have endeavoured to spot and analyse images, fables, myths in philosophical texts, when the profession takes pride in the idea that philosophy is purely conceptual. And I have disagreed with the notion of male supremacy, perhaps the major myth all intellectual fields still tend to share (though hopefully not for long!). I am doing my job as a philosopher, that's all, and *if* I am therefore seen as a heretic, it simply comes to prove that there is something most unphilosophical in our philosophical world as it is.

On the horizon of my present questioning, there is a very simple idea. Philosophy, although it is philosophy, may function as a form of religion. You can sense this in a polite comment left on 'amazon.fr' by a reader of mine, signing Jacques Thomas, about the French edition of *New Atlantis*: 'An under-recognized Bible: *New Atlantis* is a well-known but under-recognized book. It was at the origin of a large cultural movement; the creation of the Royal Society, and the refoundation of Free Masonry which followed, must be credited to it. [The French translation] comes with an introduction which is very, very good [thanks a lot for this!], perhaps a cut too feminist, which was not necessary in this type of book, the aim of which being much higher.' This is philosophy 'au quotidien', in everyday cultural life, if there is any. Now, either you truly consider *New Atlantis* as a philosophical piece of work, a fiction but philosophical, in which case I was entitled to criticize some aspects of it and to claim that the text is more convincing when 'rewritten' without its sexist components, or you see it as 'a Bible', a Bible because it laid grounds for two gentlemen-only societies and then you imply that a feminist reading of it somehow 'lowers' the text, possibly because it is critical, moreover critical of something which should not be touched by critique at all, namely the male monopoly of scientific and scholarly research! At any rate, please note how politely worded this online comment is. Perhaps we have gained that, at least: those who do not appreciate feminism dogmatically resist our views with an exquisite politeness today. I have seen much worse not so long ago. We all frequently see worse.

And perhaps, it could be suggested – with equal politeness – that Freud's book on Moses ought to be read twice. Once looking out for ideas that can help and also for pleasure, because *Der Mann Moses und die Monotheistische Religion* is not far from being a novel, and the author appears quite endearing in his way of stating that he is not competent about the material he handles, that he does not have much historical data to ground his views, but that all the same he is going to say what he wants to say. But you then need to read it a second time, with a critical eye which has been well trained by many authors you read previously, and wonder if there is not some kind of murder perpetrated here – by Freud himself. Let all the Jane Marples of this world tackle the question!

Mark Robson, School of English Studies, University of Nottingham: I would like to start from the epigraph to *Hipparchia's Choice*:

> A single sentence was enough for Hipparchia to sum up the situation of women in relation to philosophy: 'I have used for the getting of knowledge all the time which, because of my sex, I was supposed to waste at the loom.'

The question I want to ask in the light of this epigraph concerns the relation of women to philosophy in terms of time. Hipparchia gets knowledge in the time that she should have spent at the loom, and she thus seems to establish an economic relation to time – a sense of profit, loss and waste – that becomes the point of articulation between gender and philosophy. This triggered a set of connections for me to other attempts to configure such economies, and in particular I was struck by four possible paths:

a) In Plato's *Republic*, there is the famous passage (370a–c) regarding the division of time appropriate for the workers (and here I would like to link these workers to the masses that Professor Le Dœuff mentioned in her lecture yesterday who are so often linked to women and children in the philosophical tradition). Socrates tells us that the shoemaker or the weaver should devote all of his time to his profession, that he must have a single profession and that he must not miss the right moment or season (*kairon*) in which to carry out this work. This is the moment that Jacques Rancière reads as the fundamental distribution that establishes a form of philosophical elite, separating those who have the time to pursue philosophy and those whose time is to be given to something else, and this made me think that there is perhaps a link between this exclusion and that which Hipparchia invokes.

b) Jacques Derrida begins one of his texts – *Donner le temps*, translated as *Given Time* – with a quotation from Madame de Maintenon: 'Le roi prend tout mon temps; je donne le reste à Saint-Cyr, à qui je voudrais le tout donner' ('The King takes all my time; I give the rest to Saint-Cyr, to whom I would like to give all'). Derrida's text then elaborates on this economy of giving and taking, of the all and the rest, but chooses to begin from the paradoxical position allotted to the woman (and which she allots to herself).

c) In Julia Kristeva's essay 'Women's Time', she attempts to undo the traditional division between three relations to temporality: cyclical time, monumental time and the linear time of a history usually conceived in terms of 'male' events and actions. Might the resistance to expectations about how women's time should be passed best be thought of as a resistance to a particular way of conceiving of time itself?

d) Simone de Beauvoir comments in the conclusion to *Le Deuxième sexe* on the difference between male and female perceptions of time, in particular distinguishing a profitable, exchangeable male time from the inactive bored woman's attempts to kill time (as the English translation puts it), in which her gift of time is seen (by him) to be excessive.

So, I wondered whether this sense of the temporal dimension of the relation between women and philosophy might be a useful way for us to open up some aspects of Professor Le Dœuff's work. In particular, is it useful to think about philosophy as a kind of work or labour within a certain economy, or does this inevitably lead into a series of exclusions?

Michèle Le Dœuff: It is true that in *Hipparchia's Choice*, and from its very epigraph, I started with an individual history, Hipparchia making her own free choice, which was philosophy as opposed to the loom; and even though she got some blame for it, she was convinced she had made the right choice. But I believe my book moves to the potentially collective history of women's emancipation: what if Olympe de Gouges's views had been paid attention to? What if the French Revolution had not been such a backlash for women and with such long-lasting effects? I called it a *Ukronia*, after Renouvier, and suggested that, for girls of my generation, it would have amounted to being born in a better and nicer country, and to happier parents, with more freedom around them. More inner freedom too, of course, particularly to know what they truly wanted and what is still to be challenged in culture and in politics. A century and a half was lost, considering French women did not have a right to vote before 1944. With your leave, I shall concentrate on the notion of 'time wasted', in order to try and find out what it may mean.

I believe the notion of 'time wasted' is to be understood in connection with life interests. It may have at least two different meanings, an individual and an historical one, although at a certain stage, if you analyse the question from an individual or from a collective and historical point of view, you will grant that of course the two aspects are related. From an individual point of view, time is wasted when you are forced to do something that does not tally with abilities you long to develop and which, as a result, will be cramped by lack of exercise. Boredom or what other people see as 'laziness' is a fairly sure sign of it. When Plato mentions *en passant* that some women are lazy about spinning but industrious when it comes to caring for the sick of the household (*Laws*, VII, 806a), I agree, all the more so because we can now state that some women are dedicated weavers – artists in that craft, just as others are cheerful mathematicians – whereas the same people would have felt bored to death if compelled to read medicine. However, it is still a problem – in our times – that many girls are somehow manipulated into professional choices that are not their own choice. I have seen cases of nervous depression or of lasting melancholy in women belonging to our social milieu (and this quite recently), because they had been orientated by parents, well meaning or not, to study psychology or literature, when in fact they really wanted to read science or medicine, or even would have preferred a possibly hard-up life as a pianist rather than the more or less successful career they had in the Humanities. Worse, there are still women who in fact never wished to be wives and mothers, who were not cut out for matrimony or motherhood when they embraced that way of life, but who allowed the force of circumstances to press them into it, some of them far too early in life. Then you meet disenchanted and exhausted mothers, possibly still young but untimely faded. For their sake, I frequently feel inclined to challenge the very notion of gender and to state that the one thing which is good for a human being, female or male, is freedom in the development of abilities. Say a good amount of self-knowledge and free speech, combined with the basic morality which family and the schooling system ought to dispense, basic morality that must include a principle of non-discrimination. When families are generous towards their sons and mean towards their daughters, this is not just appalling. It is as immoral as training their sons into the skills of thieving or cardsharping.

Besides, parents and teachers ought to know that every human being (even among their offspring or classes) is born unpredictable. No one is pure machinery; else, gendered coercion would always happily reach its aims, because it would never bump into a vocation that had nothing to do with any partition of any sort. When stereotypes are forced on a living being, she or he will suffer, also in terms of time of life wasted. I would say the same about young men forced into military service. Considering life gives us only a meagre measure of time, a year or two spent with the army, when you tremendously dislike it, is a year or two stolen from you, to put it mildly. When you have a conscientious objection to anything military, it is much worse of course. But for many women, it is their whole life that goes against the grain.

Time may well be the adequate concept through which to theorize the dialectics between collective emancipation in history and individual conquest of freedom. At collective level, we have to create what Catharine Macaulay called – in a somehow different context – 'a system of liberties'. You could recite the agenda as fast as I could: equal citizenship, reproductive rights for all, including for women under age, access to education and all kinds of professions, political and public employments, free speech . . . the right to be protected against violence, and so on. The creation of this system of liberties is always exceedingly slow because there are opponents to women's emancipation, as Virginia Woolf already noted. They apply the brakes to our wheel, producing a constant delay; also they do not mind spending time and energy preventing younger women from knowing about the very existence of their 'foremothers', those who have created rights for all. I agree with Catharine Macaulay when she states that a system of liberties cannot be properly maintained when people have no knowledge at all about how it was historically produced.

As a result, I am convinced that giving younger women a knowledge of how the rights they found in their cradle were won will help them maintain and develop women's rights in general. This might sound like a paradox, considering that my generation in France successfully struggled for reproductive rights without the faintest idea of what women of the past had achieved for us. We had access to higher education: some of us were medical doctors or lawyers, which really helped. We were voters, which helped to put pressure on politicians. Moreover and more importantly, many of us had some experience of activism, in trade unions or left-wing associations, which means that we had not been utterly excluded from these groups. We drew support from what we already had in order to create what we didn't possess yet. This means that a system of liberties, and inclusion in political life, when still in progress, allows individuals to be creators of more freedom for themselves and younger generations. It is splendid to meet younger women who are fully aware of the fact that we laboured for increased freedom for all. Even those who will never need an abortion in their lives know how important it is to have this possibility and to see the validity of their judgement recognized in the law – 'La femme qui juge que . . . ' (The woman who judges that. . . .), that's the wording of the 'Loi Veil'. And they love it, even those who do not presently have the use of contraception. It is not just ordinary gratitude: they enjoy the idea that their bigger sisters worked hard for that and were successful. At an emotional level, reproductive rights mean more to them than if this form of freedom had come as a godsend.

Perhaps those who are philosophers will overcome and/or disregard the mild and gendered disagreement I could express, as a woman of my generation of course, with the most important French philosopher of the twentieth century, I mean Henri Bergson. And I should like to state that French philosophy, as you know it, would not have happened if he had not been around. In *La Pensée et le mouvant*, he explains that the essence of time is that it flows, but also that you are sometimes kept waiting: if one wants a glass of sugared water, one is forced to wait until the sugar melts . . . 'force est d'attendre que le sucre fonde'. When in my kitchen, I frequently think about that, because it is not just about waiting for a lump of sugar to dissolve. You have to wait for the butter to turn the right shade of brown, then for the meat to reach the right degree of absorption, etc etc., basically to control your haste, and then to be very brisk. I sometimes whisper that Bergson's only connection with domestic activities was occasionally to make a glass of sugared water for himself, he never cooked a stew, this well-esteemed colleague! Did it affect his way of philosophizing? Well, you may want to carry on reading until section V of *La Pensée et le mouvant*, which is the text of a lecture delivered at Oxford in May 1911. 'Avant de philosopher, il faut vivre', before philosophizing, it is necessary to live, great, this is not just an apt translation of the good old saying *primum vivere, deinde philosophari*, it is a splendid springboard but let us go on reading: 'And life demands that we put on blinkers' – really? His thesis is that intelligence, perception, brains, memory (etc.) are organs of attention to life and that life (from humble survival to elaborate social life) demands that we concentrate on what is useful for action, hence the blinkers. Except that some men [sic] are 'born detached', Nature having forgotten to attach their perception to action. Artists, musicians, poets and philosophers are like that. It means that they have a more direct vision and a more complete perception of reality. Ah? No one will want to make a cheap remark about Bergson's audience at Oxford, certainly full of male colleagues who never had to put a meal together for themselves or do anything to survive day after day. They must have felt gratified to understand that their 'detachment' from practicalities helped them to have a broader perception of things. They may even have guessed that Bergson was implying that utilitarianism is not the ultimate answer to everything, which may be a matter of discussion. But there is something really the matter in that piece, say male elitism that you occasionally see also in others books by, again, the philosopher to whom we owe a great deal, perhaps the very philosophical liberation thanks to which we were in our turn able to philosophize and to enjoy it.

Almost a century after Bergson, I gave a series of lectures at Oxford, to a knowledgeable audience, mostly knowledgeable in post-1960 French philosophy and, I hope, in cooking (I didn't check). I insisted on the importance of pre-1960 intellectual events. An American colleague who had attended philosophy classes in Paris around 1950 endowed me with a wonderful remark made by one of his teachers, whose name he could not remember: 'When you read Auguste Comte, you have feeling that you are walking in a sombre and endless tunnel; but when at last you arrive at Bergson, you have the feeling that you emerge in a garden full of flowers.' It is true and this is one of the sharpest things I ever heard about the history of philosophy in France. No, Mark, I have not lost sight of your question about Time! It is not a good idea to read only post-1960 French philosophers, when in fact a great deal of our stamina, along with the questions we sometimes endeavour to sort out, does come from breakthroughs that took place much earlier. Both Simone de Beauvoir and Simone Weil had read Bergson (and also Lucretius, and quite a few others). Look at this, by Simone Weil: 'We are living beings; our thought comes with pleasure or with pain', she writes in *Science et perception* (second part). But then in *La Science et nous*: 'Between any desire and its fulfilment, there is for us a distance which, in a sense, is the world itself. (. . .) If you imagine, instead of me here, an idiot, a criminal, a hero, a wise man, a saint, it will not make any difference' (*La Science et nous*). Hero, wise man and saint: that's the trilogy in *Les Deux sources de la morale et de la religion*. A reader of Bergson, but she didn't take up his male elitism, quite the opposite, for she puts these three figures in the same boat as an idiot, a criminal and herself. It is a reply actually. Time is wasted indeed, for the recognition of women's involvement in philosophy, when we do not take into account that, many years before we were born, some women tried to have a dialogue with their male colleagues, paying attention to what they contributed but also having their own say.

Alison Martin, Languages and International Studies, Nottingham Trent University: I have two questions.

1. *Hipparchia's Choice* is a text that successfully develops several arguments; one that I found particularly interesting is the claim you make for the reorientation of philosophy, which marries with your rigorous representation of Beauvoir as a philosopher. We know that Beauvoir was not a system builder, and that is one of the reasons why she did not see herself as a philosopher. However, as you argue in *Hipparchia's Choice*, philosophy cannot lay claim to being a monumental system, nor even to being a single tradition with a common standard of rationality. Rather than aiming for a unified system of thought capable of eradicating all others, you propose that philosophy becomes a looser discipline, one that recognizes all thought as polygenetic, and embraces the notion of 'thought-on-the-move'. These are stimulating and quite freeing ideas, and they open up pathways to interdisciplinarity, which you also advocate. Now, interdisciplinarity has been adopted as a desirable aim, at least, by many in Anglo-Saxon academia, but that is generally between disciplines in the arts, humanities and social sciences – it does not usually extend to the natural sciences. The emphasis you give to science in *Hipparchia's Choice* and in your work generally is quite distinctive in feminist philosophy. Do you think that engaging with the natural sciences is

a particularly fruitful direction for philosophical thought at the present time, especially for a woman philosopher? And, almost twenty years 'downstream' from the publication of *Hipparchia's Choice*, do you think that it is possible to say that Beauvoir has now been recognized as a philosopher?

2. The 'Fourth Notebook' of *Hipparchia's Choice* is dedicated to concrete, socio-political questions where you discuss the hazards that the political ideal of equality still faces, over two hundred years after its revolutionary affirmation. You show in some detail how the concept of equality is betrayed in France by laws that allow their provisions to be qualified on the grounds of gender and by systems that perhaps inadvertently perpetuate or reignite gender inequalities because other political factors prevail in decision-making. You also raise concerns regarding the persistence of 'others' in society: children, foreigners, and so on – those whose potential for equality continues to be denied or questioned. Given the concrete historical difficulties equality encounters, would you say that nevertheless it still represents the most effective rallying cry and political ideal for progressive politics, or might it be preferable to call upon other concepts, such as justice, for example, to provide the political momentum?

Michèle Le Dœuff: Engaging with the natural sciences is one important direction, among several, for feminist philosophers today. I would not claim it should become a norm, of course. We do not aim at creating 'a single tradition with a common standard of rationality', as you rightly said, Alison, except when paying attention to the future, to major values like freedom, dignity and equal access to basic commodities, which means recognition of every human being's needs, like food, clean water and a good amount of free speech, not to mention the central issue of reproductive rights for all women.

One of the reasons why I insist on the importance of engaging with natural sciences is that I have known a time when feminists in France (and in other countries) would have gladly forbidden any woman to be involved in scientific work, and this in the name of sexual difference, with or without a famous misspelling. And by the same token, they were quite inclined to throw away philosophy as well, unsuitable for a woman if she is to nurture her own femininity. This is reactionary in my view, and most unfair to women scientists, who already have to face a life in a somewhat misogynist environment, unfair also to those who work hard to attract more girls into scientific careers. In recent years, I have found a new source of stamina for this defence of sciences, through becoming more aware of the crucial question of the 'sciences of the environment', and the connection between a 'sustainable planet' as a most desirable objective, women's rights and scientific research itself. I had known a time when Green politics greatly disregarded intellectual life, particularly science, deemed guilty of horrendous technologies. I have been sometimes confronted by feminists who would state that the Pill, ugh! it's chemical, abortion is against Nature and so are nursery schools. Etc. I am glad to note that, in many countries, a dramatic change in the Greens' way of thinking has taken place. Some women have played an important role in bringing this change about, which could be summarized like this: instead of hating science or despising it, let us reorientate scientific research so that it can work to explore the real threats bearing on the environment, and we shall then devise adequate solutions. I could feel that this important turn had been taken when I participated in a conference held at Göteborg in 2001. There was a roundtable entitled 'Knowledge and Learning for a Sustainable Society'. Our late Beauvoirian friend Eva Gothlin had asked me to be there. I was a beginner as far as environmental scientific research was concerned but could broach a critique of both anti-intellectualism and of male-dominated scientific communities, particularly in relation to carelessness and waste. There was a paper by Cornelia E. Nauen that amazed me: as a specialist in research for development at the European Commission, hence not a beginner at all, she gave a talk which tallied with mine at the level of values. And we both mentioned the question of grandchildren, yours and ours. Technically speaking, I shall never be a grandmother but it does not prevent me from feeling concerned; what a disaster if they were born with no planet to speak of! Does one have to be a woman, with or without children, to pay attention to future generations' well-being? Let me amend this straightaway. Some of us have made an effort to become detached – and from many things. Which things? Perhaps you can figure this out for yourself.

At the end of the afternoon, I was chatting with Eva in the university garden and could see out of the corner of my eye a young Viking looming and hesitating. There was a pause in our conversation and then he seemed to make up his mind, came forward blushingly, said 'Today, I've heard two good papers, both by women', and then he ran away! As for me, I should like to mention two more women. One is Wangari Maathai, who received the Nobel Prize in 2004 for her work in favour of environmental sustainability. Her approach has been praised also because it involves democracy, human rights in general and particularly women's rights. Any discussion about women and science today ought to take her into account – her work and her books. And the other one is Catherine Bréchignac, a French physicist who, as president of the CNRS, managed to create from scratch a whole department of 'sciences de l'environnement' in our well-esteemed institution. If my memory serves me rightly, she achieved such a necessary decision during a summer recess, while some were holidaying, and then a few male scientist colleagues were heard grumbling that they had not been consulted, and that surely this new department would be funded through a reduction of their own funds. Needless to say, I felt proud of my president, proud by proxy, if you like, an emotion I seldom allow myself to experience.

The domains connected to environmental research are today and tomorrow sciences and they already tend to generate works and surveys which owe a good deal to our political and philosophical efforts over the years. Just one example. In September 2009, *The Lancet* published a piece about overpopulation and global warming, explaining that 200 million women in the world do ask for contraception but have no access to it, with 76 million unwanted pregnancies a year as a result. According to *The Lancet*, if that human problem were taken care of, it would dramatically help keep global warming down. Since the 1960s, we have been stating that women's free choice is part of human rights, that to be denied access to reproductive rights is to encounter a severe form of violence and that generally speaking women's rights are good for society at large, while people on the opposite bench were doing their best to maintain guilt around these questions, sometimes even enforcing the idea that it is shameful to broach them at all, thus basically working to maintain inhibitions, including at an intellectual level. They never cared about what happened to women who are poor. Some would even consider forced sterilization more favourably than women's free choice.

A silly side effect of all this took place in Paris around 1990, when François Mitterrand organized a jamboree for Nobel laureates. I was lucky enough to have a chat with an American scientist and philosopher who had just been in charge of taking notes at a few sessions. He mentioned that many participants had been thrilled no end, and in a boyish way, at being driven from their hotels to the conference in fast, official cars, with police on motorcycles opening the way and blowing hard on their whistles. Also that some pretty nonsensical questions had been seriously discussed, such as 'Will AIDS take care of the problem of overpopulation?' At the close of the conference, a French biologist – himself a Nobel laureate – was heard exclaiming: 'It is just as I always said, the proportion of blockheads (*imbéciles*) is the same everywhere', possibly an apt comment on the whole event. A silly gathering indeed, dominated by men who were not detached at all from a certain gendered identity – laddishness – and who had thoroughly internalized the idea that contraception is not something you mention favourably in public. Contrast this with the 2009 piece in *The Lancet*, which at last considers women's freedom and dignity as a factor, and a positive one, in global calculations. And our first step to save the planet will then be a trip to our local post office, to send a cheque in support of the International Planned Parenthood Federation.

Anyhow, and not to draw too sharp a contrast between the future and the past, I still think highly of the natural sciences I enjoyed at school. In *The Sex of Knowing*, I tried also to point out the importance of intellectual pleasure in pedagogy in general. Now, we could simply adopt the 'liberal view' that it would be a good idea if those of us who take a special interest in sciences and/or the history of scientific questions laboured and ploughed these fields, and wrote about these matters in a clear and unbiased way, so that all of us might then read the results. But there may be more at stake here than what liberal views tend to disclose. It is never sound for philosophy – or a particular school of philosophy – to dismiss a whole section of human endeavour. It always means some kind of contempt for humankind in general. Think of the Heideggerians quoting from their Master things such as 'Science does not know its object; it insults it.' Who is the insulting agent in that story, I wonder? More importantly, the way they repudiate science and technologies may well mean: leave all this, and all decision-making, to the *Wehrmacht*. Considering there is a cultural background which still enforces a rigid distinction between what is suitable for girls and women, and what is suitable for boys and men, it is our responsibility to address the fixity of this division, if we have in view – and we do have in view – the well-being of women of future generations and their involvement in the decisions that will be made.

Today, I tend to reason more in terms of 'background' or of the 'mental universe' you endow people with. Alison, if you want to know if engaging with natural sciences is a particularly fruitful direction for a woman philosopher, I would say that the most fruitful background we can give to women starting their own philosophical life is as good a knowledge as we can of the foremothers we potentially have in common, in order to help them develop their own capacities to the full and feel less lonely in a section of academia which may well be particularly tough. In the French-speaking world, I would recommend reading Simone Weil. She was very knowledgeable in ancient and classical science. Read her piece 'La Science et nous' (Science and us) written in 1941 but published only in 1966. She is interested in finding out what classical science may mean to human beings in general. Well, read it – perhaps you will love it as much as I do and will want to offer it to students.

From Simone Weil to your question about Beauvoir: in France, the former is more clearly recognized as a philosopher than the latter, though not recognized by all, I'm sorry to say, or not wholeheartedly, but more. Basically, Beauvoir is seen as a philosopher by those who have read my work; this began with one or two articles I had published even before *Hipparchia's Choice*. Those of my readers who accepted my views about her are mostly colleagues who had taken – before reading me – a special interest in Greek philosophy, or in British philosophy or in Montaigne, *plus* some of my former students, whatever their favourite cup of tea these days. Only one Sartrean in France, namely Michel Kail, explicitly accepted my views and to the point of working in the same direction. With Marie Ploux, he also translated Eva Gothlin's book, *Sex and Existence*. What had been crucial in *Hipparchia's Choice* for Eva as a starting point for her own work was my claim that Beauvoir's philosophy was not the same as Sartre's. In a sense, for me too, because if someone is not creative in philosophy (meaning does not produce a set of concepts not-the-same as anyone else), why bother seeing her or him as a philosopher?

As for the interest some specialists of Greek or early to classical British philosophy have shown: I would analyse this in terms of background again, which would mean that the books you read before – sometimes long, long before – you open a new one stating that Simone de Beauvoir's work is philosophical indeed, may well determine your reaction to it. I don't think I shall ever meet a specialist in medieval philosophy who would have a kind word to say about Beauvoir or, come to that, about me. Now, the key factor could be whether you like your philosophy with or without institutional power in it. Bacon or Hume were not university men; that was their main connection with colleagues of ancient times, who could afford to be playful – not taking themselves seriously – and labour on questions they had themselves chosen, as they list. It may well be the case that Beauvoir's near future in France is to be recognized on a par with Montaigne and the authors we call 'les moralistes français', all widely read as essayists. Don't forget that French academia is fairly restrictive at times. Here is a quotation from Bréhier's *Histoire de la philosophie* (still in print) which ought to give you the measure of the problem: 'Pascal (1623–1662) is not a philosopher: he is a scientist (*savant*) and an apologist for the Catholic religion.'

As for your question about equality, justice and what would provide an adequate political momentum, I suggest we keep it for another time because there is substance in it for a whole conference or a whole book.

Suzanne Dow, Department of French, University of Nottingham: I wanted to ask you about the question of philosophical style. You spoke yesterday about Simone de Beauvoir's paradoxically 'ascetic' stance with respect to the imaginary

– 'paradoxically' that is, given that although she never wanted to identify herself as a philosopher, she was always happy to identify herself as a creative writer. And it struck me that that is not something you share with Beauvoir. Your own work not only shows how philosophy – contrary to this ancient opposition between *mythos* and *logos* – is structured around the stories it tells itself, but that philosophy too is something about which one can tell stories. Your own writing often tells stories about philosophy – whether it be elucidating a concept, providing the biographical context for the elaboration of that concept or telling anecdotes from your own life. Your philosophy has a strong narrative aspect to it. One thinks, for example, of the dialogic relation you establish with the reader, who is often addressed in the second-person familiar 'tu'. Or of the dialogues you stage in your work where you imagine objections to your own argument. There are also the humorous asides, and the running metaphors and imagery, plays on words, colloquialisms, and so on. It seems to me that all those features of your philosophical style bring content to your philosophy, that they do some real conceptual work. Perhaps style is by definition something that is very difficult to talk about, something that is not consciously chosen. But could you say something about the status of this philosophical style? How do you situate yourself with respect to the imaginary?

Michèle Le Dœuff: And, in the end, the youngest member of the party asked the most impossible question . . . with relevance and so much grace that I must resist the temptation to reply that she should take care of the answer herself! I am serious about it: one day, Suzanne, you will write a book on the basis of this query of yours. It will be far better than anything I can suggest at the moment.

Looking forward to reading your book, perhaps I ought first of all to provide a few tips. There is an article by Elizabeth Fallaize, followed by a dialogue between Ulrika Björk and me, in the *Australian Journal of French Studies* (40:3, 2003). Both pieces signal that there is something to explore in the direction of 'philosophical style'. More generally speaking there is a book, by Gilles-Gaston Granger, entitled *Essai de philosophie du style*, which tackles the matter for seventeenth-century authors. I have never succeeded in reading it from cover to cover, although I honestly tried in my younger days. It is difficult stuff really, but you may want to have a look at it and then wonder whether something of it has lingered in what Bergson would call 'the basement of [my] consciousness'. Besides, I would claim that the process by which we produce a piece of philosophy and offer it to readers has, as Alison just stressed, a major aspect of 'thought-on-the-move': Is it possible at all to move, intellectually speaking, without making use of all possible resources? Now, to connect this with my answer to Mark, perhaps we may agree that Bergson's works are full of images and little stories, which is part and parcel of the dramatic breakthrough he brought about in the French approach to philosophizing, when he reintroduced free speech, or rather what we call 'la parole ouverte', and life interests at the centre of an amazingly well-informed *oeuvre*. And, to make a connection with the discussion with Pamela, he got away with it, he was not martyred for it and I do take pleasure in this as much as in his works. He had possibly the most splendid career French academia ever had to offer, which in itself is still a message of hope for everybody. Even for women today, although he may not have had our access to philosophy and to human rights at heart at all.

When you wonder whether style is something consciously chosen or not, I may want to take your question one step further. How do you choose a field? It may well be the case that you elect both a field and a style at the same time – along with a way of behaving, or indeed of *being*, within a field. Kindly remember that I didn't discover philosophy in a classroom, under a teacher's rod, nor as a 'subject' for the baccalauréat, with just good or bad marks as a meagre prospect. When I was fifteen, during a perhaps somewhat rainy summer, I read a few books – one by Plato, promptly put aside but with the intention of coming back to it later, which I duly did, Pascal, Alain (Émile Chartier, more widely known under the pen name of 'Alain'), Bergson's *Two Sources* (and I may still have a little disagreement with this book to clarify) and some moth-eaten volume on the history of philosophy, a passage of which made me roar with laughter. The author, whose name I can't remember, attributed to Aristotle or some other Greek fellow the opinion that sperm is a discharge of cerebral matter, and that, as a result, strict celibacy was advisable for philosophers. I never attempted to check if Aristotle really upheld such a foolish opinion but I knew straightaway that the field I was choosing contained nonsense I would address one day or another. And what nonsense, come to that! This opinion implied that philosophy was something for men, and men only, men who should keep away as much as possible from sex, with women or other men, because sex is bad for their working potential and the number of their little grey cells! I knew I wanted to embark on a discipline which would not intimidate me, in any sense of this word, a domain which otherwise could be both delightful and stimulating, particularly when you knew, thanks to biology classes, that cerebral matter is not something likely to leak. 'To make fun of philosophy, this is truly to philosophize', I owe this keepsake to Pascal. You will find it at the beginning of his *Pensées*.

The philosophy I first chose as a field was already a choice as to what philosophy can be. Something having nothing to do with boredom, just the opposite actually, something that would be meaningful – including when sorting out what makes sense and what does not. More importantly, a field in which it is not just possible, but indeed necessary, to be self-taught. When a girl has access to books which are like the genuine fountains of 'thinking', she may form the idea that 'adulthood is delightful' – well, it's just a thought, of course. Imagine I had received my first taste of philosophy in a classroom and from a Thomist teacher; such a misfortune actually befell many teenagers in the French-speaking world. As a result, we would not be together today, talking about *Hipparchia's Choice*, because I would have had an utterly different image of what philosophy can be and this image would not have appealed.

I cannot claim my choice was thoroughly conscious (no one could claim that) when I opted for philosophy, for the fun of it, for a certain mode of reasoning which eventually was to make me feel particularly at home in ancient philosophy and with sixteenth- or seventeenth-century authors. Consider the Stoics and their works, which are full of little stories, frequently about clever animals. Think of Marcus Aurelius, writing his *Thoughts for Myself*, or Epictetus, addressing himself in the second person. I am grateful indeed to Elizabeth Fallaize who stated that such a feature made reading my work 'pleasurable', when she could have rubbished it by stating that it is not so very original! And she would have been right too.

At any rate, I made my choice with open eyes and never regretted it, whatever the problems I occasionally encountered. With hindsight, I would deem all the problems I met to have stemmed from sheer unphilosophical attitudes in some people and that is all. Perhaps not quite the end, though. When you face an injustice, mingled or not with violence, it is often possible to consider that you will make something positive out of it. Like helping other women. Like writing about it in as cheerful a style as possible, because you see it as your personal responsibility to cheer up those who are most in need of moral support. Like remembering that, since there is a tide in human affairs, it is better to wait than to internalize a blow. Like deciding to become detached from the event, in order to be more available for other and more important things. And so on.

Notes

1 *The Works of Francis Bacon*, edited by James Spedding et al. (London: Longmans, 1857), volume III, 297.
2 *Ethics*, book IV, proposition 67; *homo liber* in the text.

On the sex of philosophy

Aliocha Wald Lasowski in dialogue with Michèle Le Dœuff

Aliocha Wald Lasowski: The question of the imaginary plays a decisive role in your thinking. In what sense was your work on women in philosophy the crucial occasion to suggest a different feminine imaginary?

Michèle Le Dœuff: The notion of philosophical imaginary sprang from my pen and in friendly conversations around 1977 or 1978. I was in the middle of reworking essays which would constitute my first book; I was already engaged, as you just recalled, in questioning the relation between women and philosophy. I was endeavouring to name the point at which the texts I wanted to put together converge and trying to grasp again what I could have had in mind when writing them. The notion presented itself as a potential title, when the volume was to be called, *Blazons: On the Philosophical Imaginary*. This title would have put the stress mostly on the semi-consciousness of self that our colleagues of ancient times and of not so long ago had occasionally been able to give themselves through the images and fabulous stories that they had coined. Through the making of emblems, philosophy, the way of life that comes with philosophy or the particular type of philosophical intervention an author is projecting, any or all of these aspects may well lead an author to create some kind of self-representation. It was Didier Eribon[1] who suggested that I should abridge the title to *The Philosophical Imaginary*.

Basically, my intention was to say that 'purely conceptual thought' does not exist! After all, I had been a student of Roger Martin for a couple of years; with a sympathetic professor of logic, which he truly was, I had learnt that when one wants to create a system of formal logic, it is definitely necessary to use a language which is called 'natural' (considered as lacking rigour) for stating the rules and constructing that system. In a sense, defending the idea of an imaginary *in* philosophy was for me simply stating a fact: there are stories, fragments of myths, of short histories in philosophical texts – only a denial of reality permits not seeing them. But then, a question arises: What status or what function do we allot to them?

AWL: Hence, a difference between an imaginary *in* philosophy and a philosophical imaginary. . . . And for that matter, what role does Bachelard play, in your eyes, in the relations between imaginary and rationality?

MLD: You are right to stress that the idea of a *philosophical* imaginary is noticeably different from the idea of an imaginary within philosophy. That idea came to me long after I had started working, and my real rupture is probably there because it led me to become fairly detached from Bachelard. I had been keen on his works, and by the way I still retain a genuine interest in them. All the same I stopped being a Bachelardian when I clearly saw how to construct the idea of the philosophical imaginary. While working on the pre-scientific imaginary, Bachelard makes a sharp distinction between what belongs to the order of the concept, of good science, of (scientific) method, and what belongs to the order of the imaginary – doomed to be prescientific, in other words, outside of science. That imaginary inhabits portions of learning when they are at their very beginning, and also in the way they are received when they are taught at school. This distinction brings the Bachelardian perspective close to a certain tradition that can be spotted in the way the history of philosophy is frequently taught: when a historian of philosophy recognizes the existence of segments which pertain to the genre of fables in one or another of our good authors, he or she confers to them the status of 'worthless remains (*caput mortuum*)', as the remnant of an older tradition, perforce a pre-philosophical one or the trace left by a primitive soul still operating in each of us!

The official dogma, then, wants us to think that the image, *it comes from the other*. Well . . . when there is an image, that is, when it is acknowledged that there is an image in the text, although people as a rule prefer simply to ignore it! As for me, I would concede that, in texts deemed as philosophical, the imagery is regularly introduced as a discourse which is taken up from some source or other: an Egyptian priest is supposed to have told the story of Atlantis to someone who next told it to someone else, and that would end up in a dialogue written down by Plato. Scholarly work about *Critias* has proved that actually the whole story was made up by Plato and/or Socrates, but never mind, most people to this day still assume that the narrative came from a very ancient tradition and occasionally some still think that Atlantis did exist. In the polemic between Saint Anselm and the monk Gaunilo on the demonstration (possible or not) of the existence of the most perfect being, 'a lost island' suddenly appears in the following manner: 'Some people say . . .', Well, allegedly some people claim that there exists an island in the middle of the ocean, more beautiful than all others. It is Gaunilo who introduces this motif within the friendly dispute which he had with and against Anselm. However, the two interlocutors understand each other immediately. No wonder, considering that one can trace this motif of 'the most perfect island' back to a passage of *Hortensius*, which they both knew. In philosophical texts, the pictorial motifs are attributed, wrongly or rightly, to the other, as if, when one is occupied creating a work of philosophy, it were shameful to recognize that one dreams, that one cobbles together and rewrites the stories reworked from a more ancient text, or sometimes make them up on the spot.

AWL: And so, you have disclosed that which was unacknowledged?

MLD: When I first introduced the notion of the philosophical imaginary, I endeavoured to make people acknowledge that the passages which appear as metaphorical and, say, as vignettes or little stories, contribute to the global meaning of the whole work, as much so as the passages which appear the most abstract. In brief, I wanted to leave behind the misrecognition of self which, from the very beginning, our worthy profession permitted itself. Although self-consciousness is certainly something incomplete or constantly defective, this is no reason to cease from searching for ways to enhance our consciousness of self or improve it! As it happened, I also strived to offer a less intimidating definition of philosophical thinking. The purely theoretical, come on! As for the many Colossi of abstract thinking . . . will you allow me to smile?

As for my work on women and/in philosophy, I would say today that this work provided a crucial occasion for understanding how much of consequence philosophical images are. Because whatever you say about islands, real islands themselves do not care about and will not get drowned by it. Whereas what you say about human beings may well have repercussions on these very human beings. I wanted to challenge the bogus stories being told by most male philosophers, whether canonical, ancient or quasi-contemporary. . . . I endeavoured to confront their misconceptions with the true faces of real women in the plural, because we are not all the same, you know; we do not all resemble the norm they hand to us, except when such and such among us do violence to themselves in order to fit that masculinist projection of 'woman'. My first goal was to contest the image of women which is offered to us with so much force, and also to question that very insistence . . .

AWL: Hence, 'Long Hair, Short Ideas' which was reprinted in *The Philosophical Imaginary*?

MLD: With 'Long Hair, Short Ideas', I wanted to help other women not to believe that an image with length of hair and shortness on ideas did in any way reflect the truth. And this, all the more so because I embarked on my reflections in 1976. For it was a time when almost everyone in France (including me) was still ignoring the existence and the work of a good number of our foremothers who I see today as colleagues. Basically, at the time, I knew women philosophers such as those mentioned by Diogenes Laertius, and I could perceive genuine philosophical efforts in the work of Simone de Beauvoir. I also knew of the tragic story of Heloise and I felt that many of my contemporaries fell into the same trap as her: the trap is created in giving one's total admiration to a (male) philosopher, and only to him. But limiting oneself like that is a disaster! There exists a wonderful diversity of philosophical works and thoughts, at your door, being offered to all of those who know how to read and intend to allow themselves to think for themselves; this is to say, to articulate their own questions, sometimes in the small gaps of a reading, sometimes by making connections between different philosophical works.

By the way 'Long Hair, Short Ideas' was not planned to become a published paper, but simply the basis for my seminar at the École Normale Supérieure at Fontenay. I had decided to alert my students to the dangers of focusing exclusively on one author alone, on creating an Other whose thinking is like the only option (*pensée unique*), and I warned them against the pattern of philosophical relations which, in the debates to follow, was gradually called 'the Heloise complex'. Now, to stress again how early in the day all this was, imagine also that it was the publication of that text in English in 1977, which made me meet colleagues on the other side of the English Channel and discover Mary Wollstonecraft through them! Basically, when I wrote that first piece of feminist philosophy, I thought beyond the means I had, something which happens to all of us, men and women, once in a while, and occasionally in a felicitous way! I had of course recorded dozens of observations concerning the relations between men and women in the philosophical republic, and I endeavoured to put these in perspective by reading them as part and parcel with the long duration of an undisciplined discipline which appeared many centuries ago in the proximity of 'the sea of a thousand smiles' extending from Milet to the gulf of Tarente. When one takes into account this long duration, one is at least able to uncover more than one definition for what is known as 'philosophical'.

AWL: And so, that leaves the door open to more than one image of the lived experience and the thinking of women?

MLD: To suggest another idea of the lived experience of women may imply contrasting persons we meet in reality to the mythical figure created by the clerical scholars. This constitutes a method of thinking, which clearly lurks in Simone de Beauvoir, which I personally took up, then came across again, and with joy in Christine de Pisan's *City of the Ladies*. One finds this frequently enough in the works of feminist colleagues from past centuries, sometimes alongside of exhortations ('liberate yourself; women, you have only to will it!'), of developments pertaining to the '*ought to be*' ('change yourself, and you will change the world') or of simply extraordinary analyses. 'Long Hair, Short Ideas' seems also to have brought (to those who were willing to welcome it) a different image from what is claimed to be masculine. Some women, along with some men, were glad that after having described the Heloisomorph position, I mentioned that on second thought it is more or less the same for men too. Some of them who would even elaborate: 'Your article is really great, and not feminist at all!' What??? You must add this to the record on the history of current, everyday, ideas: in the last quarter of the twentieth century, the so-called feminism 'of difference' was such a 'dominant' form (in the sense given this word, 'dominant' [*prégnante*] in Gestalt psychology) that an essay which was not located within any sexual apartheid (nothing in common between women and men) was not recognized as feminist.

AWL: As a result feminism throughout history appears, under your pen, first and foremost as a project of emancipation . . .

MLD: For me, this is obviously the case. Besides feminism is also the project of creating a world in which women and men would be able to recognize each other and to get together in a reciprocal autonomy and a shared humanity. Seeing that you are wondering about the imaginaries of knowing, perhaps we could halt and consider this idea further: whenever a particular form (for example here, the differentialism) is granted high visibility, other forms fall outside of the line of vision or are no longer completely perceptible. Without a doubt this is frequently enough the case, and not only when we discuss the position of women. Emile Bréhier must have had in mind an extremely well-defined 'form' of what is philosophy, with the astonishing result that Pascal was almost cast away into external darkness. Because the chapter that Bréhier dedicated to Pascal seems to have been written unwillingly, or perhaps under duress, and begins thus: 'Pascal (1623–1662) is not a philosopher: he is a scientist and an apologist of the catholic religion.' Generally speaking, people may have a tacit sort of imaginary which expels whole patches of knowledge outside the field of the visible, that is to say outside of encyclopaedias and of vast compilations of philosophy or whatever subject.

At any rate, if in France my work on the philosophical imaginary (including in the way it challenged the role allotted to women) was mostly perceived as a work of philosophy, as an argumentation in favour of a modification, of an enlargement of the possibilities of the philosophical, and so forth, let us not complain about this! And so much the better if some men understood through reading my work that, for them too, the relation to a teacher or to an author viewed as a 'master' is susceptible to eroticizing! There is no masculine immunity to the Heloise complex. And for them too, it would be a good thing to disengage themselves from that mental structure, in order to truly find their own freedom. By the way those who happen to understand this point are also those who – like yourself – eventually agree to read women philosophers.

AWL: *Voyage dans la pensée baroque*, which you wrote with Margaret Llasera in 1983, is published with your French translation of Bacon's *New Atlantis*. Now, I would like to take the opportunity to further discuss with you baroque philosophical writing. How could we define it? What relations are constructed by it between the project to reform the sciences and Bacon's literary illustration?

MLD: The nature of the relation between a philosophical project, for example, to reform the sciences, and the imaginary scene within which the project unfolds itself, is not necessarily fixed in advance. One should even be able to say: the relation does not always belong to the order of the necessary. Nothing obliged Bacon to make the 'House of Salomon', the name which he gives to the research institute in *New Atlantis*, a universe strictly masculine, with the exception of the servants, a category which includes both women and men.

In the first analysis, one could say that the relation in question is not a synthesis, but rather a syncretic relation: it is contingent and creates a mere contiguity between a project, namely Bacon's epistemic intervention, and the theatre on which he places it. This connection eventually appears to be something difficult to break, no matter how disastrous it is. In the second analysis, we can decipher this syncretic relation as purely tactical, aimed at seduction, from man to men of his times. Bacon carefully concocted this ploy, and considering he left some written traces of his discursive strategies, we may be sure that there was little spontaneity in there. His whole project is itself fastened to a proposition which itself might be true, or at least belongs to the order of the verifiable and of the falsifiable: Bacon claims that one human group which possesses knowledge finds itself in a situation of domination over any human groups who don't. As a result the imaginary scene he created unfolds something like a desire or say, wishful thinking, partly deliberated. To re-enforce the global power of men over women, and in the world of scientific research, to be all males among themselves which is so nice, but men having some women servants which is even better. About such a desire one must say that it has nothing to do with the wish to see sciences progress.

AWL: Today it is more important than ever to untie the bond established between the two domains, in other words to dissolve what you call the 'syncresis . . .'

MLD: It is very important for everybody! With of course, first of all, the well-being of women scientists in view, but the concern is even broader than that. For many young men tend to choose to join careers in sciences simply because they expect an increase of their male power from this, or to have their status as males enhanced that way. Later on they have to understand (but certain men refuse to move to this understanding) that they have only acquired knowledge and no increase in their virility. A small proportion among them cannot stand the disappointment; some of them blow their fuses and lose the plot. Some of them opt for any form of religious fundamentalism that they can find, don't we know that religious fundamentalism is so much more favourable to a phallocratic attitude? You will notice that, in recent years, those who set off bombs and other authors of dreadful attacks in the United States or in Europe are almost all men who did their studies in engineering or science. A critical reading of *New Atlantis* in the final year at school, carefully disentangling the various threads of the Baconian imaginary, might after all prove useful for peace today. At any rate, boys and young men should be told in advance that by learning they will not get anything but learning. However, I believe that the most effective remedy for unfounded hopes could be to have co-ed classes. But it would be necessary also to tell very explicitly to every 'he' and every 'she' that when embarking on scientific studies, women and men get scientific knowledge and that is it. It is just as futile to expect from that any development of the ego, as to fear any withering.

AWL: Yet plenty of other wishes express themselves in the Baconian imaginary, and not only in *New Atlantis* by the way . . .

MLD: Our author certainly wished for a more just world (except for women!), more peaceful, more prudent governments, and he hoped that increased wealth would be more fairly distributed. Now, would a society by and for science be more likely to achieve such a programme? It is for you to think about this and to make your own judgement! But this is the point where one might want to say that your pretty fearsome question concerning 'baroque philosophical writing' makes sense. Of course I could get away with it by simply mentioning the irregular shapes of 'baroque' pearls, and then to state, 'That is what Bacon is!' He maintains a constant polemic against the taste for regular forms that distort the facts, in order to force them into some harmony or symmetry which we long to see everywhere. He writes that *'there is no excellent Beauty which hath not some strangeness in the proportions.*'[2] Yet your initial question was directed towards something else. In fact, you seemed to wish that I explained how this pretty elating act of turning everything into baroque style is in itself a philosophical act?

First, I would reply, in a general manner, that every philosophical intervention must first create in a void, so that one can then put into play the elements which may be available, or to loosen up the most accepted intellectual structures. Such an intervention must put into question quite a number of things and produce proofs of intellectual dissatisfaction. Bacon himself is at variance with most pieces of learning of his time as upheld by the universities and by the 'learned' class coming from them. And that learning was actually maintained within an intellectual enclosure. That world of knowledges is unfortunately an all closed, little world, all stiff, with boundaries which mark not real impossibilities but prohibitions: as a result for him, an invitation to break through is the matter at hand. Besides this smallest world of learning is full of holes. His all-encompassing inventory led in *Advancement of Learning* puts into light that such and such piece of knowledge 'lacks' ('*and this I note deficient*' is the true leitmotiv of book II of that work).[3] But these lacks are not visible, because their space is filled with illusions of knowledge.

For example, concerning the question of medicine, our author has a field day. This knowledge which would be so relevant for human life scarcely exists. Now, Bacon wants that all portions of learning, whether directly useful or not, be! It is then necessary to develop everything that is or could be (with perhaps the exception of understanding the heart of kings or the supremely divine point at which profane learning and theology become one). Bacon wants knowledges to move from a static state (again perhaps carefully and authoritatively upheld as such by universities) to a genuine dynamic.

AWL: From that perspective, the putting into play of a baroque imaginary turns out to be extraordinarily effective . . .

MLD: That makes us dream differently and desire different things than the repetition of the same or the continual rehearsing of alleged knowledges. It takes a lot to unmake a world of knowledges, especially when it is a world which in itself does not contain much truth, but which presents itself as well ordered and without fault, *overbuilt* – to the point of no longer leaving a space to any wish to know more, or to explore further.

Now, if you wish an example of theoretical effectiveness of this baroque imaginary, here is one: everybody, in the Renaissance, endlessly repeats that *veritas filia temporis*, that truth is the daughter of time. Bacon takes up in turn that 'common place' of this age. But this *topos* does not function as such in his works, because it allows him to say *non auctoritatis*, the truth is not a daughter of authority. The philosophical repercussions of such a positioning are not slight.

All in all, of the Baconian philosophy, it is necessary to say that it does support a project to reform the sciences, but that it does not reduce itself to that. It is not simply a 'reform' that Bacon has in view.

ALW: Then, which word will we employ? The term 'revolution' . . .?

MLD: At the time, the term 'revolution' refers to astronomy (the revolution of the stars) and under Bacon's pen it took on the meaning of a peak or zenith. Bacon definitely wishes for a new 'zenith' of the sciences, considering that some have already taken place in the past. Let me dare use a language which is twentieth century and Foucauldian: we might say that he wants to extricate the sciences from what nails them to an 'epistemic socle or pedestal', which is fruitless, in order to put them in movement and in research. If the baroque imaginary, which cobbles together, interweaves, rewrites, makes things precariously balanced, services a kind of thought which is looking for de-totalization and for searching always farther on, then we could whisper (at least as a hypothesis) that there is no real thinking which is not baroque! Only there are other authors in whose writings this does not show as much as in Bacon.

AWL: Why does Bacon insist on the distinction between science of nature and divine word? To what extent is this, a distinctively Baconian thesis? Moreover, one finds him endeavouring to construct the notion of 'progress of knowledge', in such a way that it requires something like the State . . .

MLD: This is quite a timely question, considering that not a long while ago the State of Texas prohibited the teaching of Darwinian theories, and this in the name of the Bible! According to Bacon, God gave two books for humanity to read: the book of his Will, contained in Scriptures, and the book of his power, which is Nature. It is an image, of course (Nature as a book) which Galileo will take up again, a founding image, in the sense that it posits a radical distinction between sciences of nature and religions. Without that distinction, nothing of Baconian philosophy would have been able to take place. It is not merely a political proposition though it is certainly that because Bacon definitely hopes that the theologians, whether assisted by secular arms or not, would stop meddling with scientific work. He also hopes that scientists of diverse religious persuasions could work together. But it is much more than a political vision or a view relative to the organization of intellectual cooperation. It is the regulative idea *par excellence*. It clearly states the possible and the right: everything that is a part of the world is knowable by the human mind, and humanity has the right to seek to know the world, whereas mystery can be entirely turned over to the Book of God's Will; in other words, to the Scriptures, if you want.

Besides, this idea has an astonishing methodological corollary: the Book of God's Will is indeed contained in the Scriptures, but this does not imply that the Scriptures are entirely the work of God. God made use of the hands of human scribes and they definitely interpolated profane knowledge into the text (e.g. Moses was conversant with the Egyptian sciences; as a result, you will find a lot of that in the works he wrote down). At last count, you have the right to reject many things contained in the Scriptures. Look what the Bible maintains about some medical questions!

This regulative idea appears 'metaphysical', at its core, in the sense which we now give that term: because you are beyond *physics (phusis)* when you formulate a distinction of this kind. But once the distinction is laid down, you can make it your business to define the needs and methods of scientific research, occasionally to take a small excursion somewhere near rational theology, but by and large, leave the metaphysics on the side, as if you had succeeded in one single blow to state what is the most important and then, to take leave of it.

Now, among the needs of scientific research, it is true that there is the state's support, and this by the way implies that the state should side with any project which itself must be distinct from a religion or religions. At the beginning of the seventeenth century, this amounts to sketching a function of the state which breaks off with what, speaking of the Middle Ages, has been called Augustinian politics; that is to say, the idea that the union of the people must be based on a strong religious oneness, and that it must have an interpenetration of state power and of religious authority.[4] In any case, Bacon also had very precise ideas on the toleration that a State must observe vis-à-vis diverse confessions, hence towards minorities, as towards atheism. I just wonder if the people who made our law of 1905 (relative to the strict separation of churches and the State) were not quite conversant with Bacon's philosophy. This is most likely . . .

However, this may take us back to the beginning of our discussion. There is something which replaces metaphysics in Bacon's philosophy and is also a kind of religion without obligation: this is the imaginary and perhaps quite specifically his work of rewriting ancient myths, notably in *De sapientia veterum* (*Of the Wisdom of the Ancients*) published in 1609. Again, the fact that an imaginary takes the place of religion or of metaphysics does not bother me at all. But I do mind the content of that specific imaginary! Generally speaking, an imaginary can appear as a non-coercive religion. Consider the Greco-Latin myths; there is neither clergy nor secular arms to force you to believe them. Nevertheless, the imaginary has an impact and a hold, somewhere in the 'the innermost recesses of the human soul', to write a pastiche of a Kantian phrase, or which is more likely in the collective unconscious of a community, in this case the schooling or scholarly community which baconianism (several generations of baconians) has established.

AWL: In *Genèse d'une catastrophe*, which is published as 'Postface' to your translation of Shakespeare's *Venus and Adonis*,[5] you analyse this long narrative poem, tying together the themes of seduction, freedom and death, also the respective roles of the sexes, through the drama in which love and hunting conflict. Why this poem? In what way does it raise the question of identity?

MLD: 'That I, one Snout by my name, present a wall. . . . This loam, this roughcast, and this stone doth show, that I am that same wall; the truth is so.' At the end of *A Midsummer Night's Dream*, a play is announced: a 'tragic farce' is going to be given at the court of Theseus, amounting for us spectators, the sudden appearance of a theatre within the theatre. Some artisans of Athens are going to be the players: as for Snout, his role is to be the wall which separates two lovers. This is a limit example no doubt of a Shakespearian philosophy of the logical non-identity of the psyche, since 'I' is always something other. *Genèse d'une catastrophe* gives a glimpse of other occurrences of this Shakespearean notion of the 'subject' as a mere mathematical point at the end of a vanishing line. I have tried to show the existing bond between this great Shakespearian problematic (there is neither constancy nor consistency in the 'I') and the philosophical subject like that proposed in Descartes (the '*je*' from '*je pense*') and in Hobbes.

Politically speaking, this 'I' is related to assignment of power: if another person is able to represent you, this comes to prove that she or he is capable of being 'another'. You cannot go to a meeting in the local district concerning which trees to plant or not to plant all along the avenue; you give a mandate to someone else to represent your views, and you think that this person is capable of being other than her/himself, in this case to contain a bit of yourself, at least as far as the views in question are to be defended.

AWL: And the respective roles of the sexes?

MLD: In the work of Shakespeare, the most evident ambiguity of this 'play with the I' is indeed frequently a play with sexual identity. Consider Rosalind in *As You Like It*, a young girl who disguises herself as a man, then suggests to the man she loves to talk to her as if he was talking to his beloved girl, who could in any case be or become somewhat herself. . . . The 'I' is basically free to affirm a different sex/gender than the one which your body suggests or what was written when your birth was registered; and, as it happens, contemporary queer theory could commend itself very well as an offspring of the illustrious Elizabethan. However today a different ambiguity would attract our attention because the Shakespearian subject is made of play, and of play within a play, implying all possible delight, but if one understands the subject in this way, one does not have to imagine that there is a matter of a total depersonalization here. There is at the very most a playful and temporary depersonalization. Snout is a wall only for some minutes. Look at my little neighbour, in the yard, playing being an aeroplane, extending his arms and making a noise 'vroom' in a quite convincing fashion; but, in a quarter of an hour, when it is snack time or teatime, it is definitely his bowl of hot chocolate he wants to scoff. The highly individualized needs and desires of the child he is have not been erased by his game. In the realm of the ludic, it is not a matter, and happily so, of a depersonalization which would be actually lived as such.

When the notion of 'lived experience' springs up, in considering that the ludic can be an aspect of it, but an aspect only (a moment of the lived experience if you prefer), something changes. You cannot place freedom as the source or the very principle of existence. You can see it as a project, a perspective, an effort or else something to build, and which is meaningful for life itself. When one grasps lived experience as a dialectical engagement between a living being and her or his environment (I barely alter a formula by Georges Canguilhem), freedom takes on a much more concrete value. It is, for example, the right to take into account your body with its real needs and its well-being. Such a right is not necessarily recognized in the social and political universe (consider the bounded feet of Chinese women, the corsets of our grandmothers and the lack of access to contraception for our mothers). To fight in order for this right to be recognized constitutes, therefore, a process of dialectical and concrete re-personalization. A process because freedom conquers itself, builds itself, and it is a good idea to think out the conditions for it as much as possible.

I had concluded *Genèse d'une catastrophe* by inviting the readers to wonder then in what respect the world, life and love are not exactly as the Shakespearian narrative described them. Wish me a long life: I still have so much more to say on that subject!

AWL: *Hipparchia's Choice: An Essay Concerning Women, Philosophy, Etc.* analyses the works of Rousseau, Virginia Woolf, Simone de Beauvoir, Sartre and shows how difficult it is, when one is a woman, philosopher and feminist, to find a voice. Why was it so late that the Republic extended citizen's rights (*droit de cité*) to women? What theoretical difficulties are raised by the question of the relations between women and philosophy, the 'question of women' in general and in philosophy in particular?

MLD: Since you kindly stated that *Hipparchia's Choice* shows 'the difficulty, when one is a woman, a philosopher and a feminist to speak, permit me not to return today to that question! I definitely don't long to evoke again the pains that I had to confront and overcome in order to begin constructing a philosophical problematic. Besides I had exposed these ghastly pains at the beginning of *Hipparchia's Choice*, which hopefully have exorcized them a bit for everyone. It is much nicer to think about female and male readers who have found in that text the opening for a voice which is their own: it is a sweet experience indeed to discover that an analysis of yours helps others to think, invites them to begin to speak, and this for them to say things you had absolutely no idea, hence, to embark on their own discoveries.

As for your question on the French Republic which actually was so late in recognizing citizen's rights (*droit de cité*) for women, I could feel tempted to put to female and male historians a hypothesis for them to work on. Not first of all on the very late extension of citizen's rights to women, but on the contrary, on the construction of a Republic without women in the first place. Perhaps, we should go back far enough in the long ascent to the Revolution itself and, say, from the early eighteenth century, and then, to ask if, in France at least, the exclusion of women by a certain vision of Republicanism would not have itself been prepared across the whole length of that century when Enlightenment people just talked about the idea of a Republic without taking any practical step. Because politics, you tackle that with ideas. Now, one could be entitled to wonder if the French Republicans chose to go forward and to put ideas into action *only* when they felt well assured that Republicanism, as it was known to them, would maintain not to say re-enforce the appropriation of women by men and the monopolization of political power by the latter, that is, by themselves. Because after all, patriarchy or male chauvinism is not necessarily inbred in all forms of Republicanism, of every challenge to the monarchy, or of a highly legitimate revolt against aristocracy and clergy as they economically overwhelmed the Third Estate (meaning the class of non-privileged working people). It is possible indeed to produce a concept of a Republic which includes equality of the sexes as a principle, a Republic which would not be grounded on fraternity (after John Locke), or on the memory of the Roman Senate, that is to say, of an assembly of men, supposed to be elderly and each a *Paterfamilias*.

If you accept my description of how French Republicanism fed on patriarchal ideology – and this was in my view the founding vice of it – then you will stop us wondering why it took such a long time, plus the Second World War, for our otherwise beloved Republicans to accept women among them![6]

AWL: As a result, equality and fraternity are in contradiction, and weighing down the evolution of the concept of Republic?

MLD: The notion of 'fraternity' (which is far from being incompatible with an authoritarian paternal function within the family) is, it seems, a value which unfortunately climbed up from the seventeenth century onward. When one sees it appearing in Bacon, one may notice that correlatively the Prince of *The New Atlantis* hardly has any attributions or power. One can easily move from there to the notion of a fraternal contract – which relieves the monarch from his status of hyperbolic Father – such that John Locke will concoct it thanks to extravagant metaphors, theoretical slips and holes in the argument.[7]

Geographically more relevant, since we speak of France, there is Rousseau, who works along the same lines without even putting on kid gloves. Besides he had the Republic of Geneva in mind, that is, a Republican patriarchy well locked against women, as achieved and made real in one city alone. The *Letter to Alembert* carries a political plan dreadfully articulated, and which was probably understood as such. Not only the dogma dealt out in complete simplicity: 'To a

Republic, men are necessary' (whereas in a monarchy things can be dispatched by women or men), and the praise of male clubs deriving from hunting or military clubs, but also the polemic against women speaking and writing: 'There may be a handful of women in the world who are worthy of being listened to by a honest man; but general speaking, is it from them that he must take advice?' Or, yet: 'The written works of women are all cold and pretty like themselves.' And after having mentioned *Cénie*, 'though that charming play be the work of a woman . . .', Rousseau adds, 'It is not to a woman but to women that I deny the talents of men.' Are we to call eighteenth-century political philosophy a disaster for women?

At any rate, there seems to be a marked cultural contrast, I believe, between the seventeenth century and the eighteenth century in France. In the seventeenth century, you will find (still?) many women involved in intellectual life, admittedly often great ladies, but also Gabrielle Suchon, who belonged to the petite bourgeoisie; Marie de Gournay, who wasn't rolling in gold or Mme Dacier, who lived in simplicity in a scholarly milieu. In the eighteenth century, one has the impression that women largely lost their right to speak their minds; fewer names of women authors and of work owed to women come to mind. How was that control or that repression handled, like in advance, over the decades during which some circles were preparing, consciously or not, the French Revolution? And, for that matter, which circles?

AWL: Questions to address to women and men historians?

MLD: It would be necessary indeed to discuss these questions with specialists of pre-revolutionary history. What I am pretty sure of, however, is that whenever the word of a group purposely designed as such is stifled, then, when the major political upheaval which was being concocted takes place, those who dare to speak up can well face the executioner. Hence, the fact that Olympe de Gouges was guillotined for 'having taken herself for a Statesman'. True, in 1789, there were notebooks of grievances prepared by guilds of women, but who took account of them? Turning a deaf ear to what women say, that is certainly the decisive way to deny them their freedom of speech. And when there is neither free speech nor right to speak, there are no rights; and when there are no rights, neither existing nor in view, the right of speech does not exist either.

French culture will have a great deal of difficulty recovering from what happened before, during and after the three revolutions (1789, 1830, 1848). At the beginning of the nineteenth century, some aristocrats (Mme de Staël or, taking belatedly to writing, her friend the Comtesse de Boigne) were admittedly able to blossom as women writers or thinkers. Moreover, Mme de Boigne had a remarkable political mind, but then a monarchist, in the style of Louis-Philippe to whom by the way she was personally close. I could commend her *Memoires*, the merciless lines that she lets fly at the emigrants on return to France at the Restoration, along with her satire of Chateaubriand.[8] Nevertheless, one looks in vain for her equivalent on the Republican side. This *milieu* must have been thoroughly disadvantaging for women. The woman philosopher which the French Revolution profoundly inspired is English(!); I am referring to Mary Wollstonecraft. And when one considers women like Flora Tristan or Louise Michel, one must say they belonged to much more radical milieux (socialists or communards) than those which will create the 'Republic of Jules', as we say tongue-in-cheek, and not just by chance.[9] Honour be all the same given to Jules Ferry, Félix Pécaud, Ferdinand Buisson, Camille Sée, and so on, who created a secular primary schooling, free and compulsory for the children of both sexes, and also (but not without regrettable limits) state secondary schooling for girls. A measure of Calvinism or possibly several, a zest of positivism, sadly enough, which means hardly any sciences were taught to girls, but then, a large measure of anticlericalism which led them to want to extricate the daughters of the people from the grip of the Catholic Church. In spite of the limits of what they have created, one has nevertheless the right to feel glad that schools for girls were at last created, although, for them, it was not a matter – as would have been possible – of a deepening of Republicanism.

AWL: French civilization will decidedly have difficulty in recovering from the First, Second and Third Republics. Was the Fourth one any better?

MLD: A more positive turn was taken during the Liberation, when women were granted the right to vote. This decision had effects which were perhaps slow to appear, but quite clear from all points of view. *The Second Sex* by Simone de Beauvoir is published in 1949. The first volume sold 20,000 copies in one week. Still critical reviews were so cruel and so low that Simone de Beauvoir borrowed one line by Julien Gracq: '*la chiennerie est française*' ('*La chiennerie* is typically French'; *la chiennerie* means uttering disgusting and revolting, low assertions). Perhaps she was forgetting a bit too quickly the thousands of French readers (women and men) who had found a meaning in and given meaning to her undertaking.

At the moment I am immersed in a dossier put together by Geneviève Gennari (the first French woman ever to write a MA dissertation on Beauvoir) entitled by her, '*Littérature féminine*', press cuttings coming from the magazine *UNF, Union nationale des Femmes: the women voters's magazine* and from the *Nouvelles Littéraires*, in the 1950s and 1960s. One can feel there, or in these cuttings, real effort to make exist and re-exist women writers (*les femmes de plume*), basically from Marie de France to the contemporaries. A Marie of France of which by the way it is said that her 'admirable work is much better known and studied today' than in the eighteenth century. Let us also note a fine essay about Marguerite Audoux in *Marie-Claire* in 1963. All in all, throughout these magazine articles, one has the feeling that it is indeed to women voters (*électrices*) that an invitation is sent out: know about your and our women ancestors, about what they wrote and about more recent sisters! The message that I hear in this dossier (admittedly put together by a woman writer who was a reader and friend of Simone de Beauvoir) could be something like this: we shall never go back. We vote and we sum up all the wonders that French thinking owes to women, and this in order never to give in.

In 2007, at the time of the presidential election the daily newspaper *Libération* made me respond to the provocation: 'Women do not know how to think, nor how to conceptualise . . .'[10] A few days later, my baker made for herself a T-shirt which she sported while selling her bread and eclairs. 'I think, therefore I vote' which was a true declaration of sentiments. The two of us fought back a little against the non-participation which could have tempted some voters whose favourite political party had chosen a woman candidate. . . . 'I think, therefore I vote'. May I invite you to meditate on the richness of this political approach which starts with a sound recognition of oneself: 'I think' states a woman. And this time, the 'Republic of Jules' is at last out of date and behind us – at least we can hope so.

AWL: In the 1950s, this was not already the case . . .

MLD: In the press cuttings put together by Geneviève Gennari, it is possible to sense that irritating attitudes were still around, which certainly showed what work remained to be undertaken in the middle of the twentieth century. Seeing that you asked me about what kind of relations there might be between the question of women in philosophy and the question of women in general, I will try in order to reply to you, to analyse a frankly restrictive interview with Françoise d'Eaubonne published in *Les Nouvelles Littéraires* in 1951. The interviewer mentions Simone de Beauvoir and Marguerite Duras, and she replies: 'If there are among the best books by women, some which are indeed very fine successes, I still wait for an authentic masterpiece.' The woman journalist reacts: 'Come on, you are being difficult! And, what will then bring about the birth of an authentic "masterpiece" by a woman?' And Françoise d'Eaubonne replies with the synthesis of the *animus* and the *anima*, and the bisexuality of the genius. Have mercy on us! This is Jung turned into a 'ready-to-think'. ... With a pre-established dogma of this sort, philosophy did not get a chance either of being or of appearing itself. Verification straightaway. And in fact when asked, 'What about Simone Weil?', The response is categorically negative: 'This case is very particular and striking; she can only be classified as "a great masculine writer". Not a line of her work discloses a feminine hand. What is virile in it is a hair breadth of genius, but does not reach that stage because of its lack of femininity.'

Thanks to this interview, discovered a long time after having started my own reflections, I understand better which beliefs it was necessary for me to suspend, in order to be able to begin discussing the relations of women and men to philosophy. Leave the notion of masterpierce and genius outside of our reflections! The pair *animus* and *anima* (the existence of which is not much more recognized as that of pigwidgeons) is only likely to scatter unnecessary epistemological obstacles on our path. The sexualization of the soul is all the more a block to thought because soul itself is not such a very well-known thing and at any rate no one knows whether it would be this 'soul' which produces philosophy. As for the adjective 'great' I know nothing more hollow than the distinction between so-called great philosophers and the others which perhaps should be called 'petits'?[11] Let us say that the common view imagines that there are great philosophers and others who are not so great. I believe that this contrast comes to us from biblical studies: there are the major prophets and the minor prophets. Whatever it is worth in its domain of origin (I will be careful not to judge), yet the distinction does not have any meaning in philosophy. In our discipline, each woman and man endeavours to think something, poses questions, lives an intellectual adventure which, in its turn, makes her or him get an intellectual life. It is an adventure, which you never lead alone but in the company of books that you have read, and with which sometimes one want to cross swords, or at least discuss, and also more importantly in the company of the people you address.

AWL: Does this adventure first spring out of something pedagogical? And then, how far so?

MLD: Well, see Simone Weil indeed! She was so devoted to her pupils at the girls school in Le Puy that, for their sakes, in 1931–2, she experimented a way of teaching sciences from a historical point of view. The volume, *On Science*, a posthumous collection of diverse pieces, outlines that experience retrospectively. She proved able to stray from the beaten track, in order to treat her students as 'ends-in-themselves'. And then, she collected as feedback these girls' views: 'Such a way of teaching can turn science into something human for pupils instead of a sort of dogma which you are supposed to believe without ever knowing exactly why.' It would equally admit of taking into account her response to a letter from Alain, in which she states, 'The adventure of Descartes turned out badly . . . something is lacking in his *Discourse on Method*.' To dare to write things like that, it is necessary not to be in league with a group (most likely fraternal) vis-à-vis a Descartes constructed as founding Father, nor to be riveted to a Heloisomorph position towards an author of whom she was a scholar.

By the way, if today we are able to see the importance of Simone Weil's endeavour, what a road travelled since 1951, when the world and Françoise d'Eaubonne were still unjust even to Simone de Beauvoir! For articulating the question of women in philosophy and the question of the lives of women in general in retrospect we can say that it took many things, first, to throw overbroad a number of notions, to produce some new ones, and moreover, to welcome a greater degree of political conscience, the sort that the movement of women at the beginning of the 1970s will put into actions. This was a mass movement, produced as such by the grass roots, which wanted to speak up and to tell what laws we wanted the Parliament adopt. This was no longer republicanism, but definitely democracy.

AWL: Within the domain of sex equality?

MLD: We did not demand equality, we lived it. We considered our judgement was vastly as good and worthy as the judgement of people who governed us or of those who endeavoured to prevail over public opinion. We thought in fact that this judgement of ours was far better than all grandees. 'Who must decide the number of children that you will have? The President of the Republic, who has the means to have his own children be brought up? The Pope, who does not have any?' Since the summer of 1968 and the encyclical *Humanae vitae* of Paul VI against contraception, we would have had some practical reasons to reconnect with the great French tradition which can be traced back to Rabelais, namely anticlericalism. This was not the case at the time: we were affirming an equality in speech, what I would call a *phatic* equality with and against all those messieurs that one would call today decision-makers; we made use of an equal freedom of conscience on questions that we believed we knew and understood better than them.

I do not want to go into detail and explain to you how my involvement in the women's movement will transform the young woman philosopher that I was. You can guess the broad lines of this, the idea of a reorientation of thinking, and a brand new joining of hands with a potential vocation for philosophy, which you could already read in Greek authors, one which consists in freely connecting with the life of the city. I would rather conclude with Deleuze, who was generous enough to read me and to encourage me, as you mentioned. In his own words, 'Already you are sketching the outline of a thought which would be free from such constraints' – he means masculinism, described here as a constraint weighing down the thinking of everyone – 'and at what price'.

Perhaps you could kindly give some thoughts to the ending: there is definitely 'a price' to pay. Now let us invite readers to wonder what this price is, and then if they would agree to pay that price.

AWL: *The Sex of Knowing* analyses the reluctance marked when it comes to free access for women to all sorts of knowledge, including by those who appear as the champions of their instruction. Any new development of your book's perspectives since you published it? And what would you say today about the place of the book in our culture?

MLD: *The Sex of Knowing* is available in mass-market paperback. Better than giving a summary of the arguments, or the analysis that I suggest of the difficulties encountered by women as to free access to learning, I would wish that our interview opened onto, that is to say, opened without concluding, towards a praise of written culture, books and libraries. Gabrielle Suchon, at the furthest end of the seventeenth century, manages more or less to console herself after noting that schools and universities remain closed to women, this is through remembering that there are always books, thanks to them one can learn everything which can be learned. In stating that, she who owned all her learning to reading, and who was then living evidence of this possibility, proves to be very precisely the heiress of the intellectual and political work carried out by a fine cohort of humanists: the Estiennes, Lefèvre d'Étaples, without forgetting Marguerite de Navarre and her brother François I at the beginning of the sixteenth century. These very creative scholars had tremendous practical ideas: to translate the classics and the Bible with care and precision in a clear tongue: to print books in characters as distinct and simple as possible, so that reading them would be easy; hence, concretely to put the best works of their intellectual inheritance, say, Hesiod or Solomon, at the disposal of a public as large as possible, at the disposal of all those who could want them and had learned how to read.

Such an idea will circulate widely in Europe. In England, it was not far from relegating magisterial lectures to the attic, as obsolete, null and void. I remember coming across an early seventeenth-century manuscript stating that magisterial lectures had indeed been necessary at the time when books were rare and expensive; but today, the anonymous author claimed, thanks to the technical progress achieved in book handicraft, books are no longer as expensive as they used to be. As a result, teachers could change their methods, and talk with their students, and so on. Because the magisterial lectures often amounted to reading out loud, for all the assembled students, chapters of works or compilations of existing works for which there was only one copy in the library.

AWL: The magisterial lectures have nevertheless survived here or there . . .

MLD: If that form of teaching has survived even the more recent and more virulent attacks, surely this is because it fulfils a function. . . . Perhaps we do not know exactly which one. It has sometimes occurred to me that it could be a magical or normative function. At any rate, I believe that a lecture does not have any real pedagogical efficiency except when we focus on hurrying the students to the library or bookshops and this by transmitting to them an inclination for always wanting to know more. Whatever it may be, it is necessary to be lucid: beyond State regulation of what is transmitted by *ex cathedra* teaching, some political control may also exist in many ways, and of course, in the first place through elections of teachers. I have been the witness of all kinds of 'underhanded tricks' ('*sourdes menées*'), I have enough experience of the *milieu* to be able to say without blushing that I feel occasionally worried. The prohibition to teaching Darwin in Texas is only one gross example, blatant enough; but from day to day, one sees other examples and which do not affect only women with advanced ideas.

Is it necessary to be more explicit? Book handicraft, as thought out by our humanist printers, will have been for a long time the great refuge, and at times clearly the privileged means for freedom to learn. This is still the case. Not long ago (2007), Juan Goytisolo told me that, when taking a walk in a public garden in Tehran, he saw some women, wearing it is true an Islamic veil, 'reading philosophical stuff', an image for him of a society which resists. Allow me to share that image with you while wishing good luck to the up-and-coming generations and to their desire for intelligibility!

Notes

1 Didier Eribon was a student at the time. He later became a journalist for *Libération* and *Le Nouvel Observateur*. In 1989, he published a biography of Michel Foucault. He is well known as a specialist on Gender, Gay, Lesbian and Queer Studies.

2 Francis Bacon, *Essays*, 'Of Beauty', *In Spedding edition*, vol. VI, p. 479.
3 Francis Bacon, *Advancement of Learning*. Book II, In Spedding edition, volume III, passim, pp. 321–491.
4 See Henri X. Arquillière, *L'Augustinisme politique: essais sur la formation des theories politiques du Moyen Age* (Paris: Vrin, 1934; second edition, 1955).
5 Michèle Le Dœuff, *Genèse d'une catastrophe* in William Shakespeare, *Vénus et Adonis* (Châtillon: Alidades, 1986), pp. 71–107.
6 Michèle Le Dœuff discussed the role of the liberation after the Second World War in at last! giving French women citizen's rights in Towards a Friendly, Transatlantic, critique of The Second Sex", in *The Legacy of Simone de Beauvoir*, edited by Emily R. Grosholz, 2004 Oxford University Press, pp. 22–36.
7 See Michèle Le Dœuff, 'On some philosophical compacts' and Epilogue of the second edition of *Hipparchia's Choice*, p. 318
8 *Mémoires* de la Countess de Boigne (née d'Osmond) first published in 1907, reprinted by Mercure de France, 1971. Her *Memoirs* stretch from the reign of Louis XVI to 1848.
9 Jules was a highly popular first name for men in the nineteenth century and beginning of the twentieth century, as a result many politicians of the Third Republic were called 'Jules'. But in slang 'un jules' is a He-man or a pimp.
10 Published in *Liberation* 10 Avril 2007, Cahier Spécial p. S7.
11 The adjective used only in French to refer to 'petits cartesians'.

10

Highly singular memories of '68, etc.
Michèle Le Dœuff 'in dialogue' with her past

> *C'était en Mai, y novel temps d'été,*
> *Chantaient oisels, florissaient arbres,*
> *Li CRS contre li Comte Bendit*
> *Estoquaient à moult géhenne.*[1]

Returned to Paris in the second half of June after six weeks in Brittany where, by the way, May had taken place too. They no longer ripped up cobbles from the streets to throw at the police, if my memory serves me well. The barricades in the rue Gay-Lussac were gone: people talked. An enormous need for expression and exchange had emerged under the most diverse forms, including a poem, devised by some medievalist friends, of which you just read a fragment above. Actors performed in factories; what today would be called *théâtre d'intervention* performances were followed by debates, which sometimes lasted for hours.[2] The need to speak, which arose in several million of our compatriots, is something I still feel around and within myself. As a need and also as a right, of course! As a will to make up the words and to coin the phrases which are lacking.... Yet I feel its existence even more sharply when taking into account how difficult it is for free speech to come about, something I discovered through personal experience at the time.

A general meeting of philosophy was announced at Censier for the afternoon. I hastened to head in that direction. Censier was an annex of the Sorbonne, probably made of prefabricated material, quite ugly, quite sad, but the children of the baby boom had in many ways seen equally bad or worse things and there was still more to come. I followed a corridor wall-papered with posters, in a way

---

Michèle Le Dœuff, 'Souvenirs singuliers des années 68, etc.', in 'Les héritages de Mai 68?', *Sens [public]: Revue internationale* (2009); www.sens-public.org, translated and revised by Kate Kirkpatrick, Pamela Sue Anderson, and Michèle Le Dœuff.

which may later on have inspired advertisers to construct bus shelters in order to paste publicity on them. And then, I chanced upon something unforgettable, a neat sheet stuck to a door reading: 'Committee for reflection on the condition of women'. Now, really? Or . . . I mean . . . oh, gosh! Because, you see, that was my first contact with '68 in the Latin Quarter. And well, well, fancy that! Fair enough, during the early days of May, at the École Normale Supérieure (ENS) at Fontenay where I was a student, I had already understood that, according to the most political of my fellow students, the movement was quite simply unhinged. They will quickly evolve, like so many others, but their very first reaction was to think that something out of joint was taking place. The Maoists showed a genuine disquiet: according to theory, a revolutionary movement starts in the working class, then students join it, following the right ideas produced by the masses. Those who were pillars of UNEF [*Union Nationale des Etudiants de France*, National Union of Students of France] seemed more like furious:

> Throughout the year, we gave students keys to a radical critique of the government and the dreadful reform of higher education which they were plotting. And we mobilized fifty or a hundred, no more, in the court of the Sorbonne! But now, an incident takes place. A few arrests after a meeting, an incident that is just an epiphenomenon of what the powers that be want to do to the universities, and here they are: everyone in the street!

Well, years later, in 1986 when other students took to the streets against some projects concocted by Minister Alain Devaquet, one saw them determined to maintain a very strict 'framework' for their movement, without ever letting it slide off-topic: the students of '86 were the true heirs of my fellow Fontenay students, as they were during the first three days of '68 but scarcely beyond. In their own way, the students of '86 stood up for a value which was ours well before the first clash in the Latin Quarter and which has remained firmly with us: the children of the people must have access to higher education.

Even from my distant Brittany, the cobbles and barricades did not have my sympathy. Sometimes I try to understand this aspect of the events too, though without any great certainty of success. Was it a 'remake' of the revolution of 1830? Because the parliamentary Republic had been sort of pinched, a teeny-weeny bit, in 1958, don't you think so? And a kind of elected monarchy substituted for it . . .? At any rate, it is possible to analyse in such a way the change of the Constitution which took place in 1958. Maybe a political frustration had been building up unnoticed over ten years (we dubbed the Palais Bourbon[3] '*le Palais désaffecté*', the disused palace), which exploded in 1968 in a style borrowed from the Revolution of 1830 or 1848, with eyes full of Delacroix. Everyone has seen the photo of a beautiful girl standard-bearer, on the shoulders of a man, a girl-allegory alluding to *Liberty guiding the people*. And I truly believe that the May of barricades made us women risk such a status (becoming allegories, indeed!), in which case there is really no reason to rejoice and deck our memory with flags! As for the radical critique, which the UNEF provided, at the time I knew it by heart; rallies occurred frequently in the courtyard of the Sorbonne, and I attended consistently – and without doubt, partly out of a sense of duty. The simple fact that today I cannot recall the first word of it (as in the case of many lectures I tried to follow) seems proof enough of a certain lack of real involvement. Nothing to parallel the real conviction that brought me to the demonstrations against the Vietnam War! I was to discover trade unionism a bit later, in a section of SNES,[4] where topics were vigorously discussed and from which concrete actions arose. Today, I can offer a belated elucidation: this 'fundamental' or radical criticism which the UNEF gave was delivered to us as a lecture, while we had an obscure desire for something else. Our professors too, by the way. I remember more than one entering the Descartes Auditorium, looking at us with a tired and discouraged air, as if he no longer believed in what he was doing. Oh, yes, before May '68!

In any case, let's retain some of the analysis my fellow students produced: '68 was indeed an out-of-line, unhinged movement, quite off the rails, which taught some of my generation that reality is often made of the same stuff as discrepancies – hence its stunning power to inspire unforeseen events.[5] It was also a movement that brought about a lot of shifts, including shifts in those who were against it or those who were wildly against it. '*L'imagination au pouvoir!*' (Let imagination rule!); it did give power to the imagination, and not just among those who participated with fervour. Witness what happened to a lady, who was already frankly bizarre and who (alas) was in a position of authority at the ENS of Fontenay. For at least a year, she had been pestering me with awkward, tiresome and assiduous attentions. She did not hide it, telling anyone who would listen that she was in love with my 'metaphysician's blue eyes' [*sic*], and I was not ready to accept that phrase any more than the rest.[6] Desiring to save my soul, she would frequently have me summoned into her office, where I was subjected to sermons: it's up to you to decide whether to add 'stupid and nasty', and simply, typical of such a genre. If I had a cold, it was because I had sinned. Because to militate against the war in Vietnam was to try to take the unhappiness of the world on my shoulders, a task Jesus Christ assigned to himself only, as a monopoly that should be respected as such. It was very wrong to want to walk on his turf! Of course you had to pay for this like you have to, for all sins! Nietzsche says somewhere that all religion is a squalid factory that transforms suffering into guilt. A secular spirit myself, and an atheist, I do see what he means. Sometimes the sermonizer's secretary, taking pity on me, would pretend that she had had my room called in vain. That lady also pestered Martial Gueroult, a historian of philosophy who was no longer young and was quite disturbed by it; she saw him as a new Socrates, but a Socrates who seriously needed to be put back on the right path. Gueroult's children knew how to handle the situation; as a result that lady who so wanted to serve as a superego to everyone was transferred to another position (research in pedagogy!) a few months later.

My own May of '68 started in a particular way: from the first days of the movement, that person who claimed to be 'in direct and permanent communication with Jesus Christ', and who was a Rudolf Steiner enthusiast, revealed herself also to have a soft spot for ultra-Gaullism – and to have fried her last fuse. She went into full mourning, sporting a black hat with a matching muslin veil, and she shamelessly started to turn up in my room. (NB: After the Gaullist demonstration on the *Champs-Élysées* and the election of a National Assembly that was beyond the Right Wing's wildest dreams, she dressed up in a cream outfit with a matching wide-brimmed hat. That was the way we saw her attired for at least one 'raid' into our general assembly, where she harangued us about the sins we were at the time committing collectively.)

Usually, it was Mme J, the philosophy assistant at the *École* (and my tutor), who told me about the extravagances she had to hear, considering the preacher didn't hide any of her intentions about me; I never had to brooch the topic or speak up. But her visits to my room were evident proof that her mental state was deteriorating and amounted to a serious aggravation for me. I thought it best to go have a word with my tutor. The next day I received, without any indication of its author, the orders of the director: 'We don't have any advice to give you but you will take the next train to Brittany', which I did. And my tutor added: 'It seems to be a mental trouble to which marriage and motherhood are, without doubt, not strangers.' It was not too difficult to figure out who might be the source of such a diagnosis: Mme J's husband was a teacher of psychology, with whom I was acquainted because he attended, as I did, Roger Martin's seminars on formal logic. At the time people teaching psychology, and even practising psychologists, were keen to improve their understanding of logic or mathematics.[7]

'You will take the next train to Brittany . . .' That the oppressed girl would be incited to leave is something that may, today, lead to gritting of teeth. We know more tragic examples, more violent and irreversible than the one which I am relating to you. As all of those who are involved in giving support to victims of domestic violence know, sometimes there is no other solution but for the woman to leave. It is better to avoid dogmatism when seeking to help someone. I simply regret that I didn't attempt to negotiate – at that moment – permission, difficult to obtain, to stop being a boarder and live outside the *École*. I took the train, accompanied all the same by the wise words of the psychology teacher, and my occasional fellow student, who had said to his own wife that marriage and motherhood can be sources of serious pathology. Quite off the rails, too, when you come to think of it.

When I arrived with my family, I sensed that it was impossible to explain why I had chosen to come and live History with a capital H in the fresh air. At the time not a couple parents in a hundred would have been willing to hear what I would have to say, that is, if the words had existed and if I'd been asked the slightest question. The typical message that parents conveyed to their daughters was to keep their worries to themselves. Women who are under thirty today could rightly to be surprised by this, for things have changed so much. My friends' daughters frequently take their mothers as *confidantes*, with some excess, if I may say in passing. In any case, at the time that was how it was. As a result, while everyone spoke and wanted to speak, I stayed quiet. May '68 in Quimper is progressing in an equally innovative and very interesting manner; among other things I'm seen as a kind of utopia work there. But the silence about my reasons for fleeing Paris weighed me down and will do so for many years.

Then, return to Paris at the end of June. A corridor at Censier, the note on the door and me glued before it, me who didn't understand immediately, or at least not fully . . . but who stands there in wonder. I only knew the image of the Parisian revolution as broadcasted by the media. I had memorized a statement by an MP (because backbenchers too were taking the floor a lot), possibly quoting from a poet: '*on croyait la chose impossible; des innocents s'en vinrent et la firent*' ('such an event had been thought impossible, then innocence came along and made it happen'). It was a beautiful phrase, probably true: those who were set ablaze immediately, not three days later, those who made the month of May something we still speak of – they hardly had any political experience. Of course, they didn't! Because groups with some political experience were also structured by a well-defined 'line'. . . . See how the Maoist and Union activists first react! Only the innocent were left to make things happen. Standing before the sheet-size poster announcing this committee on the condition of women, by and large I am an innocent too. I am certainly unaware of the fact that I am about to meet, if not my destiny, at least the life that I shall choose to work for. So unaware that pretty different feelings arose in me: pleasure, surely, and perhaps the 'etc.' which will come to play such a large role in my way of thinking. I was thrilled to note that the revolution never stuck to its 'topic' but always took place outside of the question it purported to treat; it constantly left its orbit and I found this wonderful even though my intellectual profile tended more towards *esprit de géometrie* (geometrical way of thinking) or, say, a clear preference for rigour. I am in the process of changing, like so many others at the time, and of giving myself a new dimension. By the way, my best memory of '68 will be to have seen people become more human because the relations between people had become more humane. The laundry woman at the *École* no longer focused on laying down the law; instead she told us about '36.[8] She had something to pass on to us, she who had always had a month's salary in a savings account in case one day it became necessary to hold a long strike. So, with a smile on my lips, delighted to see that the 'student-worker solidarity' had produced one more unexpected blooming, I pushed the door open.

The room was empty. Let us risk being redundant: there was no one there. For those who were born later, I have this to offer: the experience would undoubtedly not have been as strong if, behind the door, I had found a group hard at work. Imagine that you come across a new idea one day, but discover there is no one there, on that particular day, to support it. Then, another idea will mature in silence, bringing a principle of personal responsibility. If you want something to exist, you have to make it exist yourself; if you want something done, do it! And if, born much later, you regret that you missed the emergence of feminism in France, consider this empty room that is available to you; it is still there!

Very far from *Censier* (though I only heard about it yesterday), in a small town in the *Drôme*, the girls' high school was on 'active strike', like many others. These girls were all reading Simone de Beauvoir, after this had been suggested by a teacher. French feminism as it will flourish two or three years later had more than one origin in '68. I can tell you only about the one I personally lived and of which Beauvoir, whom I had read some years previously, seemed as a person to be totally absent. Perhaps she and Sartre were still in an almost péri-Stalinist phase at the time? Eventually, they will both lean towards the slogan, 'élections, traps for idiots', to which neither I nor any feminist that has crossed my path would subscribe. Voting is not just a hard-won right for us, nor even just a duty; it is a celebration, when one thinks of our foremothers at Seneca Falls and Sheffield, of the thousands of women of all conditions who demanded citizenship for themselves and for us. That year, Beauvoir gave two interviews, one in Serbo-Croatian the other in Norwegian;[9] in them she deplores the fact that 'the liberation of women' [*sic*] had not become a reality, and furthermore, that there had been a regression with respect to the economic independence of women – that's all my findings! She didn't re-become our Simone until 1971, as a signatory of the '*Manifeste des 343*'.[10] In November of the same year, she will be with us at the first big demonstration for the right to abortion. Hats-off to Anne Zélinsky and Delphine Seyrig, who went to fetch her from the sort of retreat she had adopted and to offer her the possibility of signing the *Manifeste*. But this will take place in 1971. In May or June of '68, she seemed to be quite elsewhere, in every sense of the word, while in the meantime in the Drôme a woman (*one* woman) was bringing Beauvoir's works to life, as a good 'object' for an active strike. Some people still remember the fact, which is lovely. And by the way – each and every one of us, women and men – should put our pens to paper today and recount our own '68 years from Guéret to Marseille or Calais.

In June, standing before my door, I did not make a link between *The Second Sex* and the situation such as I tried to live it. It is only later, when reading *Histoires du M.L.F.* by Annie de Pisan and Anne Tristan (1977), that I shall discover what I had missed, and you too, which means we are in the same boat in this respect: namely, that from mid-May, some women tried to put the question of women on the agenda for the '68 movement. But there, the room being empty, I carried on to the Philosophy General Meeting. There were many of these General Meetings. And I did attend them regularly, even after the summer. Now, was it really off subject, a committee on the condition of women? Or did it go straight to the heart of the problem? I slowly began to understand better: the voices which made themselves heard in the Philosophy Lecture Room were, with very, very rare exception, those of our male fellow students, or shall I say comrades? Young men whose look and style had completely changed. This one wore a leopard-print shirt, unbuttoned to the waist with a particularly hairy chest on display. That one swaggered his shoulders under a brand new leather jacket, a style which seemed to have reached the students only a minute before. As for the chair of the meeting, always re-elected, he was sporting a suit and tie, something which we had never seen among us. One day he addressed Vladimir Jankélévitch as 'Monsieur le Professeur' – unheard of! He organized the General Meeting very well, giving the floor in a well-ordered way without ever expressing an opinion himself, which came in handy for everyone. But, on top of emphasizing his gender, the tie meant something. To say the least, he was putting himself at a distance from '*spontanéisme*', a word which was coined that year, and frequently used with pejorative connotations.[11] All of them seemed to put on display a kind of accentuated masculinity, which I had never perceived in them before. Where, then, were my friends, those with whom I chatted for two minutes before a lecture or when leaving the library? Those who did not present themselves as macho, whether in conversation or in their look? Maybe they were there, hidden in the cloud of cigarette smoke, and as quiet as my women friends and myself? Or perhaps they had gone to spearhead the Revolution in other places? I was dumbfounded, all the same, but not for the last time. Some years later, when the Communist Party renounced the concept of the dictatorship of the proletariat, I heard a colleague groaning as if he had had male menopause prematurely imposed upon him. Basically, it is since '68 that I've wondered what men invest, at the level of the imaginary, in political action and in the language of politics. Is it null and void now, this question? I don't think so, and one must ask it with respect to women today. What does it mean to stage a hypersexualization in politics? In contrast, I admired Delphine Seyrig: when she came to meetings, she left her extreme beauty at home and seemed always to find this easy to do.

At the ENS at Fontenay, a single-sex institution, there were also General Meetings and other meetings for reflection: but not one on the condition of women. And yet: before and after '68, there were, and there would be, exchanges among us about contraception. At our request, Marguerite Cordier, the director, invited Family Planning to talk with us. We also invited Simone de Beauvoir to give a conference on the subject of her choice; she declined, but at least we had made the approach. We were not totally in the dark; elements of becoming aware were there. During the famous '68 Events', captivating things would happen in our southern, suburban ENS, but nothing which would develop a feminist point of view. Notably, I remember a discussion in which, little by little, an idea would be produced in a collective manner by the agglutination of light touches and certainly 'without an author': the idea that the teaching we wished for must take the form of research seminars. At Quimper, I believe that the utopian set-up of primary schools was produced in this manner. Someone had a rough idea, someone else added to it, and so on – until we had created a child-minding service for the children of activists (the strike being 'active', it was necessary that the parents of these pupils, including their mothers, could go and participate), even creating a canteen which would function for weeks without a single centime. The strikers of the EDF would borrow the vans of the PTT strikers (or vice versa), visit the farms showing solidarity, in order to collect the vegetables and other food freely donated by those farmers who also regularly took the lead in demonstrations. Schoolteachers on strike took turns cooking what they had collected.

If one speaks of the legacy of '68, and you will have guessed that I am more an instantaneous inheritor than an actor, I want to pass this inheritance on to you. That ideas can emerge from a group, developing when everyone listens to each other, and in this way, ideas can truly be designed without any clearly identifiable author. But it is always necessary that someone begin: that there is a catalyst. My best memories of the women's movement, of my two years teaching at high schools, then at Fontenay where I returned as assistant, and eventually at Geneva, correspond to this. I am certainly not saying that I have always taught in this style, certainly not. But there were privileged moments. When all at once a group would be formed of my students and me, we would function creatively as a collective and generally finish in this manner: my students would place an order for a lecture on this or that for the following week. A lecture responded precisely to a need after which we, together, threw a few ideas around; this was completely different from the all too visible sadness of our mandarins who wondered what in the world we would do (if indeed we could do anything) with the speeches they were going to deliver.

And it is perhaps in this fashion that the inheritance of '68 will come back to me, like a boomerang, at the beginning of November 1971. I was then teaching at the Rodin secondary school in Paris, where the students had not yet finished their own May '68, as they themselves said. They bragged about having 'worn out' four headmasters the previous year, and so on. The school had entrusted me with a *Terminale C* (where the most highbrow scientist learn) in 'active internship': it meant pedagogical self-training on the job, they gave you a classroom and you had to sort things out for yourself. All in all, it went rather well. The students certainly had a tendency to be a little agitated, but they were good, almost all hyper-political as a matter of course. I never knew if a selection process through 'constant revolution in the classroom' was harsher than a selection on the basis of ability in Latin or maths, and therefore, that only the best had survived, or whether frequenting the committees of the Far Left developed their intellects in a spectacular manner. One autumn day, the youngest of them all approached me at the end of a class and handed me a tract, saying, 'if you agree with this text, could you put it up in the teachers' room?' I read it on the spot: it was a call to the demonstration of 20 November 1971 for the right to abortion, the one which would launch the women's movement as a mass movement. I agreed with the text.

'There are several girls from the class going. Would you like to come with us?'

I said, 'yes', and this was my entry into the women's movement. I did not immediately seek to analyse the situation. I contented myself with laughing a little bit: officially, the students' parents feared, or so I heard, that the teachers might 'indoctrinate' their children. But this did not at all correspond to my experience. Look: it was one of my students who had just done a bit of consciousness-raising work and made me aware of a just cause; sometimes rivers return to their source. To me, the deep significance of this step she had taken was that my younger sisters needed my help. And by the way, throughout that year I had to understand what is truly the position of parents during years which were politically 'hot' but not so keen on schooling. Parents could be conservatives, or even reactionaries, but what they all really wanted was for their children to study, to work, to turn in their homework. If you achieved that, they all blessed you. If, moreover, you succeeded in making your students read some books in the year, a pupil's mother, who happened to be a Royalist, would invite you to lunch to thank you – and I am not making this up! There, too, the constructive side of May '68 had passed, maybe unconsciously. The parents of the Rodin students sensed that teaching based on relations of authority had broken down in this establishment, which a bit earlier, *Le Nouvel Observateur* had graciously qualified as a 'rubbish school'. Once authoritative relations in teaching were no longer acceptable to these students, their parents understood that it is still possible to capture their *libido sciendi*. For *libido sciendi* exists potentially in almost everyone; and we had seen it in '68, when the masses were so jubilant to be given theatre plays analysing society, followed by debates. All you have to do is gently to help this *libido* awake; at Rodin, the headmaster (the one who was to survive) made the teachers understand that, because we were a 'pilot lycée', we could do what we liked, on the condition that we kept the interest of our students.

Today it would be about time to analyse the fact, in itself minuscule, which took place between a woman and a woman: a schoolgirl of fifteen invited her philosophy teacher to a demonstration of the *Mouvement de libération des femmes* (MLF), and thereafter, the teacher will regularly turn up at those that followed, eventually getting fully involved in the MLAC (*Mouvement pour la liberté de l'avortement et de la contraception*) as soon as this association was created in 1973. I will launch the local group in Colombes with colleagues from the SNES [trade union] and on this point, I can claim the initial push that set the story in motion, but hardly more than that. We organized a public meeting without asking ourselves if it would attract more than fifteen people. As it turned out, the room was reasonably full and the following week we shall have joy in seeing the nurses and carers from the city hospital arrive and join our little group. Serious matters were beginning. Look and behold what she had catalysed, this young E . . .? Well, yes and no, because traces of the real political benefits of '68 were there, in Colombes, which were human acquisitions, personally gained by people. The know-how to mobilize, and how to get an agreement within a trade union chapel, half with some affiliation to the Communist Party, half belonging to *L'École emancipée*,[12] with at least one member of *la ligue communiste* (a Trotskyist). A majority of colleagues getting along well from these diverse backgrounds, we ended up listening to each other and reaching an agreement, because we wanted to.... And the idea of organizing a meeting, without wondering for a minute whether it would be a flop or not, was a far cry from traditional politics. Last, but not least, those who worked at the hospital, don't you think they had lived May '68 themselves, too? They, moreover, knew exactly how a miscarriage, whether spontaneous or provoked, was actually handled in practice in the context of a hospital. Threads left waiting were there, which it sufficed to pick up again and knit together.

In the same manner, it was probably the shared heritage of '68, guessed as such, which had allowed a high school student to feel that she could make me read a tract, that her initiative made sense and would probably be kindly received. Yet, in class we had only studied *Les Enfants Sauvages*[13] and *The Profession of Faith of a Savoyard Vicar*;[14] things like that – which the Trotskyists of various persuasions, the anarchists and those who swore only by the 'base committees' liked – a fact which only goes to prove that philosophy is a marvellous discipline, able to capture the interest of young people by bringing to them what they had not expected and moving them to where they are not already: here are an outside, a detour through the outside and, perhaps, the joy of conceptualizing beyond the questions which one is accustomed to discuss. It was not the content of my teaching in 1971 which could have made my pupils guess about my as yet very modest political experience, but rather the attitude which I had towards them. I left much of the speaking to them, as long as they stuck to the text we were reading together, and then there was often an *ex cathedra* synthesizing, in which their own discourse was taken into account. May of '68 – a month, which lasted several years – proved a tremendous school, even for learning how to teach.

In fairness, the high school girl who revealed to me my latent feminism was surely a member of some group on the far Left. It is certainly thus that the information concerning the demonstration had reached her. Within more than one circle of what is now called 'Leftism', some women had developed a critical approach, which allowed them to understand that the relations between the sexes, including those within the proposed revolution, were terribly wrong ... or, even that the organization to which they belonged failed to call into question an enormous aspect of social oppression, and that masculine domination functioned there as elsewhere. We all have a considerable debt to them, if only for relaying the initiatives of what the press had christened the MLF (Mouvement de libération des femmes) in August 1970. The name was in effect invented by the journalists reporting on the happening at *Place de L'Étoile*, when nine friends placed a wreath of flowers dedicated to 'someone more unknown than the soldier: his wife'. This was followed by meetings in a room of *L'École des Beaux-Arts*; but it was only thanks to the press that this really received the large public attention required;[15] and thanks also to various far Left groups which passed on information to their grass-roots activists. At Rodin, I had one communist student; he had me sign a petition for the liberation of Angela Davis, an excellent idea too, but also one that shows the willingness of the Communist Party to give its young people legitimate tasks, which were clearly different from what the emerging feminist movement focused upon. Roughly speaking, in '71, the 'traditional left' – meaning the Communist Party (PCF) or FGDS (the future PS) – was suspicious of us; I would like to be able to say that this is no longer the case at all today, even in a veiled way. I would indeed!

In all fairness too, we must remember that the Americans were a step ahead of us. They had been active since September '68, and this partly on the basis of a critical analysis of the relations between the sexes within the mixed organizations in which they had been involved. The 'happening' at *Place de L'Étoile* was intended, among other things, to be a symbolic gesture of solidarity with a day organized across the Atlantic by the Women's Liberation Movement. History is quite a complex story, don't you think! And if you want to learn things in greater detail, and therefore even more complex, you must read books. For my part I have only wished to testify to the singular experience which was mine, to share with you the irreplaceable lesson of the empty room, and perhaps in passing to tell you where my vigilance for 'abbesses' comes from, and my radical rejection of the role St Paul imparted to '*presbytera*', the 'older' woman who has no existence except to teach patriarchal morals to younger women. Kindly do not think that my work on this character, and its function, is solely autobiographical in nature. That would be too bad, because I think that even today women let themselves be used by patriarchy to repress at least certain forms of feminism. What forms? Look around you, and you will know.

Notes

1 'It was in May, when summer was new
  birds were singing, trees blossoming
  the riot police against Count Bendit

hitting hard and creating much agony.'
   (A patchwork of medieval French)
2 Adrien Zammit defines '*théâtre d'intervention*' this way:
   Le théâtre d'intervention : un théâtre engagé dans la société, inspiré par les mouvements contestataires européens et américains d'après 1968, descendant ou cousin du théâtre d'agit-prop, du théâtre politique, du théâtre populaire, du théâtre documentaire, du théâtre de rue . . . Le théâtre d'intervention témoigne d'une volonté de sortir du champ clos du théâtre : sortir des théâtres institués pour partir à la recherche de nouveaux espaces collectifs; sortir du répertoire dramatique pour produire une autre culture; sortir du clivage acteurs-spectateurs pour créer une parole collective.
3 Seat of the French National Assembly.
4 *Syndicat National de l'Enseignement Secondaire.*
5 Later on Michèle Le Dœuff developed a theory of the unforeseen, see 'Occasionally the Unforeseen Happens', Keynote Address at the SEP-FEP (Society for European Philosophy and Forum of European Philosophy) Conference, 2011; published in *Paragraph* 37, no. 3 (November 2014): 314–25; reprinted here as Chapter 11.
6 Half of the horror is lost in the translation. This person is referring to Michèle Le Dœuff as a *métaphysicien*, hence using the masculine noun and for a type of philosophizing which is not her favourite cup of tea: metaphysics! Besides there may well be a racist aspect in this phrase: '*regard bleu*' literally, 'a blue gaze': a metaphysician with blue eyes who is 'able to look at essences' excludes quite a lot of people from this capacity.
7 Under mainly Lacan's influence the French psychoanalytical and psychological milieu had started believing in modern mathematics, contemporary logic and also, crossword puzzles.
8 The year 1936 in France was marked, first, by *Fonds populaire*, a coalition of Left wing parties, intellectuals and human rights activists, holding in common a programme of social rights reform, the banning of far Right leagues, and so on. None of this was achieved without phenomenal strikes, which have left good and joyful memories with many. Also, by the government headed by Leon Blum, because they limited the working week to 40 hours, introduced two weeks paid holidays per year, created a policy for retirement and unemployment benefits, not to mention positive reforms in education, and so on. Blum became, and is to this day, the beacon of what a Left-wing regime can achieve. On the other hand, if they failed to give women the vote or any new form of rights (although some women were members of the government) and also failed to give colonized people their legitimate rights, what they left undone became the important agenda from the end of the Second World War and on to the 1970s.
9 See *Les Écrits de Simone de Beauvoir*, edited by Claude Francis and Fernande Gontier (Paris: Gallimard, 1979). For the Zagreg interview, 12 May 1968, pp. 234–6; for the Norwegian interview, 22 August 1968, pp. 233–4.

10 *Manifeste des 343* is a text published in *Le Nouvel Observateur* (5 avril 1971) and signed by 343 women who stated they had had an abortion (a statement which could have started legal proceedings against them) and wanted it to be made legal and safe.
11 '*Spontanéisme*' means 'believing in collective spontaneity'.
12 *L'École Émancipée* is time-honoured current within teachers' unions.
13 *Les Enfants sauvages*, by Lucien Malson (Paris: *Union Générale d'Éditions*, 1964) was constantly reprinted in cheap – mass-market – paperback editions.
14 An essay in Rousseau's *Émile*, pp. 943–1098.
15 The *Manifeste des 343* was published in *Le Nouvel Observateur* (Spring 1971).

11

Occasionally the unforeseen happens[1]

Michèle Le Dœuff

It is clearly a paradox to offer a keynote about the unforeseen and about occasions – not to say accidents, happy or not, lucky or not. Because the keynote *genre*, to my knowledge, has something to do with planning a future for a subject, 'this is where we are and this is where we should go'. Now, do you ground such a project on a reassessment of the value of events, unforeseen and unforeseeable, which may well have brightened the life of a given field or dulled it? No, of course not! Except, perhaps, when prospects are so gloomy, and circumstances quite unmistakably dire, that you must try – at the very least – to show that circumstances are not the whole story. Besides, a well-considered hope may help to alter the circumstances themselves. At any rate, where there is no hope, the worst aspects of a context are earmarked to win. Perhaps we all grew up with a Roman saying at the back of our minds: *Quos Jupiter perdere vult prius dementat*, those whom Jupiter wishes to destroy, he first makes mad. For my part, I would rather suggest that, when an era tends to eliminate a certain form of intellectual questioning, the most formidable strategy it can use might well be to bring despair to the people who want to carry on. But we can at least address and oppose such a strategy. We don't need to bypass our own charming and so very necessary sense of humour in order to maintain that, if philosophy still means so much to us after so many years, surely there must be one or two good reasons why.

First-hand knowledge and lived experience will form part of my method today as I explore the highly difficult and complex question of how philosophy may bring relevant things to people in other fields. And first of all, we must respect the complexity of the question, even if the small matter of funding appears to invite hurried answers claiming that philosophy is like a river in a desert irrigating all the surrounding fields. If we want it to be a good river, which is certainly the main thing, it's better for us to forget about facile publicity straightaway. Real hope must entertain a connection with lucidity, and this requires also an inventory of potential stumbling blocks.

Now, if you wonder what philosophy may bring to people in other fields, the immediate temptation would be to sing the praises of something that has been the big idol for many years, namely interdisciplinarity. Issues around interdisciplinarity may appear different in various European countries. I shall describe what I understand of recent French history and then it will be up to you to see if parallels or contrasts in other countries can be suggested. At any rate, in France, interdisciplinarity was never a forbidden delicacy for philosophers, even many years before the word itself was coined. Have a look in standard dictionaries printed in the 1970s. I doubt you will find the word there. True, some brave archaeologists of language have indeed managed to find two occurrences dating back to the 1960s, one in an obscure treatise of sociology and one in the proceedings of a conference of 'applied geography', but that's all: 'The geographer will act [*oeuvrer*] within an interdisciplinary team'. . . . I already had the feeling that interdisciplinarity was first introduced in the saddlebags of a new obligation (which appeared in the mid-1970s, when geographers in France took over at government level), an obligation bearing on us all in the humanities, namely to be engaged in teamwork. All of a sudden, it was no longer enough to be a productive or interesting philosopher. You had to be a member of a team and this team had better be interdisciplinary. One could sense straightaway that this would increase the amount of coercion and game-playing in a field where coercion is not supposed to be welcome and in which games should not exist at all.

On the other hand, the idea of interdisciplinarity itself looked innocent enough because, without using a particular word to name it, this is what we had long been doing in perfect freedom, as naturally as breathing or walking or indeed, after the fashion of Molière's Monsieur Jourdain, speaking in prose without being aware of it – at a time before the introduction of codification. This was particularly true in mainstream French philosophy. I don't want to overstress the fact that I come from a most classical region of the French philosophical map. There is no point hiding it either: Fontenay was an École Normale Supérieure, where people were trained for *l'agrégation de philosophie*. . . . But you must take into account the fact that, when I was a student or a young academic, the system was mostly run by people who had behaved courageously during the war. And it was my choice anyway to look up to those – among my elders – who had been involved in the Resistance. As a result, the mainstream I may describe is historically and politically located in the post-war era, which roughly speaking lasted until the mid-1970s. If you find my description a shade too vibrant, you may qualify it thus: something which didn't come from the internal dynamics of philosophy, but from a kind of wisdom acquired by the best people during the war, was indeed among the key factors. Let me give the floor to my old director, Marguerite Cordier, then in her late eighties: 'Our Maoist students, well, of course they were trouble sometimes, but at least, they were truly alive [*elles vivaient*].' True, Maoist friends, along with those simply involved in opposing the war in Vietnam, were living their lives to the full and this is exactly what the best people of the previous generation had wanted for the baby boomers, which implied an enormous amount of tolerance.

At any rate, here is a quick description of interdisciplinarity as it existed at student level in French philosophy before the word was first introduced. You could insert whatever you wanted in an exam paper, provided of course it made sense. That might include bits of mathematics or physics you had just acquired thanks to your scientist friends who enjoyed teaching you what they had just learned. For they came back from Laurent Schwartz's or Roger Godement's lectures with glittering eyes and could not wait to pass on the best morsels of what they had just understood. A lot of what I acquired in this way through peer teaching ended up in my exam papers and examiners apparently loved it too. There is something to be drawn from this: intellectual excitement, real mirth in learning and teaching, is the best vector for transmission. Perhaps we could discuss that with colleagues who are in charge of training teachers-to-be, as well as our younger colleagues. In my view, there is nothing like an ounce of passion, or like finding pleasure in an intellectual activity, to convey what Rabelais called the 'substantific marrow' of anything. I would say the same of Jean-Marc Lévy-Leblond, a physicist who described himself as a non-believer – he claimed that he merely practised physics without believing in it [*pratiquant mais non croyant*]. Perhaps, but he taught the history of Einstein's work with so much *gusto* that it was unforgettable.

Roger Godement and Laurent Schwartz were deeply involved in the movement against the war in Vietnam, as I was. Highly demanding intellectual work was never incompatible with a commitment to radical politics. On the other hand, radical politics were not seen as an outcome of intellectual achievement. The two things were independent, just as, during the war, Georges Canguilhem had been very active in the Resistance, while nothing in his work had announced such an involvement. Just as Bertrand Russell could produce philosophical work which had little to do with his commitment to pacifism – and the other way round. The idea that could be imbibed from being in contact with certain people of that generation was that life is manifold, which means that totalization is not necessary. This is at least what I understood. In the meantime, other people certainly felt otherwise. Mostly men, you may ask? Yes, but never mind! We are not going to broach the issue of gender straightaway! Besides, some people, who also happened to be men, were nostalgic for the medieval Sorbonne and looking for models in Germany.

I'm not talking in the name of my whole generation when I note with pleasure that you could make use of examples taken from literature, from the history of science (good old Claude Bernard!), plus whatever you wanted to borrow from psychoanalysis, provided you didn't turn it into a simplistic catechism: apparently there was no ban on imports into mainstream philosophy, no border police on duty to stop immigrant bits of learning. Perhaps we had not all read Democritus ('In wanting to enclose a vast domain, one ends up by demolishing one's own finances'), but you could maintain that the enclosure of our field might well be pointless to begin with and would in the end lead to a great exhaustion. On the other hand, there are always questions that remain blocked, invisibly blocked as it were, because it does not occur to anyone to raise them. One of them, as far as I understood, could be at the core of the present conference: if it is clear enough that philosophy may thrive on fruit imported from other fields, what can philosophy provide reciprocally to other fields or in relation to them? What do we have to offer to scientists, historians, psychologists and so forth? Had such an impossible question been raised at that time, it would have left our minds blank, but no one raised it. There was a keen and sincere interest in what was taking place in other fields, yes, which meant recognition, both of these fields and of the otherness of the work carried out there. Yes, but apart from that? Well, of course, today, we could say that recognition in itself means a lot, particularly whenever there is a trend among other philosophers to speak ill of science. At a personal level, I could claim that I repaid my scientist friends by publishing material they enjoy reading, and not least because it contains the aforesaid recognition of an equal dignity of their fields. Fine, but apart from that? Well, apart from that, perhaps it's time to confront the blank mind syndrome.

There was another question which would have left many minds blank in the 1960s, namely the status of women within philosophy or, more generally, in learning. As a question, it was not raised at all, although, as a problem, it was blatant enough, except that it eluded us. It was unforeseeable that one day, and not long afterwards, it would become an important topic, discussed at international level. Now, when many women – and some men too – started reading the classics of feminism with the great joy of discovery, then a contrast with what I have just described appeared. For I have said that in philosophy there was no border police for things borrowed from elsewhere. And this was true up to the point when some started borrowing from feminist classics. I even know of a case of blatant censorship, when a student of mine quoted from Virginia Woolf's *A Room of One's Own* during the *agrégation* oral examination. Imagine: you grew up in a context in which quoting from Stendhal is always welcome – how are you going to guess that Virginia Woolf is not acceptable? The jury called it '*élucubrations*' – 'ravings'. To make the story worse: the subject she had drawn was: 'What do we mean when we attribute genius to a man?' ['*Que veut-on dire quand on attribue du génie à un homme?*']. At the end of her presentation, which I attended (for *agrégation* orals are public) and found very good, she discussed the ambiguity of the word 'man' in the light of Virginia Woolf's views. There might be an ounce of nationalism, male nationalism, in the way the jury reacted. Had she borrowed her inspiration from Stendhal, '*Tous les génies qui naissent femmes sont perdus pour le bonheur public*' ('All geniuses who are born women are lost to the happiness of the public'), she might have gotten away with it.[2] A French male author has a right to be illuminating to the point of being a bit of a feminist, at least occasionally, whereas a foreign woman is certainly raving.[3]

So, on the one hand, all those who were keen on feminist classics or feminist recent research were reading all we could in history, sociology, Greek anthropology, you name it, with a splendid appetite, and it certainly brightened our intellectual lives. But, on the other hand, and this even within interdisciplinarity, the ban on feminist culture – or about women in philosophy – was clearly there. Those of you who kindly read *Hipparchia's Choice: An Essay Concerning Women, Philosophy, Etc.* may remember the story at the beginning about a defence of a thesis on Kant.[4] It's time for me to acknowledge that it is a true story, which took place at the Sorbonne. Now, the member of the jury who blamed the candidate (who was my senior colleague, by the way) for not having mentioned Nabert was a man who had not trained in philosophy. He was a specialist in eighteenth-century French literature. Why he was on the jury at all, I never guessed. At any rate, he was a bit of an outsider there, and then he had to prove that a woman – fully trained in philosophy – was more outlandish than himself in philosophy. Interdisciplinarity does not in itself help put an end to sexism.

It was a pity that it never occurred to us, while being students at Fontenay, that our friendly mutual understanding took place at an all-women institution. It would have been such a good idea to compare what we were experiencing, my scientist friends and I, with something we knew through hearsay to be taking place at the same time in rue d'Ulm, which was an all-men École Normale. There were no blank minds there, nor unforeseeable and unsolved questions: some philosophers upheld the view that in scientific fields, scientists produced their own philosophizing, the problem being that this 'spontaneous' philosophizing was wrong, and perfectly ideological. For such a view, it was important that real philosophers, with proper training, should go and do some spring cleaning by refuting all the scientists' views.

Let us pause here a moment: Is this the form of philosophy we truly want, an activity which needs someone else who is in the wrong, so as to justify its existence by setting this someone else to rights? For me, the answer is no, because among other things, it is only too facile to imagine that there are people who are mistaken in their ways of reasoning, and this even before you take the merest glance at what they are actually doing – to deem them in error without even a hearing. As a predefined project, it's simply a form of the time-honoured arrogance to which philosophers have been so prone – and as such, a pure waste of time. In rue d'Ulm in the 1960s, it also started a little war, as young scientists reacted on certain occasions by criticizing in detail what epistemologists taught about modern physics – and they certainly knew how to be devastating – and on other occasions by staging practical jokes aimed at exposing the mundane aspect of some seminars, such as spraying Lacan's seminar with a hose.

In retrospect, we could deem the arrogance of male philosophers who started this war a real pity because, if it had not been an all-encompassing *a priori* project supported by philosophism, if it had left set theory and thermodynamics alone, perhaps they would have spotted one field in which real discoveries were taking place, but with bizarre political ideas attached to them. I am referring to biology, the scientific success of which carried in its wake the idea that genetics are all and that your physical brain your destiny. Meaning, among other things, that IQs are hereditary and that women's marginalization is an outcome of the double X chromosome: not good news indeed, except perhaps for some. And all this passed unnoticed to begin with. As far as I know, you have to wait until 1980 to witness a proper reaction to that. When Alain Resnais's film *Mon oncle d'Amérique* stirred both enthusiasm and outrage, then some of us suddenly understood that there was something the matter in biology, but it also came to light that a small informal group of biologists in Lyon had been concerned for a few years with what was going on in their colleagues' heads, in terms of discourse and fantasy. They had been working on it and teaching the results of their discussions to their students. A special issue of *Raison présente* was published – all contributors being scientists, and this will not prevent me from saying that the volume is in itself a philosophical operation of the critical sort.[5] Contributors are looking for limits – where do you draw the dividing line between valid scientific findings and the political/phantasmagorical exploitation of them?

Besides, within the field of biology itself, something fairly drastic took place in the 1970s. The powers-that-be decided that there was no longer anything new to be discovered in virology. As a result they closed down one research lab after another, an upheaval of spring cleaning again, and probably not without the help of colleagues in trendier areas of biology. Then, suddenly, the AIDS epidemic broke loose. Occasionally, the most unfortunate unforeseen happens! My institution, *Centre National de la Recherche Scientifique* (CNRS), had to rebuild virology teams from scratch, an uphill task because, when you destroy a domain and then have to recreate it, you face a shortage of senior specialists able to train younger people. Such a crisis should never be forgotten. At the time, Pierre Joliot stated that it should be among the vocations of the CNRS to be like a conservation area, a wildlife reserve for disciplines considered as spent, so as – if needs be – one could draw enough yeast from it to start a new batch. You never know when you will need botany again, he claimed in the mid-1980s, something which may well have been perceived as a provocation at the time, because there was (and there still is) a silly hierarchy of research domains. Pierre Joliot, Marie Curie's grandson, himself active in high-tech biology, praising moth-eaten downmarket botany! But he was quickly proved right, partly by pharmacologists, and more importantly when the environmental sciences took off. Was this utterly unforeseeable? I would not go as far as that. In the early 1960s, there was at least one lab in Paris already working on ecology. But the importance of this domain of research was not recognized until much later.

Anyway, even without the idea of usefulness – which already introduces the view that things may well be unpredictable because problems always are – one could stand up for Montaigne's idea that it is simply silly to consider that a discipline (whichever) is spent: '*Meshui, tout est trouvé et tout est vu . . .*'[6] If you say 'today, everything is known – there is nothing more to be discovered in that area', sooner or later, you will be proved wrong! Occasionally, there is a bit of wisdom to harvest from the long history of philosophical works, along with more contemporary explorations. This page by Montaigne should be compulsory reading for pupils during their last year at high school. I know, it is specific to the French educational system to teach philosophy in secondary schools, but, and to make a clean breast of it, when we wonder what philosophy may bring to other fields, the real answer – at least in my country – would be to envision young people who will be taught some philosophy without necessarily wanting to specialize in it and regardless of whether they will go on into higher education or not. A quick word about this: I taught at *lycées* for two years after the *agrégation*; at the time, it was considered the right thing to do, possibly a norm first introduced by Bergson, whose yet-unpublished opinion reached my ears through Jankélévitch: *c'est là qu'on apprend le métier* ('this is where philosophers learn their trade'). Meaning: a philosopher's trade is to talk to, or to talk with, people who are not all specialists. Of course, it was not the only opinion around; there was another one – namely that teenagers have mud their heads and that we were paid to be like Hercules cleaning Augias's stables. In terms of first-hand knowledge, I never noticed that my pupils had very muddy minds, but I quickly noticed that they had a keen appetite. They wanted me to furnish their minds and I was only too happy to oblige. All in all, in my experience, Bergson was right. You learn a job – a certain version of our job – while teaching young people who will not – except perhaps for a few of them – turn out to be specialists in philosophy. Bergson himself was a *lycée* teacher for many years. I believe you could reread his complete works in the light of one idea: it is as if, while teaching, he had learned the sort of generosity you need to provide food to those who are not specialists, nor about to become specialists. His books never stopped being widely read by people who trained in all and sundry subjects and also by many who never went into higher education. A well-deserved reward, and so appropriate.

Since I mentioned Pierre Joliot standing up for botany, perhaps I may acknowledge that I have sometimes tried to whisper that the CNRS in philosophy should also have at least one wildlife reserve for those, in the humanities, who are not so keen on well-organized teamwork. For individuals, including colleagues from universities, who would agree on sharing a coffee machine, informal chats and strictly occasional collective projects. Although this was met with sarcastic smiles only, I maintain that there is a problem to explore there. As young academics, we have enjoyed tremendously the opportunity to work together, sharing questions or bibliography, valuing objections and lively debates, sometimes over a dinner table. At a conference a few years ago, Sabina Lovibond, who had just reread 'Long Hair, Short Ideas', expressed some surprise at having found in it some remarks in praise of group work – and asked what was their relation with the teamwork which has been imposed on us since then. Sabina was right: although it is quite possible to argue that there is a drastic difference between what I was talking about – a cheerful cooperation, my lively seminars where I treated my students as my equals so that they would become my equals – and the big programmes, sometimes rigidly defined from above, into which you are supposed to insert your work, all the same we must admit something: we didn't oppose teamwork at once because the idea itself seemed in continuity with what we enjoyed so much. Perhaps bad things come around as lookalikes and then caricatures of what you first enjoyed. At any rate, lack of freedom is pretty lethal for philosophizing. Besides, gender power may show through it: since Frédéric Mitterrand has been in office as Minister of Culture, you must use the word '*patrimoine*' (patrimony) in the title of your project, else it will not be accepted; however, if you do so without perhaps enough stamina, your project will be accepted in a category to which no funding is attached. How could we be amused? And by the way, some men in my immediate environment are resenting the word '*patrimoine*' as much as I do, though 'not for the same reasons', they claim. Don't worry for us, we shall survive that. But what a waste of time! And why do they insist so much on their not sharing my reasons for finding it repellent?

A war between philosophers and scientists at all-male rue d'Ulm, a cheerful mutual understanding at all-women Fontenay: one could feel tempted to jump readily to the conclusion that gender, a word which was not in use in the 1960s, was a crucial factor in the story. And a factor it certainly was, if by gender you mean that some young women, at the time, were less encumbered by conceit or by some unconscious duty to stand up for the supremacy of a field. But it is not as simple as that. Because the structural view which makes philosophy an activity needing someone else who is in the wrong, so as to justify its existence by setting someone else to rights, has been upheld by women too. Besides, it was a man, namely Dominique Lecourt, a former student of Althusser's but also of Canguilhem's, who discovered a good use of philosophy for scientists. For there is a worldwide problem with some young – up to now male – scientists, crazy about their work to start with and then having a fit and bursting out of it, basically because of the division of labour within scientific labs and the effects of overwork. They are allotted a tiny bit of an object and as a result they see no meaning in their hard work. In the United States, sometimes they end up in sects, as anti-rationalist as they can find, in Islamic countries they can be recruited by fundamentalists, and this for anything and everything. In France, I have heard once (but only once) that the far right is frequently present on scientific campuses, looking out for discontented people. But the more widely known phenomenon in France is that many 'disappointed' young men transfer to departments of philosophy, demanding to read Heidegger or to write a dissertation on him, because he at least was against sciences. Dominique Lecourt had the idea that one way to take care of the problem could be to teach the history of science, and the philosophy of science, within scientific departments, at undergraduate level. Because there is always a meaning when you see things in the general framework of history. Now, if you want to know more, kindly invite Lecourt himself to tell you all about it. My point is mostly that devising such a use for philosophy (in this case the philosophy of science) as perhaps an apposite remedy for a painful lack of meaning would not have been foreseen at the time we were students. And it is a nice idea, to focus on the notion of a protagonist who is in need, and not on someone who is in the wrong. True, it is a moral point of view, but – after all – what's wrong with that?

A moral point of view: considering Pamela Sue Anderson is in the audience, she may discuss the account I want to give of our – quite unforeseeable! – cooperation. Pamela is a specialist of philosophy of religion, educated in analytic philosophy as well as in Continental philosophy, teaching Christian ethics, whereas I am a third-generation happy atheist. All the same we have things to say to each other. True, we do have feminism in common, and this means that feminism is a good bridge between intellectual contexts which otherwise would ignore each other or would be connected by some kind of antagonism. After all, the word 'parochial' implies that such things as parishes do exist. As a result, you must know to which one you belong and stand up for it. Well, down with parishes – let us rather focus on the fact that there are human beings in need of more freedom, including at the level of cultural representations and intellectual tools. Perhaps it is a lucky accident if an atheist philosopher and a philosopher of religion can work together. None is standing up for her own parish, nor putting the other one in the wrong. But this may well come from the fact that we are both a little unsatisfied with what is still going on in philosophy, whichever side of the Channel you may want to consider. At any rate, we might want provisionally to conclude that philosophy could be seen as the proverbial *auberge espagnole* (Spanish inn), at which you will find only what you brought with you.[7] You – who is that? Not just you yourself, but many who were there before your time, including some who were women and/or foreigners, and moreover all those who will be there in the future. Therefore, I would suggest that [throughout this conference, which I hope will be a happy one] we all consider what we may bring together, so that the up-and-coming generation will be able to develop in as good an environment as possible.

Notes

1   This piece was first presented as the introductory lecture at the Annual Conference of the Society for European Philosophy and the Forum for European Philosophy in conjunction with York St John University in 2011, entitled 'Philosophy and . . .'

I should like to thank Gary Peters, who kindly invited me; Stella Sandford, who chaired the lecture and the lively audience which gathered there; and this version of the essay is reprinted from *Paragraph: A Journal of Modern Critical Theory* 37, no. 3 (November 2014): 314–25.

2   Stendhal, *De l'amour* (Paris: Garnier-Flammarion, 1965), 219.
3   Don't worry too much for my ex-student: she made a brilliant career in something which has nothing to do with philosophy, but I rue the day she decided to turn the page. If my memory serves me right, the jury's unfairness to her was the event which triggered my decision to run a seminar on women and philosophy, and hence to start writing 'Long Hair, Short Ideas' in order to launch it (see 'Long Hair, Short Ideas' (1977), in *The Philosophical Imaginary*, translated by Colin Gordon (London: Continuum, 2002), 100–28).
4   Michèle Le Dœuff, *Hipparchia's Choice: An Essay Concerning Women, Philosophy, Etc.*, translated by Trista Selous (London: Basil Blackwell, 1991), xi.
5   'Le Matin des biologistes', *Raison présente* 57 (1981).
6   Montaigne, '*Apologie de Raymond Sebon*', *Essais*, II, 12.
7   '*Auberge espagnole*', literally 'Spanish inn': a French proverbial expression referring originally in the eighteenth century to the allegedly inadequate catering of Spanish inns, to which guests had to bring their own food in order to ensure their own sustenance. In current French, it may mean either literally a 'potluck dinner' or figuratively any phenomenon that can be interpreted by each individual projecting her own presuppositions onto it ('finding only what you brought with you').

12

A joyful dialogue with Spinoza and others
Le Dœuff, Deleuze and the *Ethics*
Pamela Sue Anderson

Let us give her a chance to tell us what we perhaps do not already know, to provoke us to change to a greater or lesser degree our vision of the world.[1]

Introduction

Conducting 'A Joyful Dialogue with Spinoza and Others' will require three steps, in order to create a distinctive, practical approach to our interlocutors.[2] The first step is to analyse our manner of 'dialogue', unpacking a positive practice for use in philosophy; the second step is to interpret this practice of philosophical dialogue as 'joyful'; and the third step is to appropriate 'a joyful dialogue' for the task of changing our view of ethical life for women as much as for men. To demonstrate this approach, I will focus on a dialogue with specific dimensions of Benedict de Spinoza's *Ethics* (originally published in 1677) as ideally suited to a distinctively 'Le Doeuffian' practice for women in philosophy.[3] Note that one of the features of this Le Dœuffian practice is a collective exploration of what makes dialogue productive in opening up new possibilities for women's living and thinking.

In the end, a Le Dœuffian dialogue with Spinoza's *Ethics* will uncover concepts for increasing in affective knowledge, and so, in bodily power.[4] To achieve this, it is necessary to strive actively to learn, first, in Michèle Le Dœuff's terms, 'what we perhaps do not already know' (EB, 13). Second, in Spinoza's terms, we increase in knowledge of what our bodies can do (*E*, 174, 312–13). Third, we come to know how to increase in joy (*E*, 173).[5] From this dialogue we will gain knowledge of Spinoza's philosophical account of cognition, affection, bodies and joy, in order to increase in the power to affect and to be affected by other bodies (*E*, 255).

Basically, in the *Ethics*, the endeavour (*conatus*) of a lover to increase in pleasure, at the same time as the thing loved increases in pleasure, is a kind of knowledge (that of imagination) in a thing's striving to increase in the power both to affect and to be affected by others. In turn, this increase in pleasure (i.e. in power to affect) means an increase in affective knowledge in body and mind (*E*, 175–84). It could be said that ultimately, in Spinoza's terms, we strive together to increase in knowledge and so to participate in all of nature.

Le Dœuff herself reads Spinoza as she would any other philosopher in the history of philosophy; that is, she adds the possibility for a woman as much as a man to learn to think philosophically in dialogue with a philosopher and, if necessary, in solitude. So, for this positive practice it is not necessary that the philosopher-author be physically present; a philosophical dialogue can take place between, say, a woman and Spinoza's text. This possibility according to Le Dœuff makes philosophy more inclusive: women and non-privileged men will be permitted to think philosophically, as long as they learn practically in dialogue with the ideas of a philosopher. Thus, 'A Joyful Dialogue with Spinoza and Others' is indebted to both the feminism of Michèle Le Dœuff and the *Ethics* of Benedict de Spinoza, for the distinctiveness of the proposed freedom (of a woman) to increase in knowledge, power and joy.

It has been necessary to agree on certain assumptions for a productive dialogue with a written text. By its very nature a text is, as Le Dœuff stresses, exterior to us. In the present case – of a dialogue with Spinoza's *Ethics* – I have already noted the three necessary, practical steps of analysis, interpretation and appropriation. Yet in actual practice these steps are not always easily distinguishable. Nevertheless, they do guide a significant, threefold movement for both this philosophical thinking in dialogue and the Le Dœuffian-inspired practice of discovering what we do not already know.

In the dialogue's final stage of appropriating core concepts from Spinoza's *Ethics*, I will also seek to 're-vision' gender as it appears in the text;[6] and this means re-visioning the 'power' to increase in knowledge as a cognitive and conative capability, whatever the gender, of a mind and body. Yet, before this, let us consider Le Dœuff's exploration of a unique text written jointly by the well-known, twentieth-century philosopher, Gilles Deleuze, and a woman, Claire Parnet, in 1970s Paris. Note both that Deleuze himself informs Le Dœuff's practice of dialogue and that Spinoza's *Ethics* informs Deleuze's philosophy.

'Women in dialogue and in solitude'

In 1976 Michèle Le Dœuff drafts an essay for her students to read about what it is to write as a woman in philosophy.[7] Le Dœuff herself later describes how she had hoped to have 'a sort of [preliminary] dialogue, in this case a half-imaginary one, between myself and my students'.[8] And as she goes on to explain:

> During the summer of 1976, I was preparing my seminar for the following year at an all-women institution, and thought it useful to write down a sort of theoretical contract; a minimalistic basis to offer my students, with the idea that people need to have a handful of assumptions in common in order to begin to talk to one another. (WD, 3)

Thus, Le Dœuff prepared students for the philosophy seminar which they would have with her, and she thought it necessary for them to create 'a theoretical contract' if they were to begin to talk to one another – that is, to have dialogue(s) in philosophy.

In 2005, Le Dœuff argues that it is still not unusual to find women learning philosophy in dialogue and in solitude (WD, 5). Why does she explicitly add, 'in solitude'? How can we have both solitude and dialogue? This *prima facie* contradictory relation is at a deeper level consistent once we understand the less obvious point: that at least for those women and men traditionally excluded from the academic institutions of philosophy, dialogue and solitude are reconciled when the 'dialogue' is between a woman (or man) and a philosopher's text and when the (other) philosopher is not physically present. Such dialogue in solitude is necessary, if excluded women and non-privileged men are to develop their own philosophical skills (WD, 1).

In 'Women in Dialogue and in Solitude', Le Dœuff recalls that in 1977 Deleuze and Parnet presented the 'becomings' of philosophers who were both in dialogue *and* in a so-called populous solitude.[9] This is the same year as Le Dœuff's essay, initiating a dialogue with students who would be in her seminar, was first published as 'Women and Philosophy'. In retrospect, Le Dœuff reflects that this was a time when some men in philosophy seemed to think it urgent to restate their own existence through 'their brand-new, not to say still to come' ability to talk with women (WD, 3). To be able to have a dialogue with a philosophical text which exists exterior to the reading self is, according to Le Dœuff, a crucial philosophical skill for those women who have endeavoured to make learning philosophy gender-inclusive.

In addition to *Dialogues* by Deleuze and Parnet, Le Dœuff points out that in 1978 Vladimir Jankélévitch and Béatrice Berlowitz publish *Quelque part dans l'inachevé* (*Somewhere in Incompleteness*) (WD, 1).¹⁰ Le Dœuff asks provocatively, 'when was it that a French male philosopher had last spoken with a woman?' (WD, 3). As far as she knew, the philosopher Deleuze speaking with the woman Parnet in print was a 'first'. But then, Le Dœuff wonders whether the dialogue between Jankélévitch and Berlowitz was the last! This rhetorical point challenges women in philosophy to investigate the practical and theoretical presence of dialogue.

From this point, I will refer to *Dialogues II* when necessary, in order to explore the idea of a philosopher-becoming something new: the possibility of new dialogues with women (*EP*, 230–3).¹¹ Admittedly, my reader might understand 'dialogue' in a very different way to the practice advocated by Le Dœuff and illustrated by Deleuze and Parnet. Yet my argument is that dialogue with a philosopher and a philosophical text can and should occur more often for the sake of change, notably for the philosopher-becoming something new, and women are to be included in this becoming. Thus, the Le Dœuffian practice of dialogue cultivates the philosophical capacity to engage women in, and outside of, philosophy.

Now, my analysis elucidates Le Dœuffian dialogue in order to set out a goal: to 're-vision' gender in philosophy. Here the concept of 're-visioning' (with the hyphen) derives from the practice of transforming gender blindness into gender awareness and openness to greater inclusivity. Previously I appropriated Adrienne Rich's term 're-vision', defined as the 'act of looking back, of seeing with fresh eyes, of entering an old text from a new critical direction'.¹² 'An old text' is another name for the body of work – in this case, the key concepts of Spinoza's *Ethics* – which will be seen with fresh, critical eyes in re-visioning gender. In *Re-visioning Gender in Philosophy of Religion*, I endeavoured to look with greater attentiveness at the texts of philosophers, especially those taught by men in the field and those I have taught to my own students.¹³ But now, I see these texts from a new, critical direction informed by Le Dœuff and her European dialogue partners, especially those who have already read Spinoza's *Ethics*. As a woman-philosopher, I have endeavoured to look back on what is broadly construed as twentieth-century philosophy, including branches of contemporary philosophy where women are rarely engaged in dialogue – let alone recognized as 'philosophers'.

Dialogue with Spinoza: The body and affects

Building on the previous section, the combined Deleuze-and-Parnet and Le Dœuffian challenge encourages the 'philosopher-becoming'. This technical conception does not so much describe the becoming of a philosopher in the history of philosophy, as, in Deleuze's words, 'a parallel evolution of two beings who have nothing whatsoever to do with one another' (*DII*, 2). As Deleuze further explains, 'the thing which is the most imperceptible [is that], they are acts which can only be contained in a life and expressed in a style. Styles are not constructions, any more than are modes of life' (*DII*, 2). Instead, style 'is managing to stammer in one's own speech. (...) Being like a foreigner in one's own language' (*DII*, 3).

It is significant for my argument that Deleuze and Parnet single out Spinoza as a seventeenth-century philosopher whose *Ethics* gives us more about 'life in a body' than any other philosophical text. In Deleuze's words, Spinoza imparts to the reader 'the feeling of a gust of air from behind each time you read him, of a witch's broom which he makes you mount' (*DII*, 12). In particular, there is 'the force of Spinoza's question: "*What can a body do?*" of what affects is it capable?' (*DII*, 45). To quote one dimension of Spinoza's answer in Latin concerning the affecting and affected body:

> Omnes modi, quibus corpus aliquod ab alio afficitur corpore, ex naturâ corporis affecti, & simul ex naturâ corporis afficientis sequuntur; ita ut unum, idemque corpus diversimode moveatur pro diversitate naturae corporum moventium, & contra ut diversa corpora ab uno, eodemque corpore diversimode moveantur. (*Ethica*, 128)
>
> (All the ways in which a certain body is affected by another body follow from the nature of the affected body, and at the same time from the nature of the affecting body, in such a way that one and the same body is moved in various ways in accordance with the diversity of the nature of the bodies which move it, and, on the other hand, that different bodies are moved in various ways by one and the same body. (*E*, 127))

For further analysis and interpretation of Spinoza's 'affecting body', let us return to Deleuze and Parnet's interpretation of 'becomings'. And let us consider a salient passage in *Dialogues II*, where what perhaps appears Deleuzian is equally a becoming-philosophy of Parnet's own power to affect and be affected. In the words of the Deleuze-and-Parnet pair,

> Affects are becomings: sometimes they weaken us in so far as they diminish our power to act and decompose our relationships (sadness), sometimes they make us stronger in so far as they increase our power and make us enter into a more vast or superior individual (joy). Spinoza never ceases to be amazed by the body. He is not amazed at having a body, but by what the body can do. Bodies are not defined by their genus or species, by their organs and functions, but by

what they can do, by the affects of which they are capable – in passion as well as in action. (*DII*, 45)

In this way Deleuze and Parnet, similar to other contemporary feminist and non-feminist philosophers, turn to Spinoza's *Ethics* for dialogue about affects, increasing power, joy and knowledge of what the body can do. As Spinoza demonstrates,

> Laetitia est affectus, quo corporis agendi potentia augetur, veljuvatur. (*Ethica*, 424)
>
> (Pleasure [Joy] is an emotion [affect] by which the body's power of acting is increased or helped. (*E*, 257))

Spinoza wrote the *Ethica* between 1667 and 1675. Now, we might ask why the production of this major seventeenth-century text has come to play such a critical role in a contemporary woman's (Le Dœuff's) own thinking about life as a philosopher and a feminist, and this is the case for other women in philosophy too, who are not themselves experts on seventeenth-century philosophical writings. A clue to this mystery is that feminist philosophers take up Spinoza, since they find in his work a positive account of mind–body relations. This account overcomes a still-dominant metaphysical dualism of Cartesian philosophy, which has tended to denigrate bodies, while sustaining wider critical debates in philosophy of mind, metaphysics, ethics and epistemology today. More specifically, the Le Dœuffian practice of dialogue has inspired many different philosophers, both young and old, men and women, to appropriate Spinoza's conception of joy in, and love of, nature.

Le Dœuffian dialogue: Wit, genius, generosity

A twenty-first-century feminist philosopher has to work painstakingly, in her analysis of a philosophical text, in order to discover those shared assumptions which emerge as the necessary conditions for dialogue with that text. I am proposing that Le Dœuff creates her own original conditions for philosophical dialogue; she herself cultivates a precise degree of wit, a critical dose of genius and a touch of generosity. It is useful to see these original qualities as distinctive conditions for a Le Dœuffian practice of dialogue.

When we apply this practice to Spinoza's *Ethics* we both discover and create reciprocal expressions of joy. The active affections of wit, genius and generosity make possible a joyful dialogue with Spinoza's text. If we sustain this joyful dialogue with Spinoza and others – notably, with Le Dœuff and Deleuze – change will happen in life as in philosophy. This change will not come from the force of obligation, but from a distinctive increase in affective power; that is, insightful wit, skilful genius and thoughtful generosity.

'A Joyful Dialogue with Spinoza', then, is clearly not restricted to a mere verbal discussion between two persons: the philosopher and his or her student. Although the well-known Socratic form of dialogue requires a philosophical thinker (Y) to be in a reciprocal relation to X, where X is another person (often a learner), Le Dœuff makes it clear that Y could be in dialogue with a text (X) written by a philosopher who is not present herself or himself. This possibility of non-presence is crucial for the widening of access to philosophy, since it is not only women who have been excluded from traditional institutions of western philosophy but other non-privileged subjects. A philosopher – as one of many readers who, whether female, non-privileged, non-western or all of these latter, are determined to think with a text – could also be described as thinking in one-to-one relation with a body of work which challenges the reader cognitively, conatively and politically.

Obviously, this thinking in one-to-one relation is not merely analysis of words on a page, especially when the right amounts of genius and generosity are at play. Thinking in dialogue with a text requires the three practical steps of analysis, interpretation and critical appropriation (as outlined at the outset of this essay) of, in this case, Spinoza's text. In addition, we can imagine how these steps might be accompanied by a highly distinctive Le Dœuffian element. Cultivating her practice of wit provokes engagement with what remains exterior to, or at a distance from, an interlocutor. Together the Le Dœuffian wit and the practical steps move interlocutors towards my proposal of a feminist re-visioning of the world: the new vision is to make philosophy more life-giving for both women and men.

For example, let us consider Le Dœuff's description of the challenge posed by the philosophical text of Beauvoir. In 'Engaging with Simone de Beauvoir', Le Dœuff illustrates two of the practical steps for dialogue, those of attentive interpretation and of critical appropriation, which put women in dialogue with Beauvoir's 1949 text, *The Second Sex* (*Le Deuxième Sexe*):

> The most precious thing, in my eyes, is that a philosophical text produces in the minds of its readers, in each one, female and male, experiences or creative shocks that the author (or whoever) could not predict, and that take on at once cognitive and therefore political value. [This is a] value variable to infinity, since it is the meeting of an individual and a body of work. (EB, 16–17)

Le Dœuffian dialogue with a text, insofar as it requires the steps of analysis, interpretation and appropriation of new ideas, becomes 'the meeting of an individual and a body of work'. Yet, this dialogue is also the meeting of an individual and a singular text, which has the potential to create a cognitive shock. With this shock, or as Le Dœuff also describes it, with 'a disruption', the reader in dialogue is jolted into changing her vision of the world (WD, 6). As Le Dœuff explains, it is necessary to have both reciprocity in the dialogue and openness to being shocked by a singular text. In this way, thoughts are definitely disrupted and opened up to something new. With the example of Beauvoir's *The Second Sex*, Le Dœuff claims that:

> [Beauvoir] was a real, singular woman, anterior and exterior to the expectation that is ours, and so always to be discovered. (...) Let us give her a chance to tell us what we perhaps do not already know, to provoke us to change to a greater or lesser degree our vision of the world. (EB, 13)

A feminist appropriation of the cognitive shock as a critical moment in dialogue gives women a certain sense of autonomy in allowing them to think for themselves in reading and philosophizing. In other words, Le Dœuff's dialogue with Beauvoir as 'a real, singular woman' enables her, more generally, to confront the sexism of the Great Philosophers in the history of western philosophy.

Returning to Deleuze and Parnet's *Dialogue II*, from which Le Dœuff herself quotes, we find that she interprets the meaning of their doubt and dialogue:

> Dialogue should take place, not between persons, but between lines or chapters or paragraphs. (...) [This] certainly has to do as well with the assumption that 'les questions se fabriquent', a philosophical question is in itself made or constructed. Apparently an interlocutor is not helpful on a building site. Interlocutors put forth questions or, worse still, objections. Yet I have heard Claire Parnet say, why not?! A philosophical question is certainly something you need to produce – you assemble things and doubts; hence solitude, as a moment [of reflection], is required. But does it need to be more than a moment and, if solitude is so necessary, why embark on a dialogue, especially after deeming dialogue to be impossible? (WD, 5)[14]

So, it appears that Le Dœuff's reconciliation of dialogue and solitude is illustrated in her critical appropriation of *Dialogues II*.

To this need for reconciliation, Le Dœuff links the feminist issue of women's exclusion from institutions of philosophy and the challenge for women in learning how to practise philosophy in solitude. A Le Dœuffian solution follows the Deleuzian idea of populous solitude in which women can dialogue with philosophers and their philosophical texts. But then, an interior freedom is discoverable as the source for philosophical cognition and political motivation. To explain this freedom, Le Dœuff cites Vladimir Jankélévitch to the effect that '[l]a liberté n'est pas seulement libre, elle est libératrice' (freedom is not just free; it is liberating) and that '[l]a liberté fait don aux autres de la liberté' (freedom grants the gift of freedom to others).[15] Le Dœuff holds to these assertions on freedom for herself and for her students, having learnt them from Jankélévitch.

In dialogue with Spinoza's ethics: *Conatus*, affections, joy

Let us now turn to central concepts in Spinoza's *Ethics*, which will serve a very particular purpose in re-visioning gender. To be consistent with a feminist vision of dialogue with philosophical texts, I have attempted to see women in philosophy as more confident in how they act both rationally and passionately. This acting is informed by contemporary philosophical appropriations of concepts found in Spinoza's *Ethics*. Most important of all is the concept *conatus*, which can be translated into French as *effort* and into English as 'endeavour', but often French and English editions of the *Ethics* keep the Latin, *conatus*. This original term keeps the highly distinctive sense of Spinoza's concept, referring to an effort, endeavour or striving to persevere in existence. Now, to capture the Spinozist sense of *conatus*, the noun, and *conatur*, the verb, consider Spinoza's text in Latin and English:

> Conatus, quo unaquoeque res in suo esse perseverare conatur; nihil est praeter ipsius rei actualem essentiam. (*Ethica*, 226)
>
> (The endeavour by which each thing endeavours to persevere in its being is nothing other than the actual essence of the thing. (*E*, 171))

From this, we find *conatus* to be what strives to increase in knowledge of the whole of nature. In turn, *conatus* as this striving creates the potential to increase in cognitive and affective activity, as distinct from decreasing activity in sadness; and this increase in activity leads us to the opposite of sadness, and hence Spinoza's concept of joy (*Laetitia*). Joy accompanies and makes possible a Spinozist perseverance-in-being; the latter is already (as in the above quotation) integral to striving for life in its fullness.

Life's fullness generates the power, understood as an affective and conative activity, through which each of us has to affirm her or his own existence, at the same time as we approve of another's. A Spinozist exercise of imagination is essential for the corporate picture at the heart of a feminist re-visioning of Spinoza's philosophy. Roughly, this means that bodily power requires imagining simultaneously a collectivity of human individuals and a grouping of bodies in one substance. Human subjects are imagined as individuals, yet parts of one body: their bodies are a multiplicity in one. So, corporality (in Spinoza) has more than one dimension actively at play: that of the body of each individual with that of the collectivity of bodies. To grasp this corporate conception of the body and its power, Deleuze and Parnet raise questions and introduce the term, 'assemblage', as follows:

> What is a body capable of? What affects are you capable of? (. . .) It is not easy to (. . .) increase the power to act, to be moved by joy, to multiply the affects which express or encompass a maximum of affirmation. To make the body a power which is not reducible to the organism, to make thought a power which is not reducible to consciousness. Spinoza's famous first principle (a single substance for all attributes) depends on this assemblage not vice versa. There is a Spinoza-assemblage: soul and body, relationships and encounters, power to be affected, affects which realize the power, sadness and joy which qualify these affects. Here philosophy becomes the art of a functioning, of an assemblage. (*DII*, 46)

Dialogues II take us back to Spinoza's *Ethics* where he discusses the 'affections of the body'. Affection – along with *conatus*, its power and joy – becomes a crucial concept for re-visioning Spinoza's *Ethics*. For instance, Deleuze and Parnet, so to speak, 're-vision' Spinoza's affecting and affected bodies–minds as 'an assemblage' of 'organism and consciousness', of 'soul and body', like that in *Dialogues II* (as in the above quotation). The English translation of the title of Part Three of the *Ethics* uses the term 'Emotions', but Affects and Affections appear closer to the Latin *Affectum*. Consider the following:

> Per Affectum intelligo Corporis affectiones, quibus ipsius Corporis agendi potentia augetur, vel minuitur, juvatur, vel coercetur, & simul harum affectionum ideas. (*Ethica*, 212)
>
> (By emotion I understand the affections of the body by which the body's power of acting is increased or diminished, helped or hindered, and at the same time the ideas of these affections. (*E*, 164))

One of Spinoza's 'Propositions' in the *Ethics* is extremely significant for the references which I have just made to *conatus*. This is one of his best-known assertions: 'Each thing, in so far as it is in itself, endeavours to persevere in its being' (*E*, 171).

Spinoza again gives a role to the imagination: this time it is in the free exercise of 'the affections of the human body' (*E*, 132–41). Affections can equally be 'ideas' in the sense of images of things, like corporeal traces, which impinge on the affected body. However, a potential problem emerges in that these images may remain passive affections in the mind. As such, it is not always clear how the affections can take on the required positive role in the active process of philosophy becoming more life-giving and hence, joyful.

At this point, we could ask, is the present appropriation of Spinozist concepts able to ensure optimism in active, corporeal relations? The difficulty is that our analysis eventually stops at Spinoza's imagining of 'inadequate ideas'; he explicitly describes inadequate ideas as existing passively in the mind; thus, these are at the very lowest level of knowledge. For Spinoza, an inadequate idea in the mind is fragmentary and confused: it does not fully make sense. Further analysis reveals that imagination could, like *Affect* and *Affectum*, be driven by *conatus*. If or when this happens, then the activities of the imagination would become caught up in the dynamics of *conatus*, that is, in the movement and impetus of the mind in its struggle to express its nature as a finite individual. The mind's joys and sorrows, its loves and hates, are inseparable from this effort, or endeavour [*conatur*], to imagine: 'The mind endeavours to imagine only those things which posit its power of acting' (*E*, 205).

Yet in his general definition of the affects Spinoza describes the passions of the mind as 'confused ideas'. Here it is necessary to presuppose the striving (*conatus*), 'by which the mind affirms of its body, or of any part of its body, a greater or lesser force of existing than before, and which when being given, the mind itself is determined to thinking this rather than that' (*E*, 223). The definition of the affects incorporates both the passive and the active states of mind. So, Spinoza understands the natures (i) of pleasure as 'a man's [*sic*] transition from a lesser to a greater perfection' (*E*, 213); (ii) of pain as 'a man's transition from a greater to a lesser perfection' (*E*, 213) and (iii) of desire as 'the very essence of man, in so far as it is conceived as determined to do something from some given affection of itself' (*E*, 212). Thus, pleasure or joy, pain or sadness, and desire are at the core of Spinoza's account of the affects, or emotions. Pleasure, pain and desire are integrated into what it is to be a passion. Spinoza concludes that the more the mind's activity increases, the more knowledge we acquire and the closer we get to a sense of joy.

The crucial point for feminist and Deleuzian philosophers alike is that Spinoza himself overcomes a traditional philosophical dualism of mind and body. As we have seen, the increase of active ideas in the mind is equally an increase in bodily activity and in bodily relations as collective activities of individuals. Yet a feminist issue still arises: Are women, like men, part of the corporate joy in the affirmation of life and intellectual love of nature?

Conclusion

In this essay on dialogue, I have moved from the dialogues of Le Dœuff to those of Deleuze and Parnet, and gradually, to a feminist appropriation of Spinoza's *Ethics*. Le Dœuff, Deleuze and Spinoza have each guided the working out of a distinctive practice of dialogue for women in philosophy. A Le Dœuffian practice applied to Spinoza's *Ethics* has guided us to concepts, which are useful for educating affections (as active) and passions (as passive).

Affirming the power to persevere in being and meditating, as Spinoza advocates, on life, not death, adds to a feminist legacy in philosophy. Contemporary feminist appropriations of Spinoza's *conatus* have become part of a philosophical legacy which is distinctive in endeavouring to become more life-giving. It is crucial (for a certain sort of feminist philosophy) that Spinoza's *Ethics* supports a motivation to increase active, life-giving relations. In particular, Spinoza's *conatus* expresses a rational striving of each individual body to exist fully as an integral part of a greater whole. Thus, we arrive at an inclusive philosophy of life; this enables re-visioning gender so that neither women nor men have their identities fixed by a binary of sexual stereotypes.

The process of the philosopher-becoming is at the heart of a Deleuzian ethics, which is also inspired by Spinoza. This close affinity between Spinoza and Deleuze makes possible a new vision for what might be called 'Spi-leuzian' ethics.[16] As we have seen, Spinoza's *Ethics* advocates a specific form of striving in life, within an active whole (of nature) in which *conatus* binds bodies together. Yet endeavouring to persevere in being as individual bodies is not yet the complete picture. The Le Dœuffian practice, as we have discovered here, adds a hint of wit, a dose of genius and a sense of generosity to the striving of individual bodies. This means that Le Dœuff's feminist philosophy guides us graciously beyond any exclusive picture of a privileged gender. Instead, the Le Dœuffian dialogue with Spinoza and Deleuze leads to my re-visioning gender: it is only by striving to increase in the power to affect, and to be affected by, other bodies and minds – whatever their sex and gender – that we (will) increase in joy within the great diversity of nature.

Notes

1 Michèle Le Dœuff, 'Engaging with Simone de Beauvoir' in *The Philosophy of Simone de Beauvoir: Critical Essays,* edited by Margaret A. Simons (Bloomington, IN: Indiana University Press, 2006), 11–19 (13). Hereafter EB.

2 This essay was originally written for the *Philosophie, esthétique et questions de genre* Study Day organized by Michèle Le Dœuff and Audrey Lasserre, under the auspices of the EHESS/CRAL/CNRS, Paris, 19 March 2013. I derive the idea of a 'Le Doeuffian' dialogue from Michèle Le Dœuff's own writings but also from her actual dialogues with individual thinkers.

3 References to Spinoza are to two editions: the bilingual Latin–French text by Benedictus (Bénédict de) Spinoza, *Ethica (et Éthique)*, translated by Bernard Pautrat (Paris: Editions du Seuil, collection 'Points Essais', 2010), hereafter *Ethica*, and the English translation, Benedict de Spinoza, *Ethics*, edited and translated by G. H. R. Parkinson (Oxford: Oxford University Press, 2000), hereafter *E*.

4 Here and throughout my use of the preposition, 'in' indicates the unique – non-dualist and immanent – nature of Spinoza's philosophy. In the *Ethics* Spinoza develops his original, philosophical position that '[e]ach thing, in so far as it is in itself, endeavours to persevere in its being' (*E*, 171). Further on, Spinoza explains that: 'Qui id, quod amat, Laetitia, vel Tristitia affectum imaginatur, Laetitia etiam, vel Tristitia afficietur; & uterque hic affectus major, aut minor erit in amante, prout uterque major, aut minor ets in re amata' (*Ethica*, 248). (Someone who imagines that what he loves is affected with pleasure or pain will also be affected with pleasure or pain, and each of these emotions will be greater or less in the lover as each is greater or less in the thing loved (*E*, 180).) Deleuze's own reading of Spinoza's 'striving to persevere in existence' involves endeavouring to be active, not passive, in order to participate in nature; here his use of the preposition 'in' highlights a uniquely Spinozist immanent process, see Gilles Deleuze, *Expressionism in Philosophy: Spinoza*, translated by Martin Joughin (New York: Zone Books, 1992), 230–4, 261, 269–72. Hereafter EP.

5 *Laetitia* is translated as joy (*E*, 173), but also at times as pleasure (for instance, *E*, 257).

6 Pamela Sue Anderson, *Re-visioning Gender in Philosophy of Religion: Reason, Love and Epistemic Locatedness* (Farnham, Surrey: Ashgate Publishing Limited, 2012), ix–xiii and 194.

7 The first published version of the text which Le Dœuff wrote for her students to read in the summer of 1976 appeared in English translation as Michèle Le Dœuff, 'Women and Philosophy', translated by Debbie Pope, *Radical Philosophy* 17 (Summer 1977): 2–11. For the revised version of the original French text, see 'Les Cheveux longs, les idées courtes', in Michèle Le Dœuff, *L'Imaginaire philosophique*

(Paris: Payot, 1980), 135–66; and 'Long Hair, Short Ideas', in *The Philosophical Imaginary*, translated by Colin Gordon (London: Continuum, 2002 [1989]), 100–28.

8   Michèle Le Dœuff, 'Women in Dialogue and in Solitude', *Journal of Romance Studies* 5, no. 2 (Summer 2005): 1–15 (3). Hereafter WD.

9   Gilles Deleuze and Claire Parnet, *Dialogues* (Paris: Flammarion, 1977); *Dialogues II*, translated by Hugh Tomlinson and Barbara Habberjam, also including, 'The Actual and the Virtual', translated by Eliot Ross Albert (London: Continuum, 2012 [2006]). Hereafter *DII*.

10 Vladimir Jankélévitch and Béatrice Berlowitz, *Quelque part dans l'inachevé* (Paris: Gallimard, 1978).

11 See also Gilles Deleuze and Felix Guattari, *What is Philosophy?*, translated by Graham Burchell and Hugh Tomlinson (London: Verso Books, 1994), 59–83 and 222, note 7.

12 Adrienne Rich, 'When We Dead Awaken: Writing as Re-vision', in *Adrienne Rich's Poetry and Prose*, edited by Barbara Gelpi and Albert Gelpi (New York and London: W. W. Norton & Company, 1991), 166–76 (167).

13 Anderson, *Re-visioning Gender in Philosophy*, ix–xiii.

14 For further discussion of 'les questions se fabriquent', or how questions construct themselves in philosophy, see WD, 1 and 15–18.

15 Vladimir Jankélévitch, *Henri Bergson* (Paris: Presses Universitaires de France, 1999 [1959]), 295 and 294, respectively.

16 When reading Deleuze, *EP*, with a group of postgraduate students at the University of Oxford in 2008, one of the then postgraduates, Daniel Whistler, coined the term, 'Spi-leuzian', to describe the sort of philosophy which we were learning in dialogue with this text. We learned not only about Spinoza, but also about Deleuze's highly original appropriation of Spinoza's *Ethics* in his own philosophy. So, we all agreed that taking the first part of Spinoza's name and the second part of Deleuze's name – in Spi-leuze and Spi-leuzian philosophy – captured the philosophical knowledge we were acquiring better than describing it either as Deleuzian or as Spinozist.

13

Towards a new philosophical imaginary?

Michèle Le Dœuff

I am very happy to be involved again in a SWIP/Oxford conference twenty-two years after the first one, which took place in the spring of 1992 at St Hilda's College – Meena Dhanda, Sabina Lovibond, Pamela Sue Anderson, Jennifer Hornsby, Susanne Bobzien, Susan James, to name but a few, were there and I believe, although this is just a belief of course, that we had a good time together. By mentioning this, I want to hint that the project to insert feminist thinking in mainstream philosophy (in Oxford) did not begin yesterday nor just in some exotic den, like a Parisian Café or a village in upstate New York. Our thanks to Amia Srinivasan for stating in the call for papers that 'we have a rich tradition of feminist philosophy'! This is indeed the first point to acknowledge. We are not starting from scratch, and if we already experienced some progress in the past, we may contemplate more in the future.

Not starting from scratch either in the country of Mary Wollstonecraft, Virginia Woolf and Harriet Taylor – again, to name but a few – perhaps those dearest to my heart, in which case we shall add straightaway Bridget Hill, our bold and brave colleague in History who started writing basically after she retired. Bold and brave she was, and generous in her support to younger women. Since I wish to convey the idea that we already have a lot of cards so as to insert a feminist questioning into philosophy, however classical, I want to state that we even have images to give us support, which is important, you are not expecting me to say the opposite, or do you? Here is one I would like to share with you.

Bridget, in a dining room in Osney, a small island on the River Thames at a walking distance from here, told me how, in an all-women college, she had had to rescue an undergraduate who had committed the double sin of getting married *and* pregnant. They wanted to expel her, 'they' being mostly and I quote 'the married women!' who stated, allegedly from personal experience, that you couldn't be pregnant *and* take your Finals. Bridget won, perhaps single-handed, so good she was at being vocal. The student got her baby and a First, then started publishing a good bulk of work under the name of Julia Briggs. That was Oxford in the 1960s, the story being told in the 1990s by a still angry Bridget. There are lessons to learn from this: occasionally, anger is justified, which is not what we were told as little girls. Sometimes we must drop our socially constructed gender, in order to give way to feminist behaviour, in this case stretching a helpful hand to another woman, so that her rights be preserved. Anger is justified and productive, particularly when it is unselfish, and it is intellectually fruitful. It helps challenge deeply rooted cultural attitudes, which in itself is a philosophical project if there was one, in this case assumptions about 'the flesh' as deemed incompatible with scholarly efforts. Or the idea that a mature woman's main duty amounts to being repressive towards other women, younger or not. A so-called duty, which wouldn't stand examination, if you ask me. We could turn this into a question: among socially imposed duties, sometimes imbibed unconsciously by individuals, is it possible to sort out those to which, after due examination, we could give some value from those which we can disregard as just 'so-called duties'? And who is 'we' in that story? Whatever the case, Bridget's anger could easily fit in discussions pertaining to moral philosophy, canonical discussions to boot, relative to the value of anger, and it could also illustrate the fact that it is still necessary to explore deep unconscious schemes of behaviour and perception, schemes which may even bias what is called 'personal experience', an otherwise precious point of reference.

Besides, I find it delightful to speak highly of a colleague from another field. It is a nice break from tradition and from the time-honoured [bad] habit in philosophy, to show that people in other fields are wrong or do not know what they are talking about. As if we needed such a thing, in order to prove how wonderful, how necessary, we are. Hence, although Bridget's story is a true story, it may also become part of the imaginary we want. It could prop up our efforts to consider that times have already changed and could change more, in the right direction, please! A photo of Rae Langton giving a piggyback to one of her daughters, a photo of Susanne Bobzien enjoying Spanish sunshine and emulating the statue of a young man, except that she is alive and female, both published by *The New York Times* under the heading, 'This is what a philosopher looks like', are helpful to update the iconography of our subject.[1] A lot of people may still have at the back of their minds the image of an old man with a white beard as the figure of the philosopher. Of course, you will wonder whether this beard was not a blue one turned white by ageing. At any rate, you have two ways to challenge such a disastrous image: you may offer alternative pictures, implying that a philosopher may be a young woman, with an aptitude to enjoy *also* a physical life, or you may analyse – hence dismantle – the old bearded icon. We can have both, of course, the critical point of view taking old images to pieces, images which – alas! – tend to become self-evident, *plus* a sort of Nietzschean technique, based on the idea that it is sometimes more efficient to replace things than to be critical. Both are necessary, in my view, both should be combined, in a collective effort to change some infra-rational aspects of our job. Now, it is quite possible that it does not take the same turn of mind to challenge traditional images by being critical *or* by replacing an image by another one. Great: it so happens that we do not have all the same turn of mind, we women, we feminists of whatever sex or feminist-friendly people. As a result, we can combine our talents, and let us get on with that.

[At this point, a little sarcastic voice from the back of my mind makes itself heard:

Q: Michèle, when claiming that all women do not have the same turn of mind, do you want to challenge the idea that physiology does have an effect on the brain and, as a result, on intellectual life?

R: No, 'to challenge' might be too polite a word to describe how I feel about both this idea and the political use some still make of it. Particularly those who see diversity, of minds, of theoretical views, on the side of men only, and want women to be all of the same kind.

And this could have been the starting point of some great dialogue between what I know as a historian of philosophy (see Bacon's *Advancement of Learning*) and what I explored in *The Sex of Knowing*.]

Several turns of mind in women *and* in men: by the way, any male philosopher who would want to become feminist or at least feminist-friendly could find good role models in the past, like John Stuart Mill, Bertrand Russell, Léon Brunschvicg (who, by the way, was Simone de Beauvoir's professor and husband to Cécile Brunschvicg), Vladimir Jankélévitch and, more recently, Gilles Deleuze. Isn't it great that *even* male colleagues would not have to start from scratch? Paul Lodge is one of the organizers of this conference; he will tell us whether he feels truly delighted with the idea that *he too* could find support in good role models from past or recent philosophy. At any rate, should we not feel self-confident nowadays when so many breakthroughs have taken place? Don't you think we could now envision our future as kind of '*La vie en rose*', considering we have so many cards in our hand?

Many cards indeed, but then, how is it that nothing dramatic happens? Don't begin to grumble that the cards are too weak. That all the men I mentioned, feminist philosophers, had of course their good points but also their limitations, like being just supportive towards women students, or just involved in practical issues, a woman's right to vote, birth control, more recently the struggle against clitoridectomy. I remember making Gilles Deleuze and Jacques Bouveresse sign a petition against what was not yet called female genital mutilation, after some other colleagues had published a postmodern defence of it.[2] Don't begin stressing the fact that we often find a determined woman thinker or activist behind the men who care for us. It was certainly the case for John Stuart Mill and also for Raymond Klibansky, who was so constantly helpful to women budding scholars: in his student days at Heidelberg, he had been an adopted member of Marianne Weber's household, on a par with her nephews, and he kept – up to his last years – downright respect and affection for her. Thanks to her, he knew what sort of potential there is in a woman when she is allowed to develop it. She was a sociologist, much involved in the movement for women's rights.[3] It is as if their friendship had grafted something forever in his mental development, or opened some unusual space in his way of thinking, a space seldom found in male academics educated by an all-male group of teachers. And why should it be a problem to acknowledge that, frequently, there is an enlightened woman behind an enlightened man? After all, this only comes to prove that feminism, as a way of thinking and behaving, moreover as a set of values, can be communicated, at least partly, *also* to male colleagues. We are not expecting any of them to be a real point of origin, since after all, none of us, contemporary women feminist philosophers, is utterly *that* either. We tend to learn from others, don't we? We have predecessors, we have colleagues, we don't mind borrowing from other fields and to give value to points made by others. We enjoy exchanging views.

Back to the white beard, which makes all women philosophers fail to look the part. History of art may help us repudiate it for good: Rembrandt's painting, still known as *The Meditating Philosopher* and reproduced on the cover of some philosophy books, may not have been at all what it is supposed to be. Art historian Jean-Marie Clarke suggested that the real topic was *Tobit and Anna waiting for their son's return*, a biblical theme, except that eighteenth-century French admirers renamed it *Le Philosophe en méditation*, thus increasing its popularity overnight. It is as if not so many people were keen on yet another portrait of a biblical patriarch, but *if* it could be seen as an image of *the* philosopher, then it deserved enthusiastic welcome. No comment! Sometimes, you can even get a square reproduction (while the original is rectangular) suppressing the right-hand band in which there is a woman busy at a fireplace. Oh, not even that? No space at all for a woman? Not even in the humble role of a dutiful housewife? What is philosophy, in some people's minds, if this picture is for them *the* image of what *the* philosopher is, when it's based first on hijacking a biblical patriarch's portrait and then on doctoring the original through altering the format?

Bridget Hill was not just a brave member of an Oxford college. You learn a lot through reading her books. Besides, they had a radical effect on me. Well, perhaps the penchant was already budding, but Bridget made it hatch: I find it hard these days to read a book, say in Politics or in History, which does not take into account what she called, after Kate Millett, 'sexual politics'. Fair enough, this is a personal and acquired attitude, I'm not saying it should or even could become a norm, like becoming unable to peruse a book which defines its object by first truncating it. Anyone whispering that it could happen all the same, so unpredictable the future is? At any rate, I have read the report written by Helen Beebee and Jennifer Saul, for the British Philosophical Association and the Society for Women in Philosophy, a timely cooperation indeed. This report draws attention to a discrepancy, namely that, in the UK, while 53 per cent of PhD students in History are female, and 61 per cent in English, only 35 per cent of Philosophy PhD students are. This is appalling. Who dunnit? Again, there are two ways of looking at such a discrepancy. You may choose to consider that if things are better in English and the community more advanced, this is because Virginia Woolf has been around. For *A Room of One's Own* brightened the reception of many other women authors. And if things are better for women in History, this is because brave women historians have conveyed to their community the idea that if you don't take sexual politics into account you may simply prove behind your subject, *or even mistaken*. The other way of looking at this is to consider that there is something the matter in philosophy and then impious questioning will spring to mind, concerning our chosen and beloved area.

Let us pause here: Is piety, even towards philosophy, a philosophical value? One may doubt it. We must of course respect obligations and have moral values, like honesty, fair-mindedness in our perception of anyone's work, intellectual integrity, goodwill towards our students and towards our readers, moreover a basic esteem for them. We must constantly assume that they can understand it all, provided we do not choose to speak or write in an obscure way or behave like gurus. We must have respect for our students and readers, and also for facts and texts. Nothing taxing, nothing special in upholding values like that. Then each of us may refine them in her own way and develop her or his own set of values; even add open-mindedness somewhere. But is it necessary to wrap all that in an idea of piety towards philosophy or towards a school of philosophy? I would rather assume that it is a good thing to be constantly unsure about the ultimate worth of our subject. And perhaps we could offer a sort of non-symmetrical way of reasoning: the idea of a society which would utterly exclude philosophy is terrifying, to put it mildly. On the other hand, the fact that there is philosophy in a given society does not prove that life in that society is good, and for everybody.

If a certain lack of piety is permissible, then the still inadequate insertion of women and of the rich tradition of feminist philosophy within the field may bring up impertinent questions: Are we a gloomier domain? More resisting Enlightenment? I would hate to accept such a hypothesis, so contradictory it is with philosophy self-image. Hang on, what is a self-image worth anyway? But we invented Enlightenment, didn't we? How could we resist what is basically ours? Well, that's a good question for historians of philosophy. For you can spot at least two waves of Enlightenment and Humanism, one in the Renaissance and one in the eighteenth century. It is a good exercise to read Sir Thomas More and Francis Bacon with the project of seeing in which respect they got it wrong. In Sir Thomas More's *Utopia*, true, women have access to learning and learning is deemed the real delight of human life. So far so good, provided you do not become a wife, because – within the family – wives are submitted to husbands, who have a right to punish them. It seems that Thomas More was able half to think against patriarchy and half not. With Bacon, it is much worse, of course. He didn't try to address patriarchy at all: he enhanced it by creating a strictly male scientific community and by singing the praise of the highest possible birth rate, thus offering a fantasy island in which women are reproductive mares or laying hens. On the other hand, Bacon was quite good on questions like welcoming foreigners or the merging of nations; also in opposing wars of religion. As if insertion of women and insertion of foreigners, or mutual understanding between people of various creeds, were incompatible. They are not! Here we have two authors who were committed to improving human affairs but could not really address patriarchy. Then, you may have the same critical exercise with Rousseau. If you do not end up acknowledging that you gained a lot from these exercises, I shall be most disappointed. The existence of sexism within works pertaining to history of philosophy is like a stone on which you can sharpen your wits, if this is what you expect from doing philosophy. But perhaps you expect much more than that. In a more constructive way, you could consider *how* the great matter of birth control, of the right to remain single, of women's right to education, and so on may have a positive impact *against* jingoism, warlike attitudes, religious intolerance, xenophobia, homophobia, and so on. The highest possible birth rate, as a political project, is never very far away from the minds of warriors, colonialists or imperialists. Think of Napoleon after Eylau battle, looking at the field littered with corpses, and stating 'A night in Paris will mend all that'. There is a future for feminist political philosophy inasmuch as it could explore the connections between all the things we do not like. An image again: I was in Washington acting as a translator for the French Planned Parenthood Association at a rally for A Woman's Right to Choose. Someone at the World Bank was happy to house me because he was convinced, he said, that sky-high birth rate baffled all efforts to help development take off in the Third World and become an autonomous development. Besides, I'm pretty sure that the project to maintain the highest possible birth rate is among the roots of common homophobia.

Now, if you say that questions like that are not philosophical enough to be included in political philosophy, I shall say you have a strange idea of what theory is, as if it ought to be utterly severed from discussions about practical issues and human life. And I shall resume my coining of impious or impish questions: Are our male colleagues more blocked in their heads and behaviour than colleagues in other fields? Not all of them, of course! But I sometimes wonder. Or more ruthless and shameless game-players? No, I have seen worse or equally bad in other fields. More unable to see good points in a woman applying to a place as a doctoral student? Or applying to anything, come to that. More full of themselves, hence more prone to corner and put in the wrong anyone whoever does not look the part? More marked by mental cruelty? Which could indicate something went wrong in an otherwise normal process of sublimation? Etc. etc. The notion of a fraternal social contract was first invented in our field (John Locke and Rousseau) and it still shows. For centuries, philosophy faculties were run by men among themselves, men celibate *ex officio* to boot, and it still shows. Etc.

What is the status of these questions and of all those you may want to add? I can't honestly claim that any of them is well founded, although, after spending fifty years in philosophy, I would not rule them out altogether. They tend to bubble up at the back of my mind sometimes, when instead of reading peacefully at home, I encounter some situations. That's a fact, and the real status of my impish questions could be just that – a little turmoil, which I feel obliged to overcome. I'm not the only one to wonder about the personality of some of our colleagues, by the way. Once, surfing on the internet, I chanced on a lovely account, by Dave J. Allen, of a paper I gave at York. Lovely of him indeed, to state that I'm insightful, sharp, pleasant and amiable – thanks a lot! – in contrast with other philosophers who, though intellectually sharp, appear 'a bit emotionally stunted, if not downright vicious'. Perhaps we could agree on the optimistic idea that there is nothing wrong with philosophy in itself, but it so happens that some colleagues seem to have turned it into a bitter fruit. I would not be French if I didn't add straightaway that it isn't the sharpest who are like that. Beware of those who are neither bad nor good. Those who have ambitions well in excess of their potentialities must add crafty mean tricks to their talents in order to reach the top. Or those who are not sure they can establish a convincing superiority over women colleagues. But this could be a merely French turn of mind, so let us rather consider how good international life can be.

I have learned a lot from the English-speaking world, just as some of you perhaps have learned a lot from reading Beauvoir and Gabrielle Suchon. Please allow me to mention *also* the Bodleian Library, in which I spent happy days, and read – among other things – *History of Woman Suffrage*, the well-documented saga of our American foremothers. Big volumes, perhaps not as carefully preserved as some Elizabethan manuscripts, but let us skate over this little difference. At least they are there, donated by the authors and kept. Our American foremothers launched the mass movement for women's right to vote and to gain access to all professions, including being President of the United States. Besides they saw their efforts as philosophical. For they claimed that it takes a lot of courage and philosophy to rise above the opinions of most men. Do we have anything philosophical to object to such a view? I doubt it. And it could be a good question to wonder about the phrase 'courage *and* philosophy'. Some people have both, of course, but are philosophy and courage distinct enough – even if sometimes they nicely add up – for us to assume that there are people with philosophy but no courage? Then you can discuss Montaigne's opinion about lack of courage as a road to cruelty. At any rate, when you assess an epistemic situation, never forget libraries and librarians. They are an important part of what students can get when attending a university.

Needless to say, any discussion about inserting feminism within the field of philosophy should in my view broach the topic from an international point of view, as well as a trans-historical one. But here we meet a difficulty. On paper, of course, it would look ridiculous to accept that locations or nationalities had a grip on philosophical discussions. The problem is that, up to now, location has had such a grip, and we ought to wonder why. Leave aside the facile example of the then new university of Toulouse, which advertised itself by making it public that 'here you can study Aristotle', whereas in Paris it was still forbidden. You may dismiss this fact by stating it was the Middle Ages, a period when philosophy was confronted to an external ideological regulation by the church, in some places more enforced than in other places. Are you sure it's finished? It is just a question to keep in mind. And what do you make of Greek philosophy? It was apparently organized in schools and almost all named after a location, Elea, Abder, Akademos gardens, a smaller garden, a certain porch or colonnade, a gym near a temple of Apollo. All were named not after a method or an intellectual principle which would be a feature of their ways of philosophizing but after literally a point of origin, as unchangeable as a birth place. Named after a *seat* where those involved breathed the same air, shared the same food, adored a founding father together, hence shared not just a few dogmas but also a closure around these dogmas and a host of implicit assumptions, as the ones you get through small talk and body language. One great counter-example springs to mind, though: the Sceptics were named after their project – namely, that they wanted to examine – not by a location turned into an emblematic site. It seems to suit them. But except for them, location was important, and the various schools had each their own axiomatic system: they didn't need to communicate one with the other, they were apart – like points or sites are apart in a geometrical space. So much for my own fantasy about philosophy being like a big harbour in which crews from everywhere could meet! Except that, when we discuss feminist philosophy with colleagues and students in Istanbul, Uppsala or London, communication does take place and the harbour is never that far away.

A quote to conclude: 'We must settle this disagreement about *mores*', I'm translating John Stuart Mill from the French. He had a correspondence with Auguste Comte, however unlikely this may seem today. A correspondence between two men who didn't have the same turn of mind at all. In addition, Mill had already been in a meaningful relationship with Harriet Taylor for ten years; Comte was recovering from a nervous breakdown and rebuilding himself like an empty fortress, with sexism as a cornerstone and racism as another one. Apparently, his marriage had been wrecked by the fact that his wife 'although much devoted of course, was not submissive enough'. The letters contain material which would be hilarious, if it were not so sad. For example, Comte says that the idea of a female monarch could perhaps be accepted in the Renaissance but would seem simply ridiculous today. So, that was his idea of progress? And he wrote this when Queen Victoria had been reigning for some years. But Comte never read newspapers. The *mores* Mill refers to are in fact the respective positions of women and men in social, philosophical and emotional life. Mill claims that 'there is room for *equality too* within human affections'. He also states that, if Comte and himself can't agree about *mores*, they can't agree about political institutions either. [Nor about anything? I should like also to ask.] But this is an enormous question: Can we all agree about *mores*? and on the idea that mores should be backed by bills of rights? and is this the unmistakable prerequisite for philosophical communication on any question whatsoever to take place?

Notes

1 *The New York Times*, 6 June 2012. The photo is still to be found on the internet.
2 Léon Brunschvicg (1869–1944), professor at the Sorbonne for thirty years, was married to Cécile Brunschvicg, née Kahn, an outstanding militant for women's vote, women's education, and so on. Vladimir Jankélévitch, an ex-student of Léon Brunschvicg and my supervisor for many years, gave valuable support to our struggle to make abortion legal and safe. See Michèle Le Dœuff, '*La Liberté*', in *Présence de Vladimir Jankélévitch*, edited by Françoise Schwab et al. (Paris: Beauchesne, 2010).
3 Marianne Weber, 1870–1954. Her husband Max Weber died in 1920.

Name Index

Altman, Meryl 4, 9, 21, 22, 155
Aristotle 68, 72, 127, 128, 131, 176, 249

Bacon, Francis 40, 77, 87, 101, 127, 142, 160, 174, 184, 187, 192, 200, 243, 246
Beauvoir, Simone de 11, 16, 25, 36, 41, 44, 47, 48, 50, 53, 55–65, 71–7, 94, 112, 131, 136–48, 156–9, 164, 169–75, 194–7, 206–8, 233–4, 238, 239, 243
Bergson, Henri 19–21, 119–24, 132, 147, 167–9, 175–6, 222, 240
Björk, Ursula 13, 24, 67, 175
Boigne, Countess of 193, 194, 200

Canguilhem, Georges 191, 217, 223
Cixous, Hélène 9, 22, 37, 50

De La Cruz, Sor Juana 88
Deleuze, Gilles 6, 7, 12, 21–6, 115–26, 131, 132, 198, 227–34
Descartes, René 24, 32, 47, 67, 70, 71, 80, 125–32, 147, 190, 197, 203
Deutscher, Penelope 22–7, 80, 83, 102, 113
Dhanda, Meena 19, 24, 25, 91, 155, 241
Dickens 79, 81
Djebar, Assia 134–6, 138–40
Dow, Suzanne 131, 149
Dreifuss, Ruth 86, 96

Eaubonne, Françoise d' 195–7

Fallaize, Elizabeth 133, 155, 175, 177
Freud, Sigmund 56–8, 148, 160, 163

Gennari, Geneviève 194, 195
Gouhier, Henri 68
Gournay, Marie de 46, 62, 193
Grosholz, Emily R. 200
Hegel, Georg Wilhelm Friedrich vii, 54, 68, 77, 115

Hipparchia 8, 87, 163–5
Hypatia (the philosopher and mathematician, not the Journal) 30, 31

Ibn Tufayl 1, 75
Irigaray, Luce 7, 9, 20, 22, 24, 25, 37, 50, 94

Jankélévitch, Vladimir 7, 12, 20, 21, 68, 70, 80, 115–207, 222, 229, 230, 235, 240, 243, 250

Kant, Immanuel 156, 189, 219
Kirkpatrick, Kate vii
Klibansky, Raymond 244
Kristeva, Julia 22, 37, 50, 164

Lasowski, Aliocha Wald 179
Lecourt, Dominique 223, 224
Lévy-Leblond, Jean-Marc 217
Locke, John 96, 98, 99, 162, 192, 218, 247

Martin, Alison 159
Michel, Louise 194
Mill, John Stuart 57, 70, 243–50
Miyoshi, Nabuko 29
Montaigne viii, X 116, 174, 221, 225, 248

O'Cadhain, Mairtin 148

Palcy, Euzhan 135
Pisan, Annie de and Tristan, Anne (pseudonyms) 207
Pisan or Pizan, Christine de 32, 38, 42, 62, 87, 183
Plato 3, 4, 30–4, 41, 67, 70, 118, 126–8, 132, 142, 156, 164, 165, 176, 180
Proust, Marcel 137, 151, 155

Rabelais, François 140, 197, 217
Ranke-Heinemann, Uta 53, 160–2
Robson, Mark 159, 163
Rodgers, Catherine 43
Rousseau, Jean-Jacques 13, 24, 30, 39, 71, 101, 191–3, 214, 247
Russell, Bertrand 217, 243

Sartre, Jean-Paul 1, 11, 20, 30, 38, 53, 54, 56, 57, 77, 121, 151, 159, 174, 191, 206
Schiller, Friedrich 40, 42
Seyrig, Delphine 48, 49, 65, 207, 208
Shakespeare, William 189, 190, 200
Simons, Margaret 239
Socrates 3, 34, 118, 126, 127, 147, 162, 164, 180, 204
Spinoza 7, 21–6, 121, 162, 227–40
Srinivasan, Amia 241

Staël, Germaine de 193
Suchon, Gabrielle 3, 13–26, 32, 37, 41, 71, 73, 86–9, 101, 103, 112, 124–30, 132, 137, 138, 155, 193, 248

Taylor, Harriet 70, 105, 241, 250
Tristan, Flora 194

Weil, Simone 29, 63, 169, 173, 196, 197
Wollstonecraft, Mary 37, 46, 71, 98, 182, 194, 241
Woolf, Virginia 14, 46, 62, 73, 74, 80, 167, 191, 219, 241, 245

Yamamoto, Tetsuji 29, 31, 41

Zobel, Joseph 135

www.ingramcontent.com/pod-product-compliance
Lightning Source LLC
Chambersburg PA
CBHW071818300426
44116CB00009B/1359